I0828372

The Civil War Missouri Compendium

THE CIVIL WAR MISSOURI COMPENDIUM

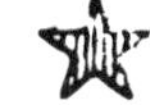

Almost Unabridged

Joseph W. McCoskrie Jr. & Brian Warren

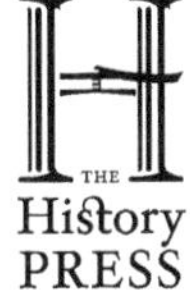

Published by The History Press
Charleston, SC
www.historypress.net

First published 2017

ISBN 9781540227461

Library of Congress Control Number: 2017948488

Notice: The information in this book is true and complete to the best of our knowledge. It is offered without guarantee on the part of the authors or The History Press. The authors and The History Press disclaim all liability in connection with the use of this book.

"The real war will never get in the books."
—Walt Whitman

Contents

Preface

The idea for this book was the product of several discussions over coffee in Fulton, Missouri. Whit had related how Missouri was recognized as the state where the third-most Civil War engagements took place (estimates range from 800 to 1,200 military actions), following only Virginia and Tennessee. As historians and the owner of a bookstore, we were amazed by the number of books, many superb in their painstaking research, on the Civil War in Missouri. But there did not exist a single book to consult, short of combing through the complete 128 volumes of *The War of the Rebellion: A Compilation of the Official Records*, published from 1881 to 1901. Although we viewed it as impractical to include every recorded military event, readers will find that this book provides a serious overview of the major campaigns and more than 300 military actions. Readers will hopefully gain an appreciation for both the immense price in blood and treasure Missourians paid and how the Confederacy's leaders throughout the war and historians today have overlooked Missouri's strategic importance.

This book is a roughly chronological overview of hundreds of the documented engagements that took place within Missouri's borders. Hence, we believe that including "Almost Unabridged" as the subtitle is appropriate and suggests that we intend to improve the book in later editions. Throughout, we have tried to represent dates, locations, actors and outcomes as accurately as possible given the source material available, some of which consists of contradictory and inconclusive information. In addition, we hope to encourage our readers to visit the historic locations to expand their knowledge of the actual engagements. In the bibliography, readers will find a plethora of informative websites and excellent travel brochures available for those interested in visiting exact locations of the engagements. Further support for interested readers includes five regional maps and three campaign maps, indicating the approximate locations of military actions and the major campaigns conducted on Missouri soil.

We view this project as one that hopefully will live well beyond the publication of this edition. One of the most exciting things about taking on a project like this is the community of historians and Civil War buffs with whom we will connect to discuss and debate our findings. We have created a companion website that will guide readers to the specific historic locations and act as a communication hub and database for new and updated information. (The website is www.almostunabridged.com and is designed to elicit your feedback.)

Welcome to that fascinating time in American history when the sobering events of the Civil War directly confronted Missouri's deeply divided population.

Acknowledgements

I wish to start off by thanking the United States Army ROTC program and Department Heads Lieutenant Colonels Malcolm Wallace, Eric Overby, Robert Boone and Eugene Snyman for providing me the opportunity to teach leadership and military history to Army ROTC cadets and students at the University of Missouri and Illinois State University.

I am indebted to Jerry Morelock, longtime editor-in-chief of the popular military history magazine *Armchair General*, who provided me with the concept for compiling a historical guide about the Civil War events that took place in Missouri.

I want to thank Barbara Huddleston, director of the Callaway County Historical Society, for providing access to the historical society's library, where we initially began our research. Local Callaway County historian Martin Northway was an important influence on recognizing the rich heritage that exists in learning the story of the Civil War and its impact on so many local towns and communities in Missouri.

I could not have gained an appreciation for the wealth of Civil War history in St. Louis without the enthusiastic support of St. Louis resident and my navigator Nathan Griffin, as well as John Maurath, director of the Missouri Civil War Museum at Jefferson Barracks.

Obviously, this book could not have been completed without the enthusiastic support and patience of the staff at The History Press, particularly Ben Gibson and Ryan Finn.

Finally, I praise the unselfish, enthusiastic support and encouragement of my wife, Virginia, and our two sons, Brian and Robert.

—WHIT MCCOSKRIE

I would like to thank Danielle Kilmer for lending her time and talent to the maps included in this book. I want also to acknowledge the people of the state of Missouri for embracing this California transplant and for exposing me to so much of your state's wonderful and rich history.

—BRIAN WARREN

Introduction

Tensions were high in St. Louis, Missouri, on May 10, 1861. It had been nearly thirty days following the firing on and surrender of Federal forces at Fort Sumter to Confederate forces in Charleston under the command of Brigadier General P.G.T. Beauregard. The attack on Fort Sumter should not have been a surprise to Federal authorities, as South Carolina's governor had demanded the handing over of the fort in a letter to then president Buchanan in 1860.

But Fort Sumter was not the only Federal property the secessionist states of the Confederacy were interested in. In St. Louis, Missouri, stood twenty-two buildings that housed thirty thousand weapons at the largest arsenal of Federal ordnance west of the Mississippi River. Just two months before, in March, Missouri's elected representatives held a Constitutional Convention and voted overwhelmingly, ninety-eight to one, neither to leave the Union nor to provide arms or men to either side. The legislators' intention was to avoid conflict on Missouri soil, but that wish ignored the fact that Missouri was rich in lead (a vital natural resource for the manufacture of bullets and ordnance) and had more industry, more miles of railroad and more agricultural production than any other state in the Trans-Mississippi region. Furthermore, the three major frontier trails—the Oregon, Santa Fe and California—originated in Missouri, making it a strategically critical state for the Federal government to control as America expanded westward.

Although Missouri's leaders made clear their desire to remain neutral, the sentiments of Missouri's citizens were not so conciliatory. Governor

Claiborne Jackson, an outspoken pro-Southern sympathizer who had earlier affirmed that he would stand by Missouri's neutrality position, chose in early May to call out the Missouri Volunteer Militia for duty at Camp Jackson. Coincidentally, Confederate president Jefferson Davis sent artillery to support the militia training. Governor Jackson soon learned that the Federal commander, Captain Nathaniel Lyon, had already moved the weapons to a secure location in Alton, Illinois, in late April.

An unsuccessful mustering trip to Belleville for the Illinois adjutant general provided Ulysses S. Grant, "Sam" to his friends and acquaintances, a few idle days to spend in St. Louis. Grant stood at the corner of Fourth and Pine Streets on that fateful day in May 1861, watching Union sympathizers outside Rebel headquarters tear down a Rebel flag after Lyon had taken the Camp Jackson militia volunteers prisoner. Earlier that day, Grant had introduced himself to Francis P. Blair, an influential Republican Union leader whose elder brother, Montgomery Blair, was postmaster general and a loyal member of Lincoln's cabinet. Little did Grant know that that chance meeting might have played a role in his meteoric rise in 1864 to commander in chief of the Union army.

Missouri also played a significant role in the issue at the heart of the Civil War: slavery. In 1819, Missouri petitioned for statehood as a slave state. Missouri's bid met resistance from northern members of the House of Representatives, but it was eventually settled with the Missouri Compromise and Maine's successful bid to be admitted as a free state.

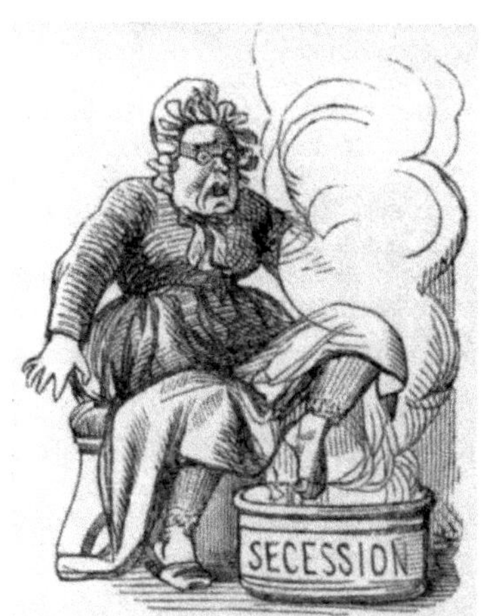

"Poor deluded Miss-Souri takes a Secession bath." *Courtesy of the Library of Congress.*

Missouri again gained national attention over the slavery issue in 1846, when slaves Dred Scott and his wife, Harriet, successfully sued in a St. Louis court for their freedom after their owner had taken them into a free state. The Missouri and federal Supreme Courts overturned the court's decision in the Dred Scott case, vaulting growing abolitionist sentiment into the national limelight. The adjudication of this controversy failed to stem the nation's increasing polarization over slavery and the matter of states' rights.

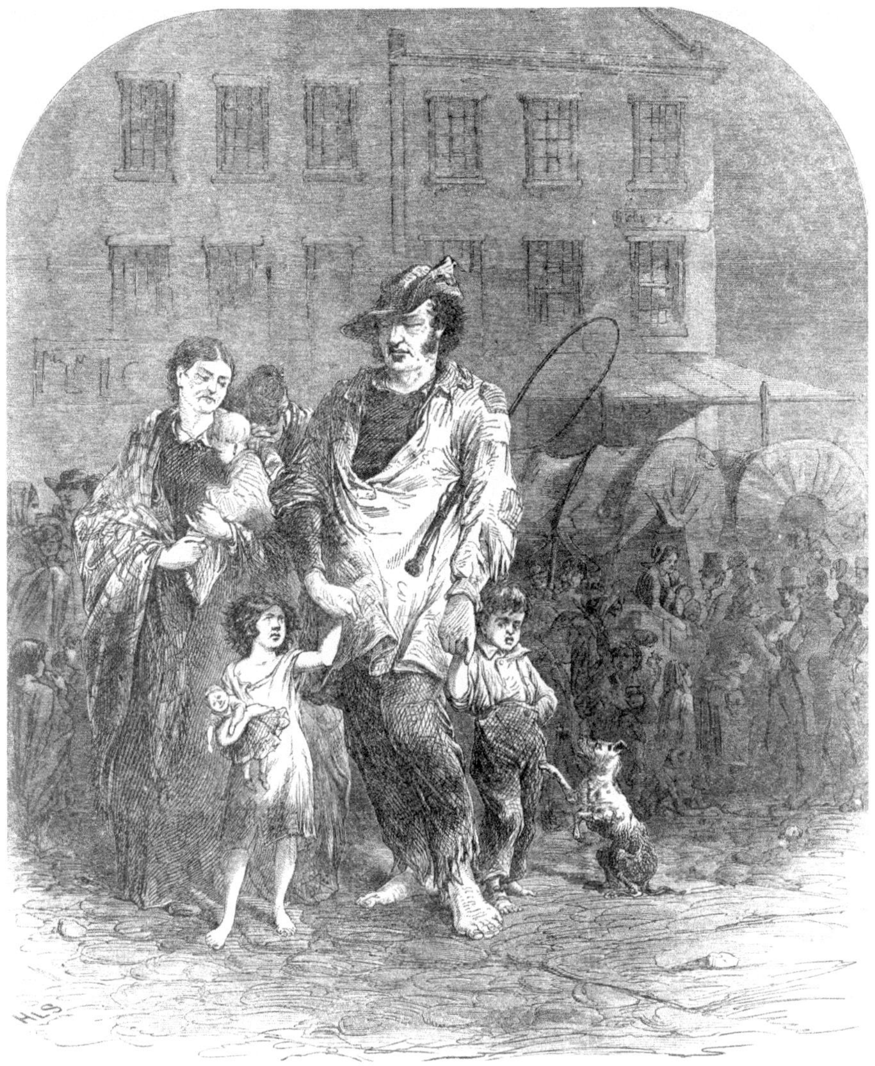

Refugees from northern Missouri entering St. Louis. *Courtesy of the Library of Congress.*

Racial injustice increased in Missouri in 1847, when the Missouri legislature banned education for slaves and freedmen alike, imposing heavy fines and jail sentences for anyone operating a school for blacks.

The southern Democratic hold on legislative power in Congress was demonstrated by the Compromise of 1850. One of the compromise's provisions, the Fugitive Slave Act, made slavery a protected institution in an attempt to fend off the possibility of further Dred Scott–like cases. The act

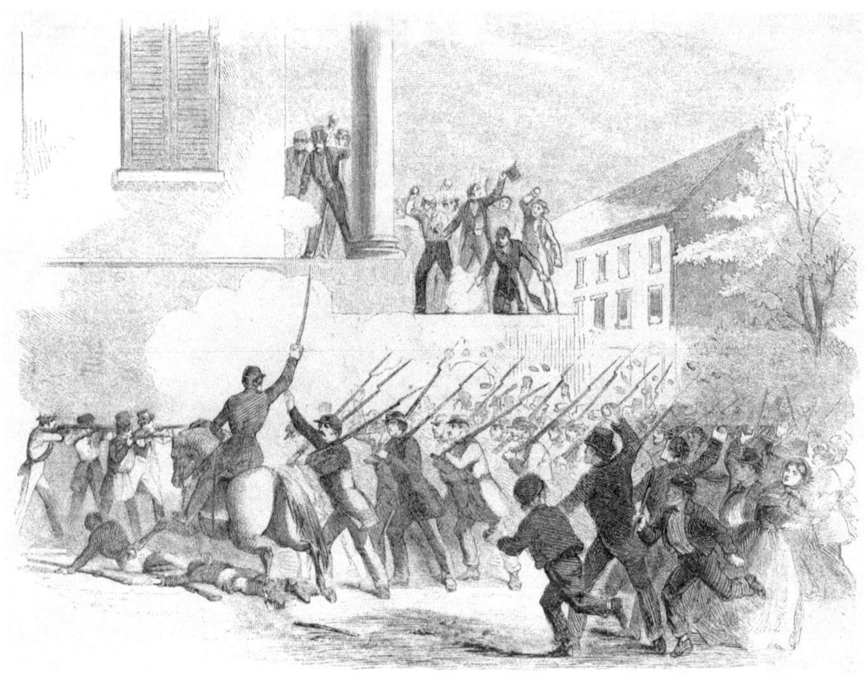

Union Volunteers attacked by the mob, corner of Fifth and Walnut Streets, St. Louis, Missouri. *Courtesy of the Library of Congress.*

imposed harsh fines on marshals failing to enforce the law and high bounties for slaves captured and returned to their owners. Meanwhile, abolitionist sentiment gained national prominence through publications like William Lloyd Garrison's *The Liberator* and Harriet Beecher Stowe's novel *Uncle Tom's Cabin*, further encouraging the moral justification of the Underground Railroad networks that aided slaves' passage from the American South north toward Canada. The passage of the Fugitive Slave Act is considered by many historians a watershed moment that made the secession crisis inevitable.

Desperate to regain some sense of national reconciliation, Congress enacted the Kansas-Nebraska Act of 1854, introducing popular sovereignty and overturning the provisions of the Missouri Compromise of 1820. As a result, violence broke out along the Missouri-Kansas border as pro- and antislavery forces vied for political control of the Kansas territory. The rise to national prominence of fanatical abolitionist John Brown began along the border when his followers murdered five settlers outside their homesteads near Pottawatomie Creek, Kansas, in retaliation for an attack of proslavery bands on Lawrence. Hoping to rally antislavery settlers, John

Brown's Kansas militia engaged in a series of raids along the Missouri-Kansas border against proslavery forces, popularly referred to as "Missouri Ruffians." The Battle of Osawatomie in 1856 witnessed John Brown and his militia of 40 men defending the town from a violent raid by John Reid's militia of 250 Border Ruffians.

The territory soon earned the moniker "Bleeding Kansas," and Captain John Brown earned the nickname "Osawatomie Brown." Brown's crusade became known as a vanguard of righteousness for the abolitionist cause and gained the admiration of prominent American intellectuals like Ralph Waldo Emerson, Henry David Thoreau and Frederick Douglass, but more significantly, it attracted supporters like the "Secret Six," who were prepared to financially embrace Brown's call to violence. Lincoln considered Brown insane, and after Harper's Ferry, Nathaniel Hawthorne stated that "[n]obody was ever more justly hanged." Brown would be lionized in a popular Union folk song, "John Brown's Body," and Herman Melville characterized him as the "Meteor of the War."

The border conflict took on a life of its own, particularly in southeast Kansas, where bands of "Free Staters" like James Montgomery preyed on and looted the homesteads of proslavery settlers and even those of Free Staters seeking to live in peace. Proslavery leader Captain Charles Hamilton retaliated and ordered the murder of five men from the village of Trading Post, Linn County, later known as the Marais des Cygnes Massacre.

Probably few Americans today know that in November 1859, Abraham Lincoln, conducting one of his stump speaking tours, traveled across Missouri to St. Joseph before giving a series of speeches in Kansas to share his views against slavery and secessionism.

Once the Southern states seceded in 1861 and their delegates vacated Congress, the Homestead Act of 1862 opened up new lands in the West, encouraging independent farmers to journey out and break the stranglehold of wealthy planters. Missouri's location at the juncture of the Mississippi and Missouri Rivers in the east (St. Louis) and a central departure point in the west (Kansas City) solidified its position as a critical strategic location for the Federal government to protect and control.

When the Civil War began, Missouri's population was approximately 1.1 million, 114,000 of which were persons held as slaves. By 1865, 20 percent of Missouri's population had fled the state; 60 percent of males living in Missouri of military age had joined a military unit; and thousands of soldiers from Iowa, Wisconsin, Illinois, Arkansas, Texas and Kansas had fought and died on Missouri soil.

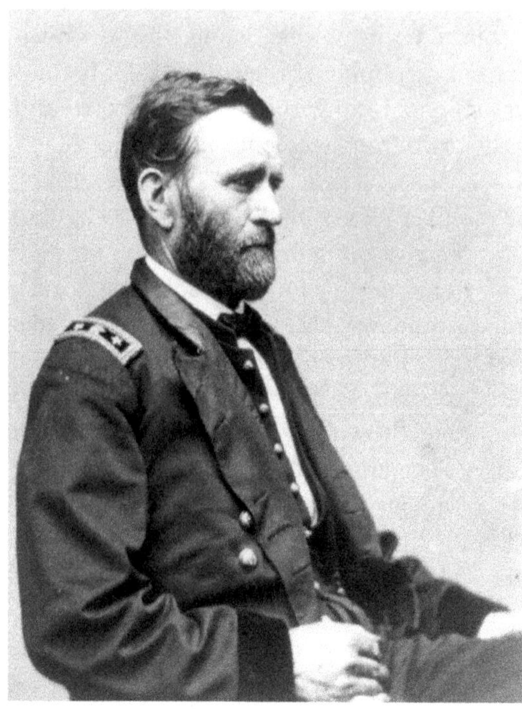

Ulysses S. Grant. *Courtesy of the Library of Congress.*

Nearly 14,000 of 110,000 men from Missouri in Union service lost their lives to fighting and disease. Best estimates suggest that more than 52,000 Missourians served on the Confederate side. Thousands more returned home missing legs or arms or having suffered some other horrible or disfiguring injury, placing terrible burdens on families and communities attempting to rebuild in the war's aftermath.

Many of the North's senior leaders of divisions, corps or armies—the likes of John Schofield, Samuel Sturgis, Grenville Dodge, Benjamin Prentiss, Jefferson C. Davis and John Pope—began their service during the early conflicts in Missouri. Several fought during the Mexican-American War alongside Union commanders Ulysses S. Grant, William T. Sherman, Philip Sheridan and Confederate commanders Robert E. Lee, Thomas "Stonewall" Jackson and James Longstreet.

Missouri's population suffered guerrilla actions too numerous to count, led by infamous guerrilla leaders and bushwhackers like Alvin Cobb, William Gregg, William Quantrill, John Poindexter, David Poole, Joseph Porter, John Thrailkill, George Todd, William "Bloody Bill" Anderson and former St. Joseph, Missouri mayor Jeff "Swamp Fox" Thompson. Many of these notorious men attained legendary status in Missouri. Post–Civil War

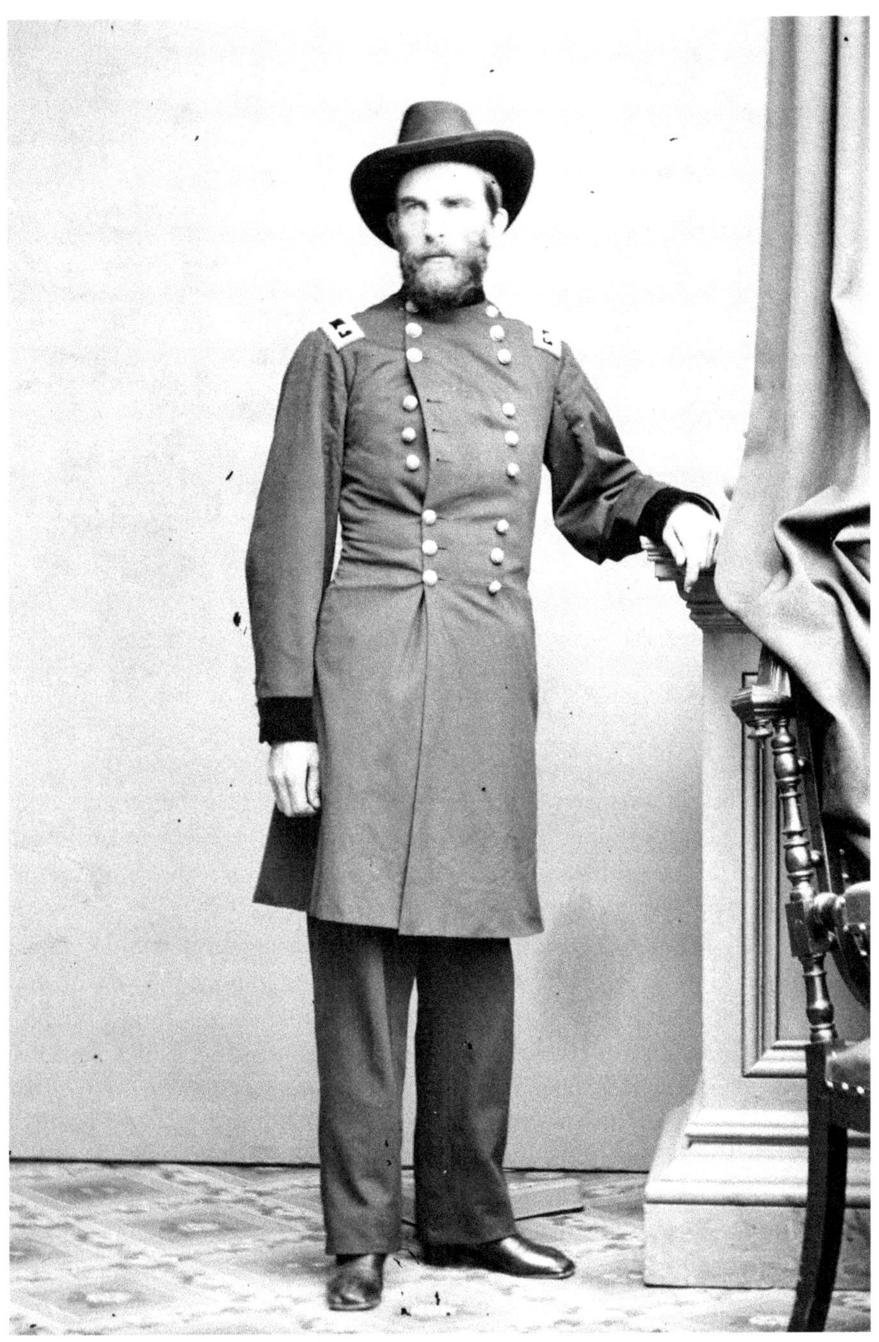

Grenville Dodge. *Courtesy of the Library of Congress.*

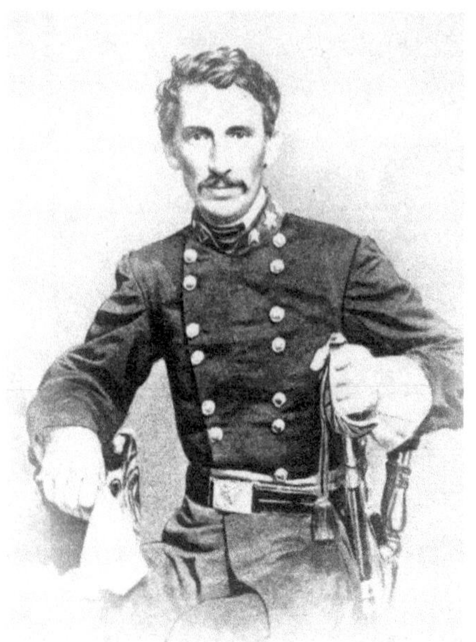

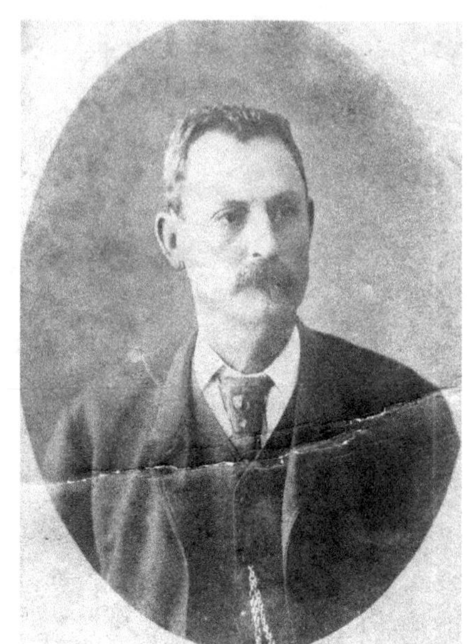

Left: Jeff "Swamp Fox" Thompson. *Courtesy of Duke University Libraries.*

Right: John Thrailkill. *Courtesy of the State Historical Society of Missouri.*

tabloids made a literary genre of tales featuring the bank-, stagecoach- and train-robbing exploits of Frank and Jesse James and the Younger brothers, who learned much of their illicit craft serving under Missouri's infamous guerrilla leaders.

Pro-Union Jayhawker "Red Legs" leaders like Senator James H. Lane and Colonel Charles Jennison customarily practiced indiscriminate robbery and murder on both proslavery and antislavery homesteaders, hiding behind the moral justification of the abolitionist cause. Raids from Federal troops and Jayhawkers led by Lane and Jennison put to the torch more than 2,400 homes and buildings, nearly exterminating the Missouri towns of Osceola, West Point, Papinsville, Butler, Pleasant Hill, Dayton, Rosehill, Columbus, Lexington, Chapel Hill, Holden, Kingsville, Morristown, Camden Point and Platte City, as well as Jackson County neighborhoods too numerous to cite. Osceola, a prosperous community on the Osage River, alone suffered the destruction of 800 buildings at the hands of James Lane's Jayhawkers. It is believed that freed slave and Quantrill scout John Noland's sentiments were influenced by a Jayhawker raid on his family homestead, suggesting that many such raids were not necessarily morally inspired or undertaken

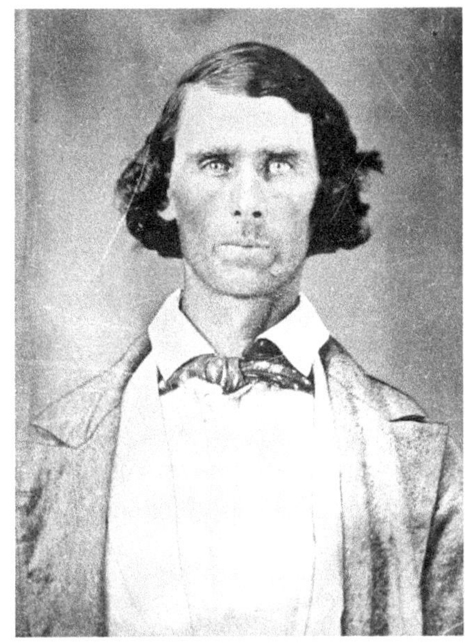

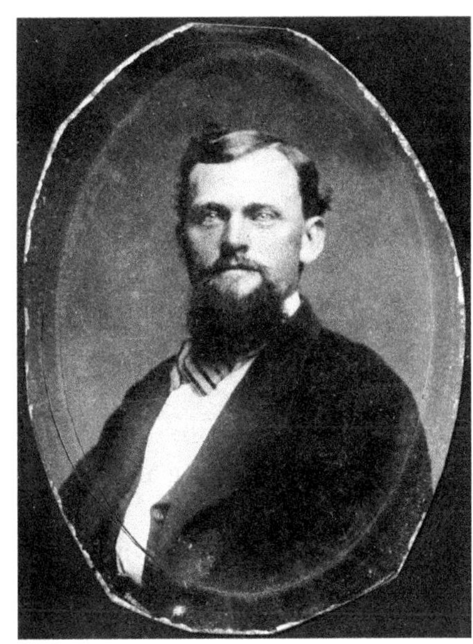

Left: Dave Poole. *Courtesy of the State Historical Society of Missouri.*

Right: Joseph Shelby. *Courtesy of the State Historical Society of Missouri.*

on official Union army orders. Missouri was the theater where Confederate cavalry leaders Sterling Price, Joseph Shelby and John Marmaduke practiced their trade and deserved the recognition afforded the more historically revered Confederate cavalry commanders like Jeb Stuart, John Mosby and Nathan Bedford Forrest.

The hilly, rocky terrain of the Ozarks offered ideal conditions for launching sudden, violent harassing actions on transportation centers, while dense foliage and fast-moving rivers and streams hindered Federal pursuit of Rebel guerrilla bands. Southern sympathizers supported and harbored bushwhackers, further enabling successful guerrilla operations of ambushing, raiding, looting and destroying bridges, rail and telegraph lines.

Atrocities committed by pro-Confederate and Union alike terrorized Missouri's population. Although Lincoln and his commanders were legally obligated to enforce the guidelines of General Order No. 100 regarding treatment of prisoners of war, by 1863, if guerrillas, bushwhackers or Union soldiers were captured, the mantra of "No quarter asked, No quarter given" prevailed. Nearly every day, local newspapers reported on casualties from recent actions and how captured soldiers were sent off to miserable conditions in POW camps and of the raiding and looting of critical food supplies, livestock and equipment necessary for the survival of homesteaders, farmers and other citizens.

Missouri bushwhacker and guerrilla reprisals reached their zenith when William Quantrill, a Confederate partisan, assembled a band of more than 400 riders near Warrensburg, Missouri, and after a two-day ride massacred nearly every male inhabitant—150 men and boys—in Lawrence, Kansas. This raid on Lawrence in the summer of 1863 convinced Union general Thomas Ewing to issue the infamous General Order No. 11, which evicted from their homes as many as 20,000 known or suspected Southern sympathizers from four western Missouri counties. Those who returned later found their homesteads in ruins. The guerrilla war between Kansas's Jayhawkers and Missouri's bushwhackers has continued symbolically for more than a century in one of the oldest rivalries in college football, between the University of Kansas Jayhawks and University of Missouri Tigers.

One of the first uses of African American troops in combat, the 1st Kansas Colored Volunteer Infantry, occurred on October 29, 1862, at the Battle of Island Mound, Missouri. African American soldiers were quickly made aware they would be executed if captured; they learned that fighting for the Union required more of them than was asked of the typical white soldier. According to the Missouri State Historical Archives, between 176,000 and 200,000 African American soldiers served in 170 regiments for the Union by the war's end. Another 200,000 African American civilians worked as scouts, spies, cooks, teamsters and even chaplains. It is estimated that nearly 40,000 African American soldiers were killed or died from wounds and disease during the Civil War. After the war, the Buffalo Soldier troop units created from African American veterans served for thirty years conducting "pacification" actions in the western frontier. Despite blatant discrimination, twenty-five black soldiers earned the Medal of Honor for gallantry in the Civil War and eighteen during the Indian Wars.

In 2012, University of Missouri–St. Louis professor of history Louis S. Gerteis, in his scholarly study *The Civil War in Missouri: A Military History*, took issue with the current state of Civil War historiography. Citing James M. McPherson and James Hogue's *Ordeal by Fire*, a preeminent textbook on the Civil War, Gerteis noted that Missouri receives scant coverage because of what the authors imply is a lack of historically significant battles with important interpretive value. Professor Gerteis pointed out that the Federal Civil War Sites Advisory Commission report in 1995 listed Missouri as the state with the third-most (29) out of the 384 important and historically

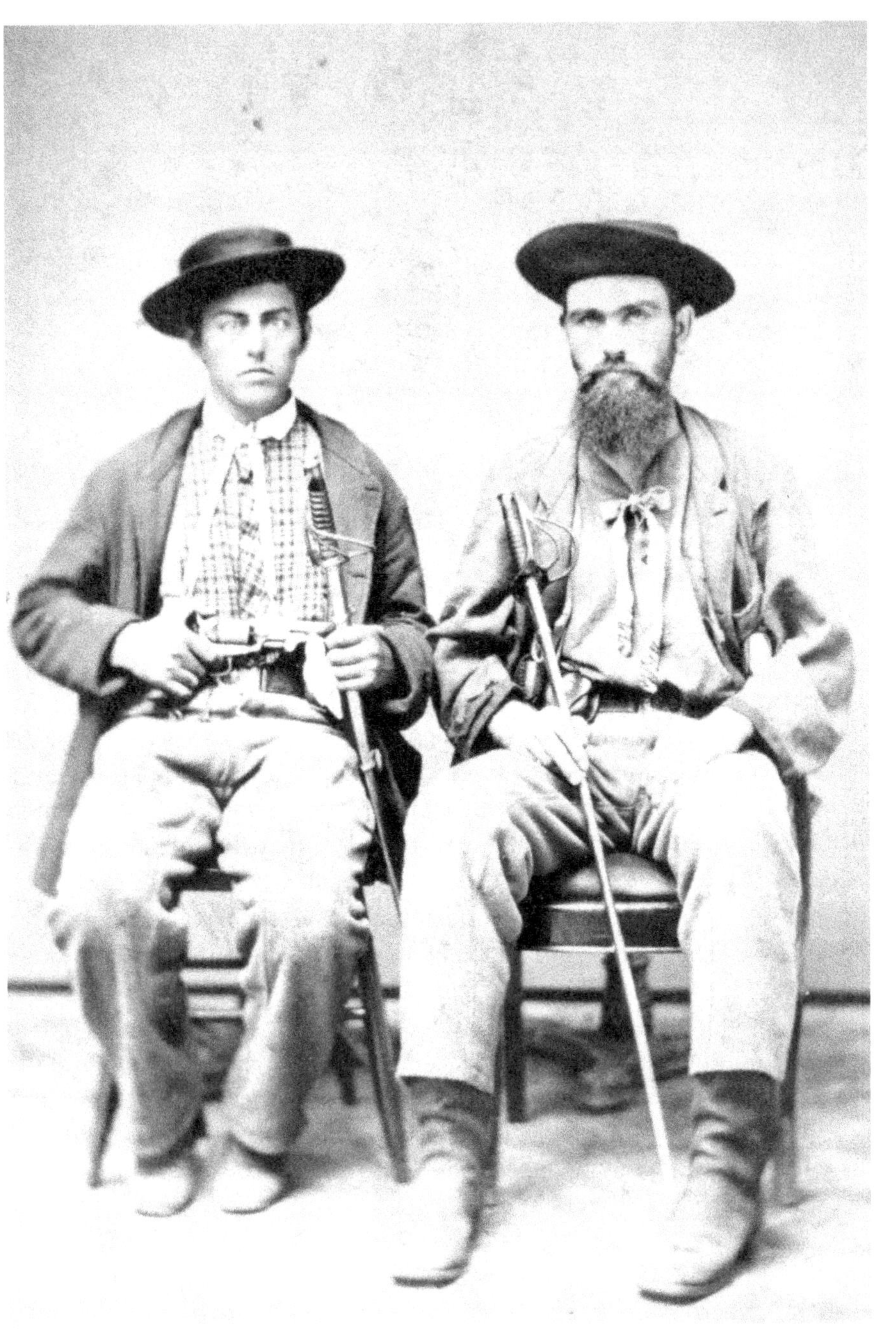

Unidentified Border Ruffians. *Courtesy of the Library of Congress.*

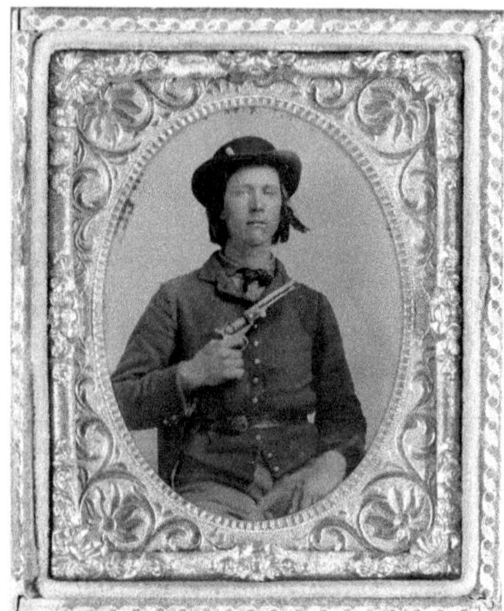
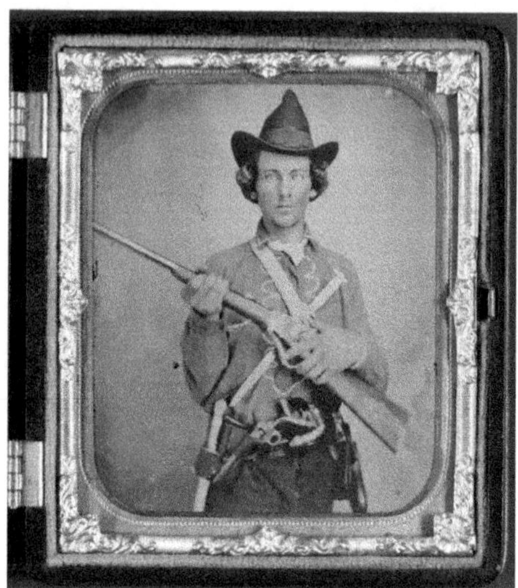

Left: Unidentified Confederate soldier. *Courtesy of the Library of Congress.*

Right: Unidentified Confederate cavalry soldier. *Courtesy of the Library of Congress.*

significant sites. Yet Missouri still garners little national attention for its important role in the causes and overall outcome of the Civil War.

Based on the commission's criteria, this book provides ample evidence of how the identification and classification of battle sites shines a brighter light on Missouri's numerous military actions and how these actions provide exceptional interpretive and educational potential for studying the conflict today. Among the commission's considerations for classification of battles are:

- loss of a significant military figure;
- exceptional casualties;
- important lessons in strategy or tactics;
- unusual importance of the battle in the public mind;
- effect on national politics or strategy;
- significant involvement of minority troops; and
- high archaeological potential

The American Civil War has provided historians the opportunity to study a new, deadlier and more destructive kind of "total war" than the wars fought in the Western world prior to 1861—wars characterized by the devastating carnage inflicted on noncombatant populations and their staggering consumption of national resources and economic infrastructure.

In particular, the Missouri experience is useful for military commanders interested in studying how to operate in a variety of terrains and climates, in rural counties and densely populated cities. The American Civil War should be particularly germane for current military planners and leaders trying to understand how modern war too often leaves the victor as battered and demoralized as the defeated.

The intent of this work is show readers Missouri's important role in this epic conflict. While some estimates of military actions in Missouri have exceeded one thousand, we chose these three hundred to demonstrate the widespread geographic nature of the conflict, the difficulties operating in unfamiliar terrain, the challenges to leadership, the suffering of the population and the often bitter and remorseless conduct among combatants.

HOW TO USE THIS BOOK

AMERICAN HISTORY TEACHERS: Provide a historical setting for students to expand critical thinking skills when examining how Americans in Missouri approached moral, political, military, economic and cultural problems leading up to and during the Civil War.

AMERICAN HISTORY STUDENTS: Enhance the understanding of the Civil War and why it was a seminal event in Missouri's development.

PARENTS: Provide a sense of ancestral connection in the role Missouri played in the history of the United States during one of its most difficult periods.

TOURISTS: Gain an appreciation for Missouri's rich history in one of the most studied and written-about periods of American history.

CURRENT AND FUTURE POLITICAL AND MILITARY POLICY PLANNERS: Unique opportunities exist to examine the nature of insurgencies, visit actual Civil War battle sites, study the terrain, analyze leadership, critique decision-making and comprehend the difficulties of preparing for war and achieving peace. Gain a historical perspective of the immense challenges that political leaders are confronted with, such as gauging political legitimacy and the security of populations and critical infrastructure during civil wars, armed rebellions, humanitarian relief and other types of irregular warfare.

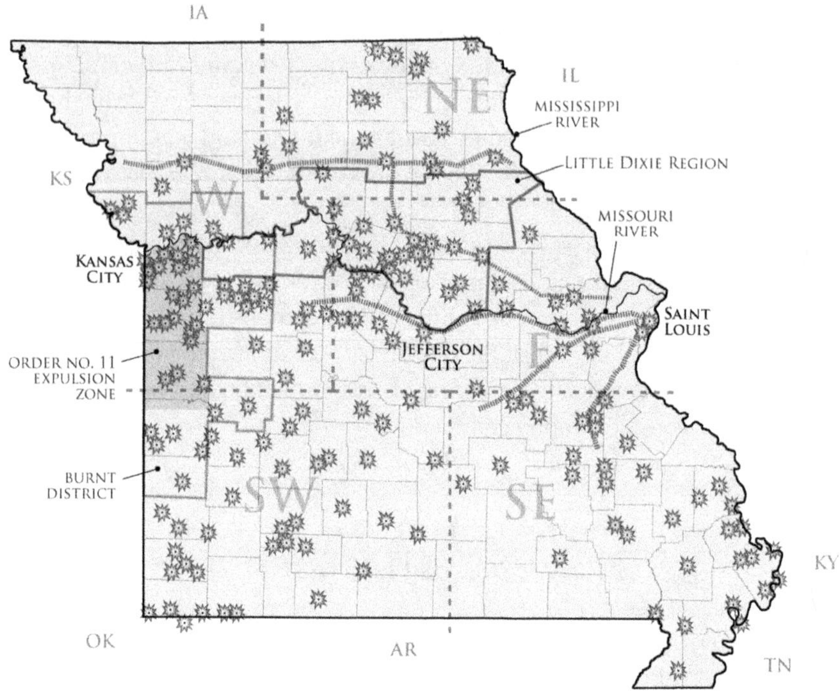

Missouri's Civil War Engagements. Courtesy of Danielle Kilmer.

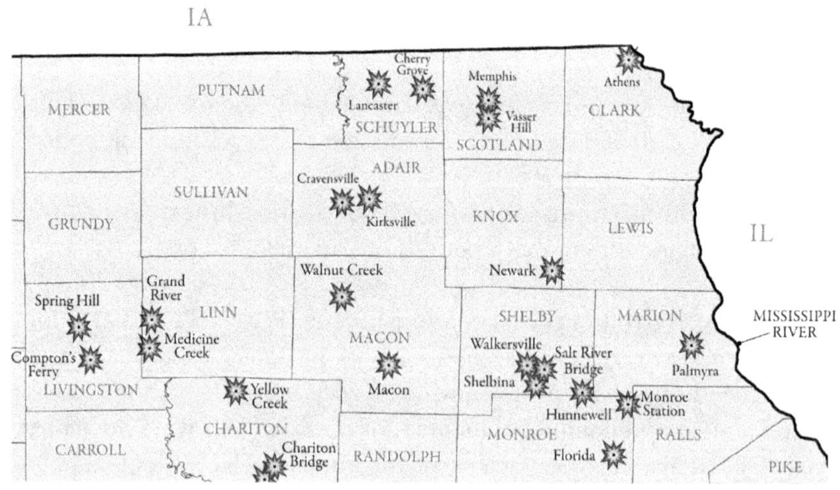

Civil War Engagements in Northeast Missouri. Courtesy of Danielle Kilmer.

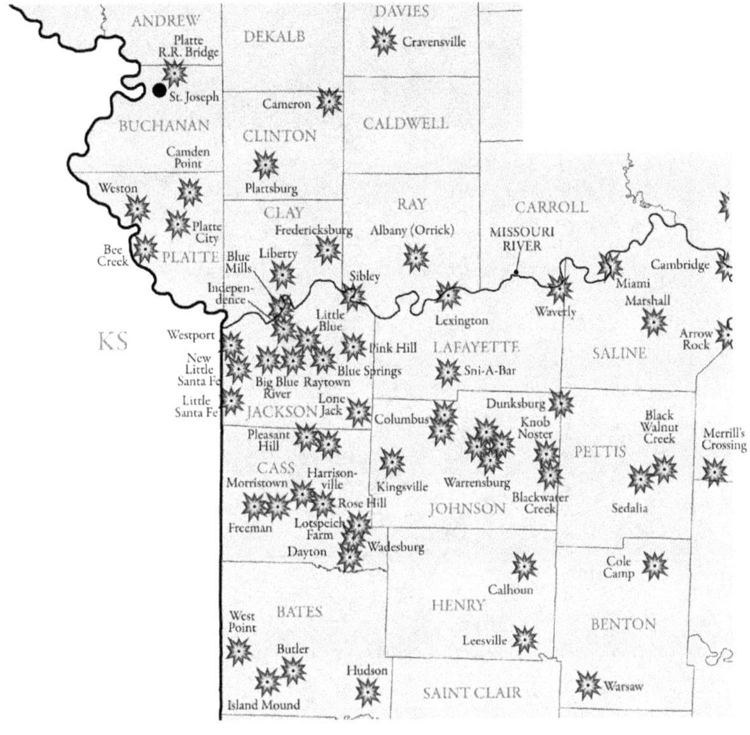

Civil War Engagements in Western Missouri. Courtesy of Danielle Kilmer.

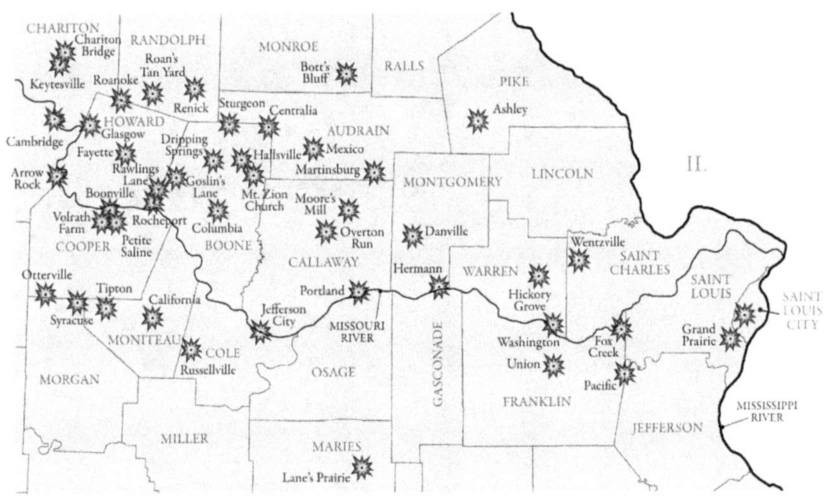

Civil War Engagements in Eastern Missouri. Courtesy of Danielle Kilmer.

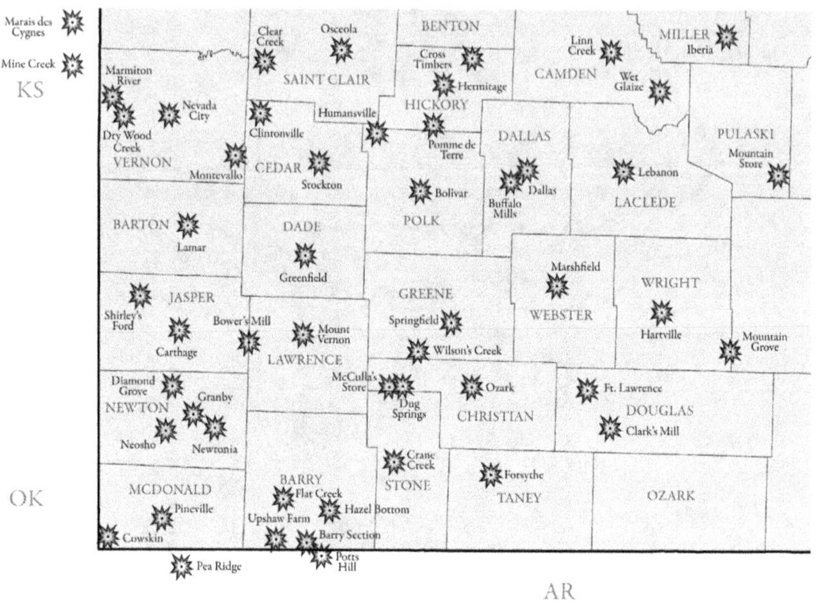

Civil War Engagements in Southwest Missouri. Courtesy of Danielle Kilmer.

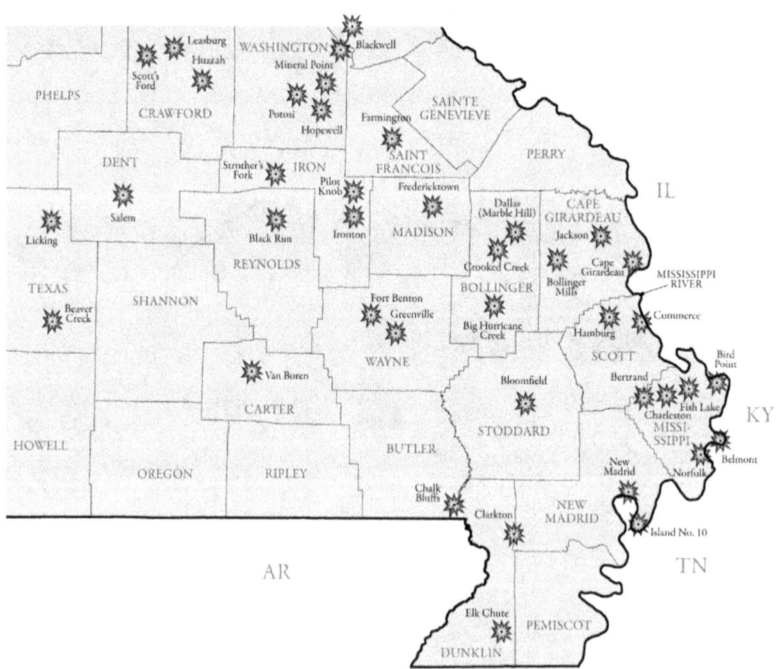

Civil War Engagements in Southeast Missouri. Courtesy of Danielle Kilmer.

ACTIONS IN 1861

FEBRUARY Captain Nathaniel Lyon arrives in St. Louis from Kansas with a company of federal soldiers to enhance defense of the arsenal. His immediate concern for the safety of the St. Louis Arsenal creates animosity between Lyon and his superior, Brigadier General William Harney, current commander of the Department of the West. Lyon persuades editor of the *Missouri Democrat* (an influential Republican newspaper in St. Louis) and Missouri politician Congressman Francis P. Blair, an outspoken opponent to secession, to assign Lyon to command the federal arsenal.

The Confederate States of America is formed in Montgomery, Alabama, by six southern states that had seceded after Lincoln's election.

In late February 1861, a Missouri State Constitutional Convention convenes to decide the matter of whether or not to secede from the Union.

MARCH 4 Abraham Lincoln is inaugurated as the sixteenth president of the United States.

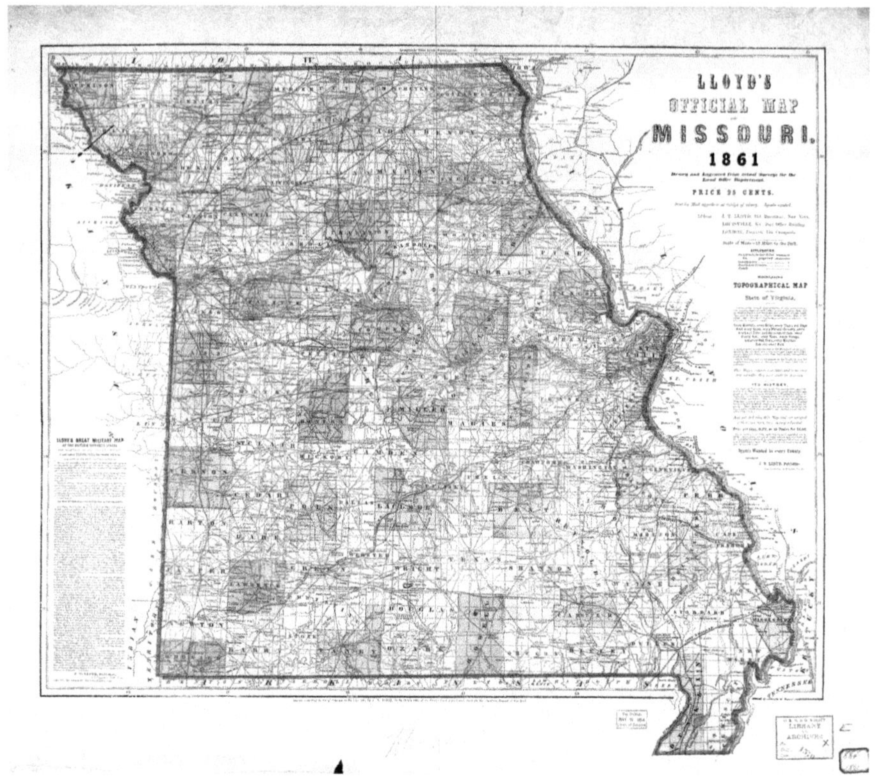

Lloyd's Official Map of Missouri 1861. Courtesy of the Library of Congress.

MARCH The Missouri special Constitutional Convention votes overwhelmingly, ninety-eight to one, to not secede from the Union and remain a neutral state. In addition, the convention decides to not supply weapons or men to either side if war broke out. President Lincoln had rejected neutrality very early in his presidency but only publicly announces it at a special session of Congress on July 4, 1861.

A Federal Relations Committee is established, and Hamilton Rowan Gamble is named as chairman. The committee recognizes the strong Southern sentiment in Missouri, but secession is considered too dangerous an undertaking.

APRIL 12–13 Union-held Fort Sumter in Charleston Harbor is bombarded by Confederate forces and surrenders the following day.

Lincoln calls on the states to muster troops to serve in the Federal army. Virginia, North Carolina, Tennessee and Arkansas refuse and join the Confederacy. Missouri governor Claiborne Jackson rejects Lincoln's call to raise troops from the state of Missouri to serve the Federal army. Jackson gains legislative authority over the St. Louis Police Board and appoints pro-Southern sympathizers. Lyon suspects that Jackson intends to gain control of the Federal arsenal.

The War Department authorizes Lyon and Blair to raise several regiments (primarily German pro-Union sympathizers). General Harney travels to Washington to protest the raising of the German Home Guard.

ACTION: The United States Army arsenal is seized at Liberty, Missouri, by pro-secessionist sympathizers, Clay County, April 20, 1861

ACTION: Governor Claiborne Jackson calls out the Missouri Volunteer Militia for "maneuvers" northwest of the St. Louis Arsenal at Lindell's Grove (current location of the campus of St. Louis University), May 1, 1861

A pro-Southern Missouri Volunteer Militia under the direction of Southern sympathizer Governor Claiborne Jackson and General Daniel Frost establishes Camp Jackson (current location of St. Louis University) for the purpose of conducting annual military training. Confederate president Jefferson Davis ships cannons and muskets to arm volunteers for the purpose of seizing the Federal arsenal in St. Louis; however, most of the weapons had already been transferred for safekeeping in Alton, Illinois.

Action: Ordnance stores are seized in Kansas City, Jackson County, May 4, 1861

Action: Pro-secessionist forces muster at Camp Jackson, St. Louis, early May 1861

Captain Nathaniel Lyon and Colonel Francis P. Blair secure the St. Louis arsenal for the Union. Correspondence from Captain Nathaniel Lyon to General Daniel Frost establishes the intent of the Federal forces in St. Louis to enforce a directive from Washington to order the immediate disbanding of any pro-Southern secessionist organization, specifically referring to the pro-Southern militia at Camp Jackson.

Action: Camp Jackson Affair Massacre, St. Louis Riots, May 10, 1861

Federal forces commander Captain Nathaniel Lyon and approximately six thousand regulars and volunteer militia surround the Missouri Volunteer Militia, at Camp Jackson. Pro-Southern sympathizer volunteers under the command of General Daniel Frost's refuse to take an oath of allegiance. Captain Lyon arrests and marches more than six hundred prisoners through the streets of St. Louis to the St. Louis Arsenal. Violent protests by pro-secessionist residents against primarily German militia volunteers erupt and cause the indiscriminate killing of twenty-eight and wounding of dozens more civilians (including women and children). Later, martial law is imposed after retributions are taken against German volunteers returning to their families. Former army officers and fellow West Point grads Ulysses S. Grant and William T. Sherman, unaware of the high military commands they would hold in the later phases of the war, observe the violent riots in St. Louis.

Union Casualties: 4
Confederate Casualties: 27

May 11 The Missouri General Assembly approves legislation to create a force for the purpose of resisting invasion and suppressing rebellion, primarily against Federal forces.

May 12 Federal forces commander General William S. Harney agrees to a truce, spelling out responsibilities for maintaining order and protecting the rights of citizens in the respective areas state and Federal forces control.

May 13 Missouri General Assembly authorizes the governor to take possession of all railroads and telegraph lines.

May 14 Missouri General Assembly enacts the Militia Act, providing for the organization, government and support of militia forces, the "Missouri State Guard," as well as the organization of "Home Guards" for local service. The formation of "armed clubs" or other military organizations is prohibited. The act further specifies that the Missouri State Guard constitute all able-bodied white males between the ages of eighteen and forty-five enrolled or liable for duty. Missouri is divided into nine military districts, each commanded by a brigadier general to be elected by the commissioned officers of the line in the district.

Home Guard forces are to be appointed by the division inspector or his assistant of the district and would remain and perform military service in the county of the district. The Home Guards consist of males between the age of fourteen and eighteen, with the consent of their parents, and those over the age of forty-five who were competent to serve. The county where these men served would be responsible for their expenses.

May 18 The Militia Act provides for one commander of the Missouri State Guard, who will serve with the rank of major general. Sterling Price, a former governor of Missouri and veteran of the Mexican-American War, is appointed. General Price assumes command, appoints his staff and forms the Missouri State Guard, with headquarters in Jefferson City.

May 21 The Price-Harney Truce—The Federal commander General Harney accommodates Jackson and Price by agreeing to not interfere with the raising of the Missouri State Guard. This will cause Colonel Francis Blair to enact Lincoln's authorization to remove General Harney from command. The War Deparment promotes Nathaniel Lyon to brigadier general and assigns him command of all federal forces in Missouri.

MAY 30 Brigadier General Nathaniel Lyon formally takes command of the Department of the West.

JUNE 11 A conference is held at the Planters House Hotel, on Fourth Street near Chestnut and Pine Streets, between Missouri governor Claiborne Jackson, General Sterling Price and Brigadier General Nathaniel Lyon to work out differences regarding purpose of the Missouri State Guard and the Home Guard. The differences prove irreconcilable and result in a break in relations between the Federal commander, General Lyon, and pro-Southern sympathizer Governor Jackson and his followers. Governor Jackson and General Price immediately depart for Jefferson City and call out the Missouri State Guard to defend Missouri against any invasion by the Federal government. An armed rebellion is on the verge of erupting in Missouri.

TOURISM NOTES: There are many informative Civil War historical sites to visit in St. Louis. Several noted figures are laid to rest in St. Louis cemeteries. Dred Scott and the Union army's second-most venerated general, William Tecumseh Sherman, are buried at Calvary Cemetery. New York City had laid claim to Sherman upon his death in 1891, but according to the St. *Louis Post Dispatch*, "while New York City wanted to lay claim to the hero's corpse, his clearly articulated wish was to be buried in St. Louis." St. Louis is where he was commissioned as a Union officer and spent a considerable part of his life.

Next to Calvary Cemetary is Bellefontaine Cemetery, with more than fifty notable Civil War grave sites exist, including senior military officers Generals John Pope, Sterling Price, Francis Blair, Andrew Jackson Smith (victor over legendary Confederate cavalry officer Nathan Bedford Forrest at Tupelo, Mississippi), Don Carlos Buell and Meriwether Lewis Clark (who is buried next to his father, famous Louisiana Purchase explorer Wlliam Clark). Other notables include Missouri governer Hamilton Gamble, Union naval vessel builder James B. Eads and Brigadier General Albert Gallatin Edwards (who introduced Lincoln to his wife's sister, Mary Todd.) A self-guided tour brochure of the cemetery can be obtained at the cemetery's front office.

The St. Louis Arsenal, the focus of the eventual outbreak of hostilities during the Camp Jackson action, is the current location of the St. Louis Air Force Station.

Jefferson Barracks Military Post is in the U.S. National Register of Historic Places and served as an active military post from 1826 to 1946.

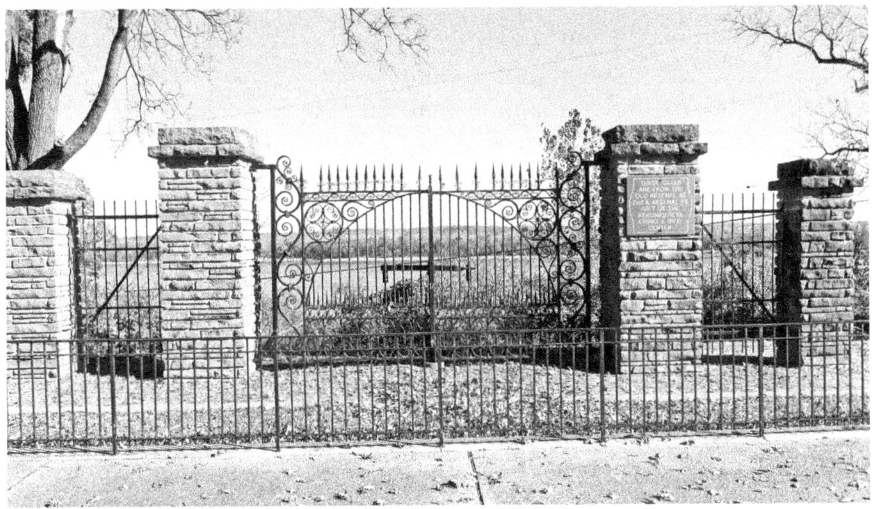

Arsenal gates, St. Louis. *Courtesy of Whit McCoskrie.*

The post was at one time the West's most important military installation, originally selected for its strategic location overlooking the Mississippi River. Two museums exist on post, including a multimillion-dollar renovation of a one-hundred-year-old three-story barracks building that houses the Missouri Civil War Museum, which opened in 2013.

Jefferson Barracks National Cemetery is the location of one of the largest national cemeteries and the resting place for more of Missouri's Civil War veterans than any other. Jefferson Barracks National Cemetery was established after the Civil War as part of a program to create a system of military cemeteries. There are more than eighteen thousand interments on 331 acres overlooking the Mississippi River. Veterans interred date back to the Revolutionary War, notably Colonel Thomas Hunt, a militiaman at Lexington and Concord, Massachusetts, and the Siege of Yorktown; Peter Cook, the last living veteran of the Spanish-American War; two Medal of Honor recipients; and veterans from almost every conflict since its formation. Both sites can be easily reached by taking I-270 south from I-70. I-270 leads into I-255, where you take the MO 231 Exit and head north on Telegraph Road to the entrance on Sheridan Road.

Downtown St. Louis, looking directly at the St. Louis Arch, is the historic Old Courthouse, where Dred Scott and his wife, Harriet, sued and were granted their initial freedom in 1846–47. *Dred Scott v. Emerson* was a landmark decision. Although overturned by a two to one vote in the

Supreme Court of Missouri and ten years later at the U.S. Supreme Court, the ruling further inflamed pro- and antislavery sympathizers, eventually leading to the passing of the draconian Fugitive Slave Act in 1850. The courthouse, restored to its original condition, is run by the National Park Service, provides an informative venue regarding Missouri's frontier history and is open daily for tours. The St. Louis Arch in the background provides a spectacular daytime and evening view contrasting old and new St. Louis. The Old Courthouse is located on North Fourth Street, just a few blocks from the Busch Stadium.

One of the oldest historic structures, the Mercantile Library, has hosted illustrious speakers like Mark Twain, Ralph Waldo Emerson and Oscar Wilde. Primarily used as a research library for faculty and students of Washington University, it later became the repository for major historical collections of books, papers and other important cultural works. In 1998,

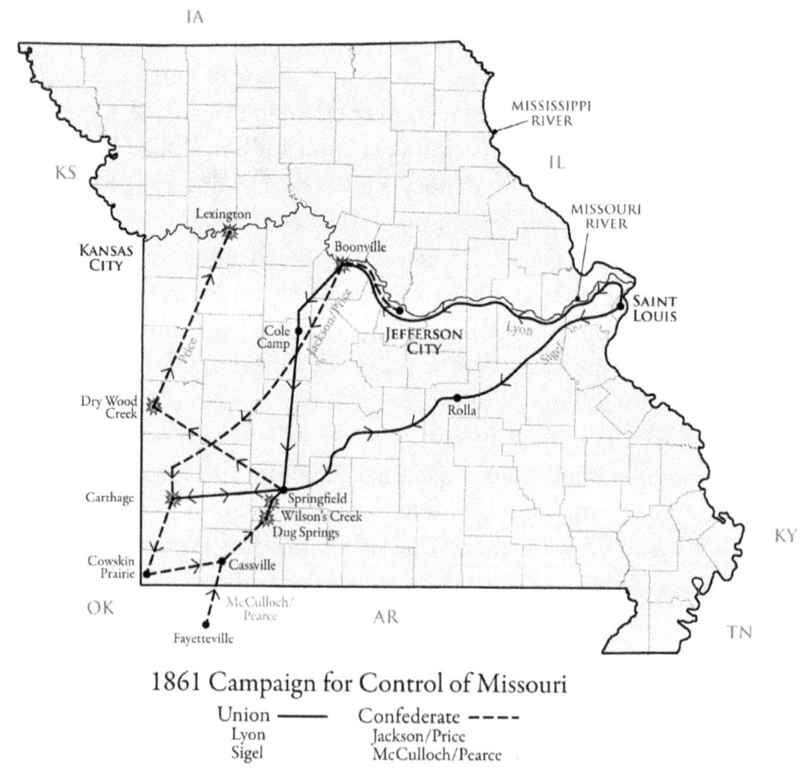

1861 Campaign for Control of Missouri. Courtesy of Danielle Kilmer.

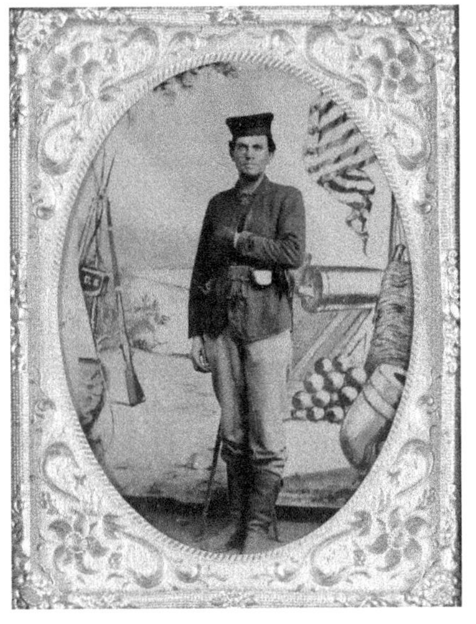

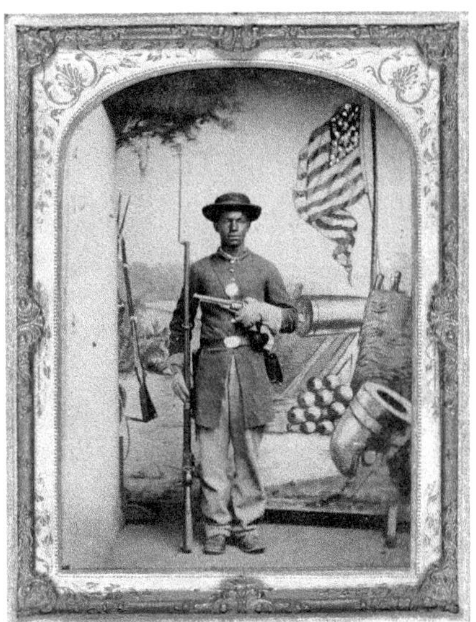

Left: Unidentified "First Scotch Regiment" Union soldier at Benton Barracks, St. Louis. *Courtesy of the Library of Congress.*

Right: Unidentified African American Union soldier at Benton Barracks, St. Louis. *Courtesy of the Library of Congress.*

it was moved to the current location in the Thomas Jefferson Library Building at the University of Missouri–St. Louis, where its collections are available to the public.

Before the war, Ulysses S. Grant struggled to operate a farm in St. Louis called White Haven, the childhood home of his wife, Julia Dent. It is now a National Historic Site administered by the National Park Service. Grant worked the farm site alongside an enslaved workforce from 1854 to 1859. The financial Panic of 1857 and ensuing Depression forced Grant to relocate his family in order to work for his brothers in Galena, Illinois. In St. Louis, the National Park Service operates an informative museum and visitor center and provides tours of five restored structures, including the Dent Home, an excellect historical remnant of how St. Louisans lived and worked during that period. The site is located ten miles southeast of St. Louis. Take I-44 to I-270, then south on I-270 to Highway 30 (Gravois Road) and follow the signs to the entrance.

An important Union army encampment, Benton Barracks, is the site of the Old St. Louis Fairgrounds Park, approximately 132 acres that later hosted the city's first zoo, horse racing and many other attractions. Later in the 1950s, a bond issue financed a new public swimming pool, baseball diamonds and tennis courts. It has unfortunately gone the way of so many inner-city parks due to a deteriorating city tax base. It is located at the northwest corner of Grand Boulevard and Natural Bridge Avenue.

ACTION: Federal forces seize state government at Jefferson City, Cole County, June 14, 1861

Federal commander Brigadier General Nathaniel Lyon transports his military force down the Missouri River, captures Jefferson City and assembles a new state government. Governor Jackson and General Sterling Price's Missouri State Guard forces had already evacuated upriver to the town of Boonville.

Union Casualties: 21
Confederate Casualties: 34

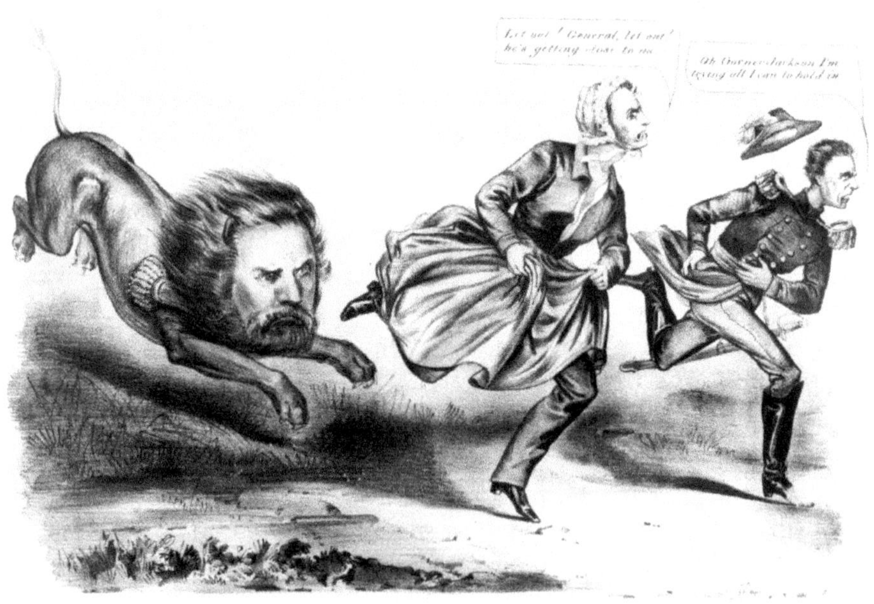

The Battle of Booneville, or the great Missouri "Lyon" hunt. *Courtesy of the Library of Congress.*

TOURISM NOTES: Directly in front of the state capitol building on High Street is an informative panel covering the tensions over Missouri's pre–Civil War and early Civil War history, along with a map of fortifications constructed by Federal forces regarding defense of the state capitol facilities.

ACTION: Battle of Boonville, Cooper County, June 17, 1861

General Lyon immediately pursues Governor Claiborne Jackson and General Sterling Price's Missouri State Guard up the Missouri River. Lyon transports approximately 1,700 Union troops to a port eight miles below the city of Boonville and disembarks his Federal forces. General Price had gone on to Lexington, leaving Governor Jackson without his most experienced military officer. Five hundred of Colonel John Marmaduke's 1st Missouri Rifles, Missouri State Guard soldiers, are positioned to block Lyon's forces approach to Boonville along the Rocheport Road. Marmaduke's poorly prepared and ill-equipped forces are pushed back by better-equipped Union forces of the 1st and 2nd Missouri Infantry accompanied by artillery support. The retreat of the Missouri State Guard turns into a rout after a feeble attempt to rally is shattered by Union gunboat cannon fire from the Missouri River. Union forces occupy Boonville, confiscating abandoned Missouri State Guard equipment and supplies. Confederate forces of Governor Claiborne Jackson and General Sterling Price depart Boonville and move southwest to linkup with Confederate forces from Arkansas and Texas.

Union Casualties: 12
Confederate Casualties and Losses: 75–95

WHY IT MATTERS: Considered by local historians as the first Civil War land battle. Governor Claiborne Jackson's desire to gain support for Missouri's admittance to the Confederacy was stymied, and he was removed from office the following month at the Missouri State Convention and replaced with Hamilton Gamble. The ease with which Lyon's forces brushed aside Governor Jackson's poorly prepared Missouri State Guard and the subsequent report by a local newspaper of the governor watching the battle safely perched on a hill away from the engagement brought his leadership in time of war into question. The Union maintained control of the Missouri River, a key center of gravity denied to the Confederacy.

Tourism Notes: Military engagements in Boonville are included in the Gray Ghost Trail Missouri Civil War Heritage Trail Maps. In addition, the Missouri Civil War Heritage Foundation and Boonville Tourism Commission have positioned several informative panels in and around Booneville. The First Battle of Boonville interpretive panel is located half a mile east on East Morgan Street on the north side of the Boonville Correctional Center (http://www.thecivilwarmuse.com/index.php?page=battle-of-boonville-historical-marker). A helpful guide to Civil War actions in this region can be found at the Old Trails Region website (http://oldtrails.net/civil-war-tour.html). A small stone marker for the Union army landing site of General Lyon, Merna Marker, is located next to railroad tracks near the Missouri River south of Boonville. Directions to the Merna Parking Area can be found at http://www.thecivilwarmuse.com/index.php?page=federals-disembark. Depending on the terrain conditions, visitors may want to take an off-road vehicle.

Action: Skirmish at Independence, Jackson County, June 17, 1861

Minor skirmish by Missouri volunteers under Captain Stanley.

Action: Battle of Cole Camp, Benton County, June 19, 1861

A Benton County Home Guard force of approximately 400 to 600 men under Colonel Abel Cook attempt to obstruct Governor Jackson's retreat from Boonville to southwest Missouri. Home Guard forces are easily pushed aside by a secessionist force of 350 "Warsaw Grays" under the command of Lieutenant Colonel Walter O'Kane, enabling Jackson's Missouri State Guard to continue southwest in order to link up with Confederate forces from Arkansas and Texas.

Union Casualties and Losses: 40–120
Confederate Casualties: 24

Tourism Notes: Just south of Highway 52, in downtown Cole Camp, the historical museum retells the events of the Confederate victory.

Action: Murder near Martinsburg, Audrain County (dates vary between June and August 1861)

According to the history of Audrain County, Alvin Cobb, a one-armed bushwhacker, and his small band ambushed a Major Ben Sharp and Lieutenant A. Jaeger near Martinsburg. Injured in the attack, the two officers flee to the nearby town of Martinsburg, where some local citizens attempt to aid the wounded men. Subsequently, Cobb and his men ride up, move aside the citizens and place Sharp and Jaeger on horses, whereupon they are transported away from town. One week later, the captured men are found in a shallow grave four miles from Martinsburg.

Biographical Sketch: Captain Alvin Cobb supposedly received a commission in the Missouri State Guard. Cobb fits the quintessential definition of a bushwhacker masquerading as a guerrilla leader. A farmer from a settlement called Cobbtown, near Wellsville, Montgomery County, conspicuously carried a hook in place of an arm lost in a hunting or farming accident. A local story that has survived over time relates that it was only the confession of Mrs. Alvin Cobb that connected Alvin with the murder of Major Sharp and Lieutenant Jaeger. The execution of Sharp and Jaegar caused a vicious response in Montgomery and Callaway Counties by Union patrols against suspected Southern sympathizers. In one such case, three local citizens were executed. Cobb continued to develop a reputation for executing pro-Union citizens, ambushing Union patrols and destroying rail lines. Cobb is also connected to skirmishes at Overton Run to Fulton, Mount Zion, Battle of Moore's Mill and probably the raid on Danville. Union forces finally drove Cobb out of Missouri, after which it is believed he met up with Stand Watie's Cherokee Confederates in Indian Territory.

Campaign: Operations to control Missouri, July–October, 1861

Action: Battle of Carthage or Battle of Dry Forks, Jasper County, July 5, 1861

On July 1, Colonel Franz Sigel with 1,100 Union soldiers marches north from Neosho, Missouri, to intercept Governor Claiborne Jackson and General Sterling Price's pro-secessionist forces withdrawing south from Boonville. Approximately ten miles north of Carthage, Colonel Sigel makes contact and commences fire on Confederate positions with his artillery. A small vanguard of 150 partisan rangers under Captain Joseph Shelby, supported by Confederate cannons, executes a frontal attack on Union positions. Sigel, fearing that he is facing a much larger force than originally believed (6,000 Missouri State Guardsmen, although only two-thirds were probably armed), orders a general retreat to the outskirts of Carthage and into the town square, where heavy fighting then takes place. Colonel Sigel, gravely concerned of the possibility of being flanked, withdraws to link up with General Nathaniel Lyon's main body camped southwest of Springfield. Historians have criticized Sigel's assessment of the situation and leadership ability when he chose to pull back without ascertaining the Missouri State Guard force's true fighting capacity. Claiborne Jackson, no longer obstructed by Union forces, moves his Rebel force south to link up with Texas forces under Colonel Benjamin McCulloch.

For more information, eleven official reports can be found in the *The War of the Rebellion: A Compilation of the Official Records.*

Union Casualties: 44
Confederate Casualties and Losses: 200

WHY IT MATTERS: This was the first major engagement after President Abraham Lincoln invoked his war powers on July 4, 1861. Carthage was also the only military action featuring a sitting state governor leading state militia troops into battle against the Federal government. The Confederate victory at Carthage encouraged pro-secessionist recruiting in Missouri.

Carthage would also be the scene of several more military actions, on March 23, 1862; November 27, 1862; January 13, 1863; June 27–28, 1863; September 6, 1863; October 2 and 18, 1863; July 21, 1864; and September 22, 1864.

TOURISM NOTES: The site of the Battle of Carthage is located on a seven-acre State Historical Site just off US 71. Take Garrison Avenue exit south to East Chestnut Street, turn east and proceed to Carter Park. An information kiosk of the battle is provided next to the visitor parking.

The Carthage Civil War Museum is located at 205 Grant Street. Tourists can view a detailed miniature layout of the battle. The museum also contains many interesting displays describing African American and American Indian involvement, among other topics. Open Tuesday–Saturday 8:30 a.m.–5:00 p.m. and Sunday 1:00 p.m.–5:00 p.m.; admittance is free.

ACTION: Raid on Neosho, Newton County, July 5, 1861—*OR*, Captain Joseph Conrad, 3rd Missouri Infantry, July 11, 1861

Union forces under the command of Captain Joseph Conrad are surprised and overwhelmed by a superior Confederate force of Brigadier General Benjamin McCulloch under the command of Colonel Thomas J. Churchill and Major James McQueen McIntosh. Union forces surrender and are subsequently released after swearing an oath to not take up arms against the Confederate States of America. The released Union soldiers march a grueling eighty-five miles to Springfield in fifty hours with little food or water, arriving exhausted and demoralized.

Union Casualties and Losses: 80

ACTION: Skirmish at Florida, Monroe County, July 8, 1861

Missouri Union forces surprise and disperse a small Confederate camp.

ACTION: Destruction of Salt River Bridge, Monroe County, July 10–17, 1861

Colonel Ulysses S. Grant's 21st Illinois Regiment departs Quincy, Illinois, to provide protection against the Confederate forces of Colonel Thomas Harris.

ACTION: Skirmishes in and near Monroe Station, July 11, 1861—*OR*, Colonel Robert F. Smith, 16th Illinois Infantry, July 14, 1861

Elements of the 16th Illinois, 3rd Iowa and Hannibal Home Guard encounter a Rebel force twelve miles south of Monroe Station. Union artillery engage and scatter the Rebel forces. Union forces withdraw to Monroe Station and prepare to defend against a larger Rebel force estimated at 1,500 to 2,000 Confederates. Union artillery prevent Rebel forces from successfully capturing Monroe Station. Rebel leaders order a withdrawal upon learning of Union reinforcements approaching from the east by train.

Union Casualties: 3
Confederate Casualties and Losses: 99

Action: Skirmish at Mexico, Audrain County, July 15, 1861

Minor skirmish involving Union forces of the Missouri 2nd Infantry.

Action: Raiding of Federal troop trains near Wentzville, St. Charles County, July 15–17, 1861

According to local historian Emmett P. Taylor, Wentzville was an important depot for the Northern Missouri Railroad and the vicinity, subject to harassing skirmishes from marauding bushwhackers. In late June, elements of the 2nd and 8th Missouri Infantry are sent west by rail from St. Louis to Mexico, Missouri, to link up with Colonel Franz Sigel. The Union troop train stops at Wentzville for dinner before continuing its journey. After departing Wentzville, bushwhackers immediately conduct harassing attacks on the train, injuring several Union soldiers. Union troops are unable to find any bushwhackers and return to Wentzville to care for the wounded at the Wentzville Hotel (the current location of the West Allen Grill).

Union troops proceed again by rail the next morning and repulse three more attacks by the Missouri bushwhackers before arriving at their destination in Mexico, Missouri.

Union Casualties: estimated at 37
Confederate Casualties: unknown

TOURISM NOTES: Cannonballs found near the railroad are displayed at the Wentzville's Historical Society Museum. A historical marker is located at Bicentennial Park west of Linn Avenue on Pearce Boulevard. Wentzville conducts reenactments celebrating this historic event periodically.

ACTION: Skirmish along Overton Run, near Fulton, Callaway County, July 17, 1861

Missouri State Guard forces under Brigadier General Thomas Harris are detected moving through Callaway County to link up with General Sterling Price's Confederate forces. Several companies of the Union 3rd Missouri Reserves (comprising St. Louis Dutch citizens) under the command of Colonel John McNeil and Lieutenant Colonel Adam Hammer heading north from Jefferson City are ambushed by a detachment of Harris's men and local Southern sympathizers. A running engagement commences two miles southwest of Fulton and reaches the town limits, where Confederate forces are dispersed. A local newspaper report of the engagement views it as a Confederate victory, angering Union forces, who retaliate and destroy the newspaper office. Local historians considered this act censorship of the local press to squelch disloyal Southern sentiment.

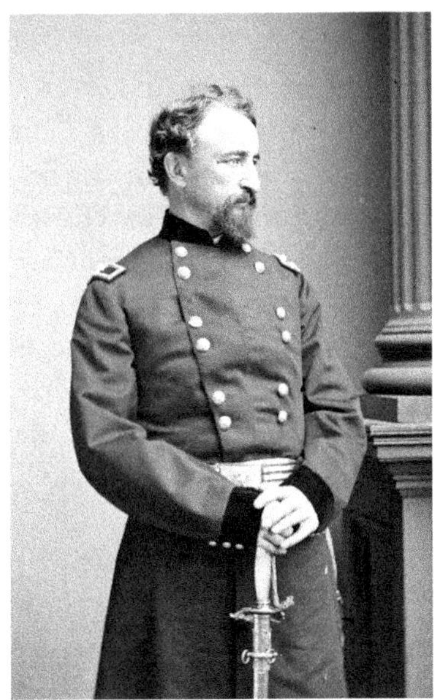

John McNeil. *Courtesy of the Library of Congress.*

Union Casualties: 16
Confederate Casualties: unknown

TOURISM NOTES: Callaway County has a very active Civil War heritage organization that has created several tourism stops in the county to educate visitors about the local history of Callaway County's involvement in the Civil War. The website www.callawaycivilwar.org has a link to these sites, where visitors will discover informative panels about the Civil War in Callaway County and its bitter aftermath.

The Missouri Civil War Heritage Foundation has published several informative Civil War map guides. There currently exists three Grant Trail Maps: northeast Missouri, southeast Missouri and a southeast Missouri/western Kentucky. These three colorful brochures and the Gray Ghost Trail Map of central Missouri can be downloaded and printed from mocivilwar.org/travelers. The reference to "Gray Ghost" symbolizes the strong Southern sentiment and partisan resistance in central Missouri that earned several counties in the mid-Missouri region the nickname "Little Dixie."

ACTION: Series of minor skirmishes at Martinsburg, Audrain County, July 15, 17–18, 1861

Union Casualties: 2
Confederate Casualties: unknown

ACTION: Skirmish at Harrisonville and Parkersville, Cass County, July 18–19, 1861—*OR*, Major R.T. Van Horn, Missouri Reserve Corps, August 3, 1861

Major Robert Van Horn's battalion, U.S. Reserve Corps, takes two companies of soldiers, approximately 150 men, from Camp Union to relieve a Major Dean of the Cass County Home Guards in Austin, Missouri. Five miles north of Harrisonville, while encamped, Van Horn's men are approached by a sizeable force of suspected Southern sympathizers commanded by Colonel Theodore Duncan from Jackson County. Van Horn is informed that Union forces are not welcome in the area and is directed to leave. Within minutes of Major Van Horn's return to his troops, now positioned along a tree line, the forces of Colonel Duncan engage the Rebel forces with rifle fire and maneuver on his flank and rear. Duncan's forces are repulsed but do not retire until sundown.

Additional Confederate forces of approximately one hundred men are next detected in the rear of Union forces. Van Horn's initial plan is to cut timber and prepare defensive positions until a shortage of ammunition makes an effective defense improbable. Major Van Horn conducts a successful evacuation of their location early the next morning and successfully crosses his force over the swollen Grand River. Union forces continue their march southwest to the Kansas state line to link up with reinforcements from Colonel William Weer.

Union Casualties: 15
Confederate Casualties: 2

Tourism Notes: Camp Union was a cavalry barracks constructed on a pasture that Kersey Coates had selected to develop a hotel. It is the current location of the historic Coates House Hotel, Quality Hill Apartments, downtown Kansas City, Missouri.

The Burnt District Museum highlights the history of Harrisonville and other communities in Cass County. The area was a site of constant skirmishing, attributed much to William Quantrill utilizing Cass County as a base to launch much of his raiding before the raid on Lawrence in 1863. General Order No. 11 forced homesteaders living with one mile of Harrisonville or Pleasant Hill to vacate their homes in fifteen days. Most homesteads were burned to the ground prior to the Union confiscation of grain, hay and other food supplies. Municipal rule was not reestablished until 1867. Cole Younger's father was the mayor in 1859.

Action: Expedition from Springfield, Missouri, July 20–25, 1861, Battle of Forsyth, Taney County, July 22, 1861—*OR*, Brigadier General T.W. Sweeney, U.S. Army, Headquarters Southwest Expedition, Springfield, July 27, 1861

After departing Springfield and traveling forty-five miles in a little over two days, Brigadier General T.W. Sweeney's advance guard of Kansas Rangers encounter and capture two Confederate pickets three and a half miles outside the town of Forsythe. General Sweeney sends his mounted units and encircles Forsyth. Initial Confederate resistance is squelched by Union artillery fire, forcing an estimated 150 Rebels into the surrounding hillsides. Forsyth is occupied by Union forces, who capture considerable contraband and supplies.

Union Casualties: 2
Confederate Casualties and Losses: 15

Action: Skirmish at Blue Mills, Jackson County, July 24, 1861—Missouri 5th Reserve Corps

Union Casualties: 13

Action: Skirmish at Lane's Prairie, north of Rolla, Phelps County, July 26, 1861

Union Home Guard skirmish against local bushwhackers and guerrillas.

Union Casualties: 3
Confederate Casualties: 4

Action: Skirmish at McCulla's Store, Christian County, July 26, August 3, 1861

Minor skirmishes of several small detachments prior to the Battle of Wilson's Creek are conducted along the Fayetteville Road, twenty-four miles southwest of Springfield.

Action: Skirmish at Dug Springs, Christian County, August 2, 1861

Confederate cavalry forces encounter a large portion of the main Union force under Brigadier General Nathaniel Lyon encamped approximately twenty miles southwest of Springfield, Missouri, and withdraw south toward McCulla's Store on the Fayetteville Road. A small skirmish takes place the next morning, but Lyon, unaware of the exact Confederate location and strength and deep in hostile territory, decides to withdraw back toward Springfield.

Authors' Assessment: Dense undergrowth, unfamiliar terrain and lack of clear intelligence of Confederate troop strength and location appear to persuade General Nathaniel Lyon to show caution and not get drawn

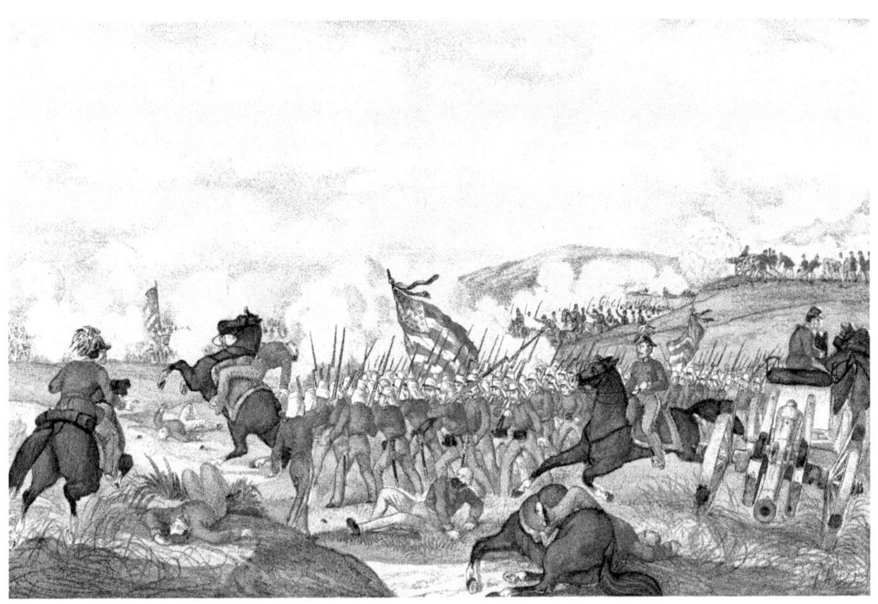

Death of General Nathaniel Lyon during the battle at Wilson's Creek, Missouri. *Courtesy of the Library of Congress.*

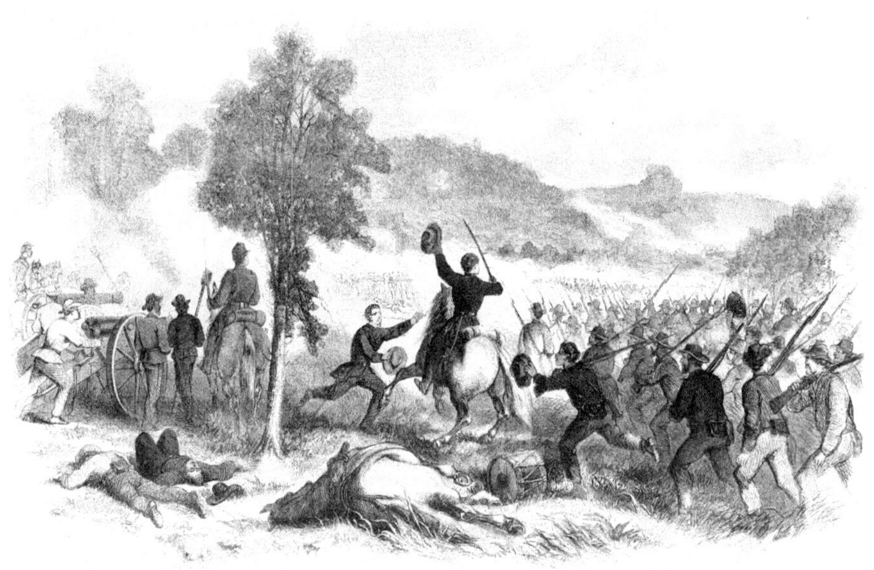

Charge of the 1st Iowa Regiment, with General Lyon at its head, at the Battle of Wilson's Creek. *Courtesy of the Library of Congress.*

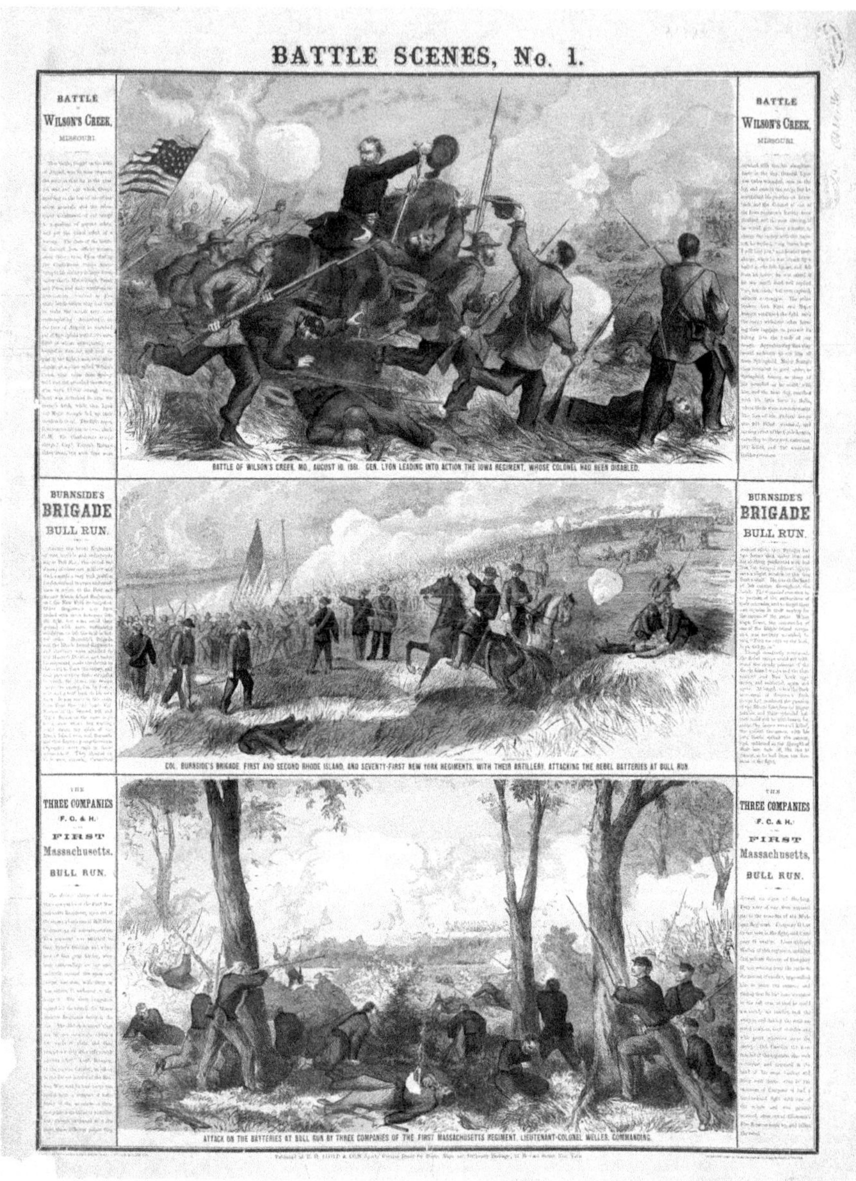

Battle of Wilson's Creek, Missouri, August 10, 1861. *Courtesy of the Library of Congress.*

into an engagement on unfavorable conditions. Lyon's initial caution dissipates as he gains more reliable information on Confederate force troop strength and location. Expiring enlistments and a debilitating bout of diarrhea from too much beef may have influenced Lyon to change course and launch a surprise attack against a much larger Rebel force five days later at Wilson's Creek.

Union Casualties: 41
Confederate Casualties: 84

ACTION: Battle at Wilson's Creek (Oak Hill), Greene County and Christian County, August 10, 1861

General Nathaniel Lyon's army of approximately six thousand Union troops conducts a surprise attack from two directions in the early morning hours on a Confederate encampment southwest of Springfield, Missouri. Approximately ten to twelve thousand Missouri, Arkansas and Texas Confederate soldiers under Generals Sterling Price and Benjamin McCulloch repulse the initial attacks of Union forces. Confederate fortunes improve when the Union brigade under Colonel Franz Sigel, attacking from the South, misjudges an approaching Confederate force for Union reinforcements and holds fire. Too late in recognizing his mistake, Sigel is driven off and fails to send word to Lyon. General Lyon is killed leading a counterattack in the late morning on Bloody Hill. Although Union forces successfully repel three Confederate counterattacks during nearly five hours of intense fighting, heavy casualties and extremely hot temperatures force the new Federal commander, Major Samuel Sturgis, to withdraw to the Union supply base in Rolla. Confederate forces occupy Springfield, but the lack of sufficient facilities for the care of the wounded and exhaustion of the remaining Rebel forces prevent a possible pursuit.

Union Casualties and Losses: 1,317 (21 percent)
Confederate Casualties and Losses: 1,230 (13 percent)

For more detail, forty official reports from regimental commanders and staff can be found in the *The War of the Rebellion: A Compilation of the Official Records.*

WHY IT MATTERS: The Battle of Wilson's Creek was the first major battle of the Civil War west of the Mississippi River and established which side would control southwestern Missouri and utilize its rich natural resources. For soldiers who had not experienced real fighting, the bloodshed at Wilson's

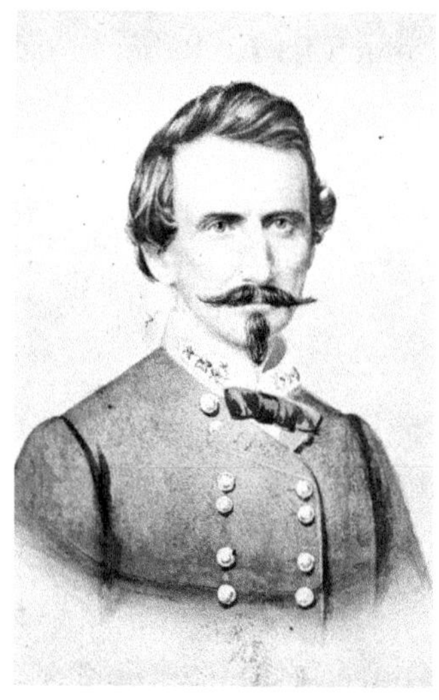

Benjamin McCulloch. *Courtesy of the Library of Congress.*

Creek is a precursor of the heavy casualties both sides suffered over the ensuing four and half years. Union and Confederate leadership demonstrated inexperience in planning by not recognizing a critical need for a medical director and ambulances to remove the wounded. Just two ambulances were all that was provided by Union leadership for a battle that produced crippling casualties to more than 20 percent of its soldiers. Communication challenges also hindered both sides' ability to control operations.

Readers may find that fate often influenced the course of many engagements. In the case of Wilson's Creek, the two Confederate leaders, General Sterling Price and Benjamin McCulloch, were eating breakfast together when General Lyon initiated the surprise attack. Both leaders quickly coordinated the repositioning of Rebel forces to counter the Union threat. Another problem that confounded Union leaders in the West was that Confederate forces wore a variety of uniforms and not all Union forces wore blue. This was true at Wilson's Creek, causing confusion for Colonel Franz Sigel at a critical point of the battle.

The Battle of Wilson's Creek provided an early glimpse at how the conflict in Missouri soon took on the characterization of "total war," as the local population experienced firsthand the occupation of their homes as hospitals. Throughout the conflict, homesteaders were required to provide food to feed both sides. Quite often, homesteaders' farms, livestock and equipment were confiscated by foraging patrols. The decomposing bodies of men and animals required the immediate excavation of mass graves that could possibly have caused the contamination of the local water supply. General Nathaniel Lyon was the first Union general killed during the Civil War. Nine Federal officers involved at Wilson's Creek would later go on to command Union corps or armies. Major General Lyon's chief of staff, Major John Schofield, earned the Medal of Honor for gallantry at Wilson's Creek and in later administrations served as the secretary of war and an influential army chief of staff.

The political challenges after the Union defeat at the Battle of Wilson's Creek are well illustrated by Civil War historian Bruce Catton in *The*

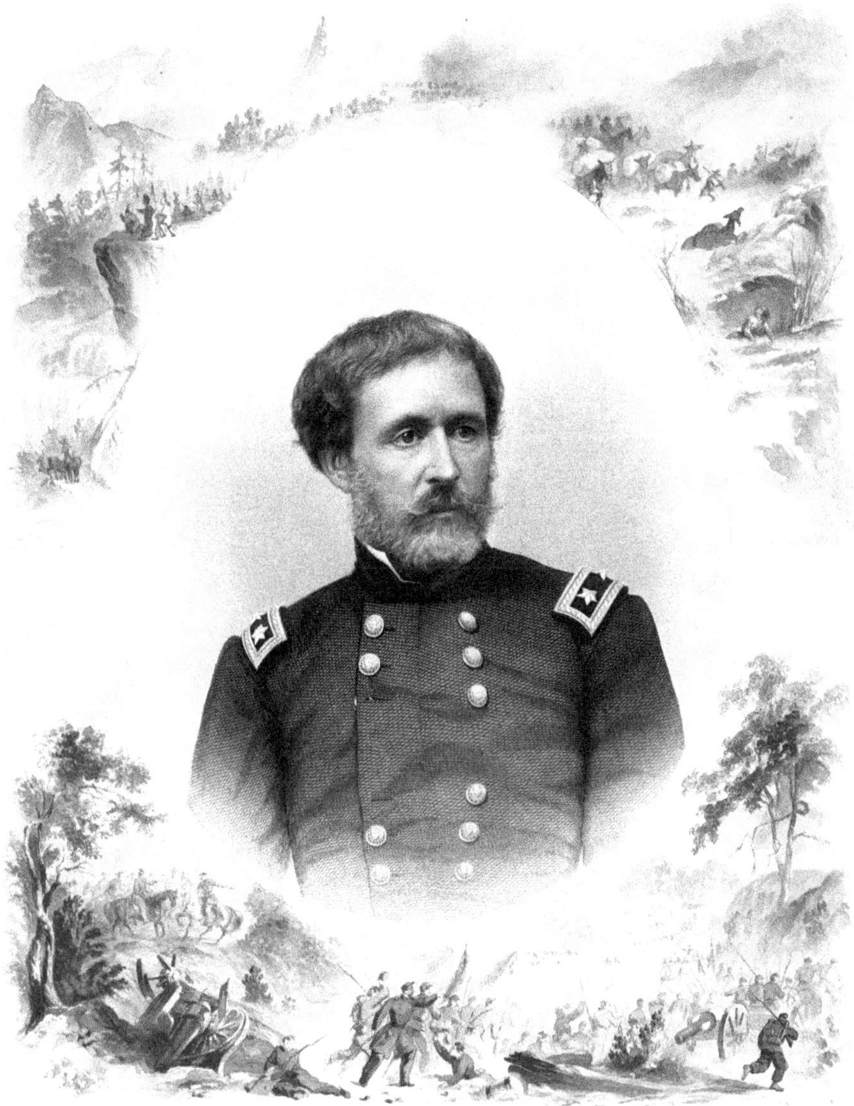

John C. Frémont. *Courtesy of the Library of Congress.*

Coming Fury. Catton highlighted President Lincoln's challenge of finding competent senior leadership. Lincoln was often placed in the position of choosing political expediency over competency in the selection of Federal commanders.

Frémont shared a common hubris with some Union commanders: buying into a narrative of invincibility that came with their celebrity status. John C. Frémont was an accomplished early explorer of the West, particularly in the Rocky Mountains, where a peak is named after him. Frémont became the first senator of California after playing an instrumental role in overthrowing Spanish rule and gaining California's statehood after the Mexican-American War. After Fort Sumter fell, Lincoln accepted the distinguished explorer and politician's offer of service and commissioned him a major general. Although General John C. Frémont was appointed to the Department of the West on July 3, he did not arrive in St. Louis until July 25. His first official action was to immediately begin throwing up entrenchments and sending out a barrage of messages to political leaders and unit commanders with little real direction or coherent strategy. After receiving Lyon's request for reinforcements prior to the battle, Frémont, believing that he was unable to spare any Union soldiers from the defense of St. Louis, recommended Lyon withdraw back to Rolla.

TOURISM NOTES: Wilson's Creek National Battlefield is a well-preserved historic battlefield site administered by the National Park Service approximately ten miles southwest of Springfield near the community of Republic. It is a must-see for Missouri Civil War buffs, particularly those wishing to further understand the circumstances surrounding the breakout of hostilities and the first major battle in Missouri. The United States Army's career officer school at Fort Leavenworth has utilized the Wilson's Creek battlefield as a case study for its military officers to glean historical lessons. University ROTC programs have utilized the Battle of Wilson's Creek for familiarizing officer cadets with the lessons of American military history prior to their appointments as second lieutenants in the United States Army. The visitor center provides numerous exhibits and a lighted three-dimensional geographic map of the battle, accompanied by several displays detailing major military actions in Missouri during the Civil War. The website (www.nps.gov/wicr/index.htm) is informative, and you can download a brochure.

The Wilson's Creek battlefield is open all year and can be reached off I-44 at the Highway 360 exit south of Springfield. The entrance is approximately 3.5 miles south. An informative National Park Service map can be picked up at the visitor center for use on a driving tour that provides numerous stops to view different parts of the battlefield and study the course of events.

ACTION: President Lincoln formally declares the inhabitants of the seceded states to be "in a state of insurrection against the United States," August 16, 1861

ACTION: Major General John C. Frémont proclaims martial law, emancipation of slaves, August 30, 1861

Lincoln grows anxious about Frémont as he learns of stories of extravagance, poor judgment and corruption. It was not unusual for the president to learn of such missteps through a source other than its author. The final straw for the president is General Frémont declaring martial law in Missouri and threatening court-martial and execution of all pro-Southern armed persons found north of an arbitrary line drawn through the state and the forfeiture of all property, including slaves who would be freed. General Frémont shows disregard for the efforts of Governor Hamilton Gamble in restoring civil government when he proclaims, "Circumstances, in my judgment, of sufficient urgency render it necessary that the commanding general of this department should assume the administrative powers of the State." Gamble had offered amnesty in early August to those pro-Southern sympathizers who had taken up arms and were now desirous of returning to their homes peacefully.

On September 2, President Lincoln reminds General Frémont that Congress had granted freedom on August 6 only to those slaves forced to participate by the Confederacy. Frémont delays six days before replying to Lincoln's request to modify the proclamation. Soon after, the Confederate commander of the 1st District of Missouri, General Jeff Thompson, issues a counter-proclamation against any pro-Union sympathizer should Frémont order the death of any Rebel soldier. After further incompetence is displayed during the Confederate Siege of Lexington and during operations to retake southwest Missouri, President Lincoln relieves Frémont on November 2 and appoints General David Hunter to command.

ACTION: Colonel Ulysses S. Grant's early military service in Missouri, June–August 1861

Biographical Sketch: Ulysses S. Grant, an 1843 graduate of the United States Military Academy and distinguished veteran of the Mexican-American War, served uneventfully after the war and retired in 1854. After army service, he struggled financially in business while living in St. Louis. The financial Panic of 1857 and ensuing depression forced Grant to relocate to Galena, Illinois, and assist his two brothers running the family general store.

Grant's remarkable rise to command of all Union armies in 1864 began in Missouri after a short tenure mustering recruits in Illinois. After the firing on and surrender of the Federal garrison at Fort Sumter in April 1861, Illinois immediately responded to President Abraham Lincoln's call for seventy-five thousand troops. After Grant mustered into the Union army a company from his hometown in Galena, the governor of Illinois recognized Grant while in Springfield, knew of his military experience and requested he volunteer for service to Illinois, reporting to the adjutant general's office.

Grant demonstrated an ability to accomplish large organizational tasks and was directed to muster into service ten new regiments from Illinois. During a short stay in St. Louis, Grant observed the first outbreak of hostilities in Missouri. He observed firsthand the bitter and divisive sentiments in St. Louis when pro-Union sympathizers tore down a Rebel flag outside secessionist headquarters on Pine Street near Fifth.

Grant returned to Illinois and was promoted to colonel and assigned command of the 21st Illinois Regiment from Matoon, Illinois. He had been encouraged by fellow West Point graduate Brigadier General John Pope to send a letter offering his service in the Federal army to the adjutant general of the United States. Washington did not respond to Grant's request. Grant also called on Major General George McClellan, headquartered in Cincinnati, but McClellan declined to see him. Grant returned to Illinois and took his first command, the 21st Regiment, to its first duty station at Quincy, Illinois, a railroad transportation hub on the Mississippi River.

Grant's initial operations into Missouri were in response to Confederate raiding in the northeast part of the state. Grant subdued the Confederate forces of Colonel Thomas Harris at Salt River and at the small village of Florida. Grant was then assigned to Mexico, Missouri, responsible for protecting the Northern Missouri Railroad.

In Mexico, Missouri, Colonel Ulysses S. Grant took command of three regiments at a military subdistrict headquarters. Union troops immediately demonstrated that they were undisciplined and poorly trained and lacked competent leadership. Grant arrived and witnessed the terrorizing of local inhabitants forced at gunpoint to take loyalty oaths, as well as the unauthorized seizing of the property and supplies of local citizens. After spending a day studying the current standard army instructional guide, *Hardee's Rifle and Infantry Tactics Manual*, Grant immediately ended the harassment of the local population and commenced drilling the units into a more disciplined military force.

Grant gained the attention of General Frémont, who recognized an "iron will" in Grant's demeanor. When Grant was one of seven nominated for brigadier general from Illinois, he commenced assembling a staff that accompanied him as he advanced to command in the West and ultimately the entire Northern army.

Ulysses S. Grant's follow on assignments of service in Missouri:

- transferred to Ironton, Missouri, and promoted to brigadier general
- ordered to Jefferson City to construct defenses around the capital and protect a large influx of German immigrant fleeing Rebel bushwhackers
- ordered to Cape Girardeau, Missouri, to command the District of Southeast Missouri

Action: Reconnaissance from Ironton, Iron County, to Centreville, Reynolds County, August 2, 1861—*OR*, Colonel B. Gratz Brown, 4th Missouri Infantry (USRC), August 3, 1861

Confederate actions threatening the critical Ironton Railroad line from St. Louis cause Union forces to push out from Ironton in search of marauding Rebel forces. About 150 men from Colonel Franz Karl Hecker's 24th Illinois Volunteer Regiment under the command of Lieutenant Colonel Geza Mihalotzy make contact with a large Rebel force, estimated at 1,700 men, under the command of James McBride. Colonel Hecker immediately dispatches reinforcements to Mihalotzy's detachment, but Union forces quickly return to the protection of fortifications in Ironton.

Action: Battle of Athens, Clark County, August 5, 1861

In the northernmost Missouri engagement of the Civil War west of the Mississippi River, an estimated 330 to 500 men of the 1st Northeast Missouri

Home Guard under Union colonel David Moore defeat approximately 2,000 Missouri State Guard forces under Colonel Martin Greene seeking to capture this Des Moines River port town.

TOURISM NOTES: Several interpretive displays and exhibits explain the action at the Battle of Athens State Historic Site. Directions to the site and a printable copy of a map can be located at https://mostateparks.com/park/battle-athens-state-historic-site.

Union Casualties: 23
Confederate Casualties: 31

WHY IT MATTERS: A Confederate attempt to control a northern port town in Missouri was thwarted by the Union victory.

ACTION: Expedition to Price's Landing, Commerce, Benton and Hamburg, Scott County, August 7–10, 1861

According to the official report of Major John McDonald, one company of 20th Infantry from Illinois and one company of 8th Infantry from Missouri are transported by the steamer *Luella* from Cape Girardeau, twenty-five miles south, with the purpose of finding General Sterling Price and approximately 1,100 Rebels, reported to have been encamped in the area. The only inhabitant of the residence was Price's son, William Price, who is apprehended. Subsequent reports also suspect that several hundred Rebel soldiers under the command of Confederate general Jeff Thompson may be operating in the vicinity.

ACTION: Raid on Potosi, Washington County, August 10, 1861—*OR*, Brigadier General U.S. Grant, August 11, 1861, and OR, Colonel Frederick Schaefer, August 12, 1861

During the early stages of the war, Union sympathizers are subject to harassment and threats from Southern secessionists. The citizens of Potosi raise a Home Guard force in May, but by early August, hostilities erupt when several local citizens are murdered and others threatened by Southern sympathizers.

Approximately 120 Confederates under a Captain White of Fredericktown and Benjamin Talbot attack Potosi around 6:00 p.m. with the intent of catching the Missouri Home Guards eating supper at Douglas Hall. The intended target is a building called the arsenal (the armory for the Home Guard weapons and equipment), defended by 20 Union soldiers. At the arsenal, Union soldiers hold their ground, return several volleys and wound many of Captain White's men. Confederate forces withdraw.

WHY IT MATTERS: Access to lead mines and rail transportation routes were key centers of gravity for Union forces to protect. Brigadier General Ulysses S. Grant sent troops from Ironton to protect this important lead mining town along the Ironton Railroad line from St. Louis.

Union Casualties: 5
Confederate Casualties: 6

ACTION: Raid on Hamburg, Scott County, August 11 or 12, 1861—*OR*, General Jeff Thompson, Headquarters 1st Military District MSG, Camp Whitewater, August 12, 1861

After a day of destroying railroad tracks, General Jeff Thompson sends a detachment of dragoons to confiscate horses and wagons nearby. Thompson's men attack and overwhelm Federal Home Guard forces in Hamburg.

Union Casualties and Losses: 19
Confederate Casualties: unknown

ACTION: Federal operations in and around Kirksville, Adair County, August 16–21, 1861—*OR*, Brigadier General S.A. Hurlbut, USA, August 21, 1861

Brigadier General S.A. Hurlbut, with five hundred men of the 3rd Iowa, moves his command temporarily to Kirksville from Macon City to find and hunt down a Rebel force estimated at two thousand men assembled

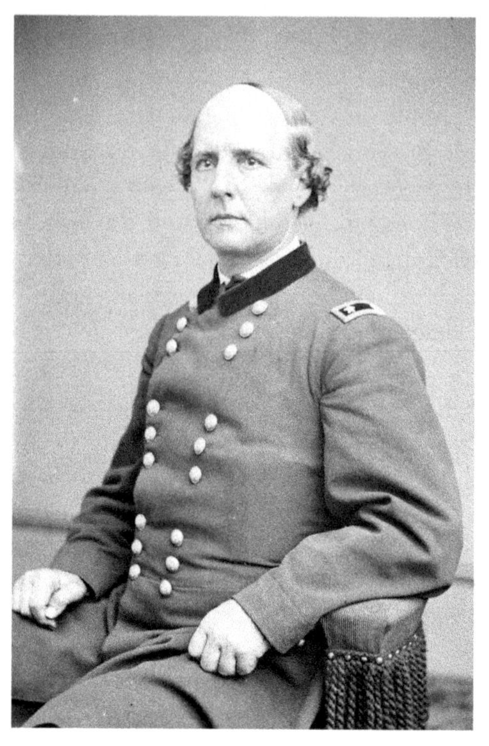

Stephen A. Hurlbut. *Courtesy of the Library of Congress.*

southeast of Kirksville. Union operations consist of reconnaissance parties encountering small bands of Confederate soldiers coming and going around a place called Bee's Branch. Confederate troops proceed into southwest Knox County in the vicinity of Monroe and Ralls Counties. General Hurlbut conveys in his report the difficulty in maintaining communications with his subordinate units and Macon City as cause for his inability to engage the Rebel forces under guerrilla captains Green and Franklin. Hurlbut sends most of the Home Guard forces home, leaving one hundred to act as pickets around Kirksville.

Union Casualties: estimated 1
Confederate Casualties: estimated at 14 or more

Action: Skirmish at Palmyra and Hunnewell, Shelby County, August 17, 1861—*OR*, Brigadier General John Pope, USA, Headquarters District of North Missouri, St. Louis, August 17, 1861

Union forces en route to Hudson, Missouri, are fired on near Palmyra and Hunnewell. Confederate forces are driven off. In a letter directed to the mayor and citizens of Palmyra, General Hurlbut threatens to move a brigade of soldiers into the area and fine the county and city a considerable sum of money if the marauders are not handed over in six days.

Union Casualties: 2

ACTION: Raid at Charleston, Mississippi County, August 19, 1861, and Fish Lake, August 20, 1861—*OR*, Major General John C. Frémont, USA, commanding, Department of the West, St. Louis, August 20, 1861

About 300 Union men under the command of Colonel Dougherty successfully attack a Rebel force of some 1,200 at Charleston. Soon after, a detachment of 50 Centralia cavalry soldiers under Captain R.D. Noleman captures 35 Rebels five miles east of Charleston.

Union Casualties: 7
Confederate Casualties and Losses: 57

ACTION: Skirmish at Lexington, Lafayette County, August 29, 1861

Union Casualties: unknown
Confederate Casualties: 8

ACTION: Skirmish at Dallas, Bollinger County, September 2, 1861—11th Missouri

Union Casualties: 2

ACTION: Battle of Dry Wood Creek, aka Battle of the Mules, Vernon County, September 2, 1861

Confederate forces after their victory at Wilson's Creek move north to the Missouri River Valley city of Lexington. Kansas Union cavalry forces under the command of Colonel James H. Lane set off from Fort Scott toward Price's Confederate army. Confederate forces are initially surprised in Vernon County, but Colonel Lane's heavily outnumbered force of six hundred Jayhawkers quickly withdraws, abandoning a herd of Federal mules to Price's soldiers.

Union Casualties: 22
Confederate Casualties: 40

TOURISM NOTES: The land of the battle site is privately owned. An interpretive panel for the Battle of Drywood Creek is located at a truck stop seven miles west of Nevada on Highway 54. In Deerfield, turn south into Emery's Truck Plaza parking lot. The marker is near the Truck Plaza sign. Details of the battle are also displayed in the Bushwhacker Museum in Nevada, Missouri.

ACTION: Platte railroad bridge tragedy, St. Joseph, Buchanan County, September 3, 1861

Bushwhackers sabotage the Hannibal and St. Joseph Railroad Bridge over the Platte River east of St. Joseph. A train carrying two passenger cars of men, women and children plunges into a shallow river, killing and injuring more than one hundred passengers. Union troops are ordered to track down and execute the bushwhackers. General Sterling Price protests this order from General Henry Halleck, who justifies it due to Confederate bushwhackers not wearing uniforms identifying them as Confederate soldiers.

TOURISM NOTES: St. Joseph contains several Civil War historic sites. Fort Smith Park, the site of a Union army fort erected in 1861 as part of the Federal army's intent to protect the railroad transportation hub, is located at the corner of Bellevue and West Michel Street. The four-story Hotel Patee House, now a museum on 1202 Penn Street, was one of the largest hotels west of the Mississippi River and served as the headquarters for the

Union provost marshal. A Civil War interpretive panel is located at 914 Penn Street across from the Pony Express Stables. General Jeff Thompson, former mayor of St. Joseph, and many other Civil War veterans are buried at Mount Mora Cemetery, 824 Mora Road.

ACTION: Raid on Shelbina, Shelby County, September 4, 1861

Confederate forces are driven out of Shelbina by Union forces under the command of Brigadier General Stephen Hurlbut.

ACTION: Operations against Captain (later Colonel) Colton Greene's guerrillas, Shelby County to Howard County, September 8–9, 1861—*OR*, Brigadier General John Pope, USA, September 10, 1861

General John Pope and soldiers from the 16th Illinois and 3rd Iowa pursue an estimated three thousand guerrillas under the leadership of Confederate guerrilla commander Colton Greene east of Macon in the vicinity of Shelbina. After Pope's men conduct a night march of twenty-three miles and surprise the guerrilla force, Rebel forces manage to quickly mount and scatter to avoid a decisive engagement. Pope continues west in pursuit of Greene. Greene continues to move west as well as to approach and engage Union forces at Glasgow, Missouri, and capture the steamer *Clara Bell.*

ACTION: Skirmish at Black River, near Greenville, Wayne County, September 12, 1861

Black River is a typical example of the hundreds of skirmishes that occurred when opposing sides suddenly met while moving throughout the countryside or along major roads. In this case, a reconnaissance patrol of the 1st Indiana Cavalry gets the jump on marauding Rebel forces. Union forces scatter the Rebel forces and capture several muskets and horses.

Confederate Casualties and Losses: 5

ACTION: Second Battle of Boonville, Cooper County, September 13, 1861

Official reports from Union colonel Jefferson C. Davis (no relation to Confederate president Jefferson Davis) to General John C. Frémont warn of General Sterling Price's Confederate column of three thousand Rebel troops en route to Boonville. Although initial reports of the surrender of Boonville are premature, the Home Guards under Major Joseph Eppstein are initially successful against an advance guard six hundred to eight hundred strong. Confederate forces break off the attack before Union reinforcements arrive from Syracuse.

Local historians' version of this engagement is that Confederate Colonel William Brown and 800 Missouri State Guard surprised 140 pro-Union militia of Boonville Home Guard under the command of Captain Joseph Eppstein while eating breakfast. The story goes that Confederate forces wrapped their battle flags in black sheathing due to adverse weather, an act considered by soldiers as a customary sign that no quarter will be given to the defeated in battle. Local historic sentiment is that this threat played a decisive factor in bolstering the Boonville Home Guardsmen's resolve against a vastly superior Missouri State Guard Confederate force.

Union Casualties: 5
Confederate Casualties: 52, including Colonel Brown

TOURISM NOTES: An informative interpretive panel is located at the Boonville Thespian Hall at 522 Main Street. Built in 1855, Thespian Hall is one of the oldest theaters in the West and was used extensively during the Civil War as a barracks and hospital.

PRELUDE TO THE BATTLE OF LEXINGTON: By the end of August, seasoned Mexican-American War veteran Colonel Jefferson C. Davis had succeeded Colonel Ulysses S. Grant as the commander of Union forces in northwest Missouri, now headquartered in Jefferson City. A large contingent of Missouri State Guard forces under the command of Confederate general Sterling Price moved through the area to possibly threaten St. Louis or seize Jefferson City. Union leadership prepared for

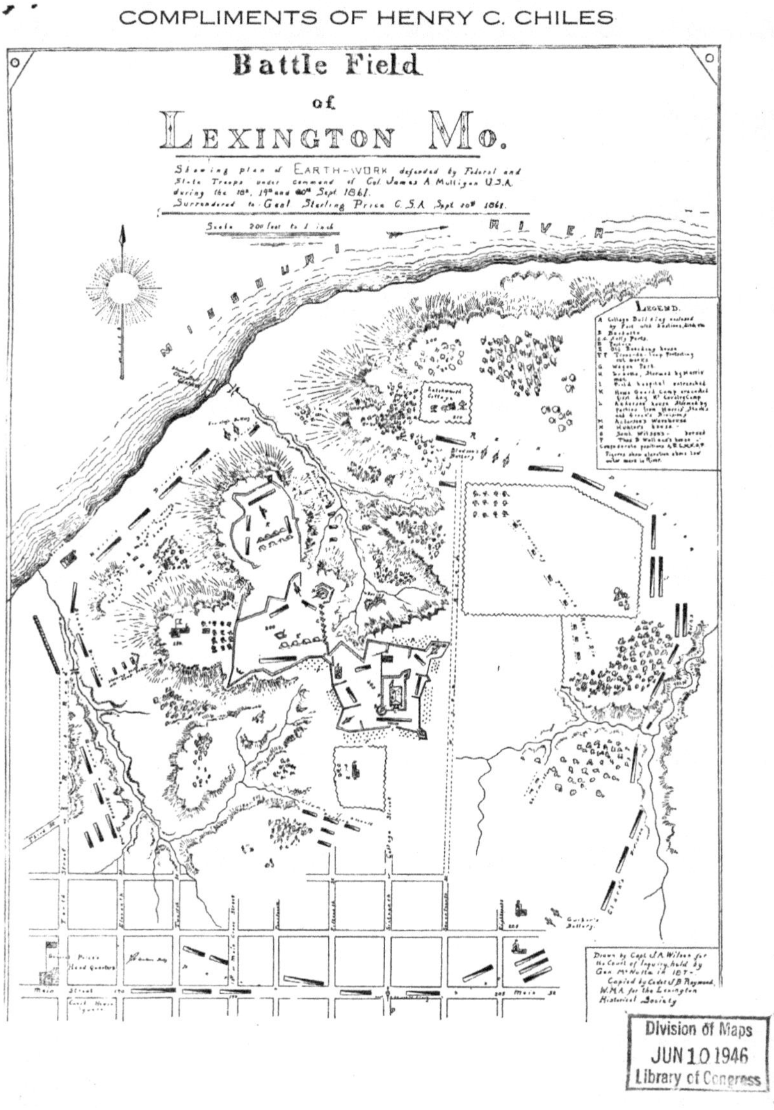

Map of the battlefield of Lexington, Missouri. *Courtesy of the Library of Congress.*

a siege by building extensive fortifications at Jefferson City manned by a force estimated between eighteen and twenty thousand Union soldiers. The Confederate strategy also sought to break the Union blockade of the Missouri River and provide support to the numerous Rebel bands north of the river.

Missouri governor Hamilton Rowan Gamble had raised the importance of Lexington when he communicated his concern to Federal commanders of a sizeable amount of money, estimated as much as $900,000, residing in a local Lexington bank. The money had allegedly been confiscated by the federal government to deny its use by the pro-secessionist government.

ACTION: Siege and First Battle of Lexington, aka Battle of the Hemp Bales, Lafayette County, September 13–20, 1861

General Sterling Price's Rebel force, estimated at 12,000 Missouri State Guardsmen, marches from Springfield through Warrensburg to seize Lexington, guarded by a Union garrison estimated at 3,500 soldiers of Illinois and Missouri regiments under the command of Colonel James Mulligan. Price's fellow commander at Wilson's Creek, Brigadier General Benjamin McCulloch, differing with Price on the importance of Lexington, refuses to accompany Price's Missouri State Guard, believing it exceeded his orders to protect Arkansas from Union invasion. Price's forces, estimated at 15,000 to 18,000 (including many unarmed and poorly equipped new recruits), accompanied by support of thirteen artillery pieces, lay siege to Lexington, culminating in a three-day pitched battle September 18–20. Mulligan's defenses initially repulse the Rebel attacks, but additional Rebel reinforcements and resupplies arrive to continue the attack on Lexington. Confederate forces eventually advance and capture the Union defensive positions, protected by portable hemp breastworks. After suffering heavy casualties, Union forces surrender in the early afternoon of September 20. The Battle of Lexington is considered one of the largest engagements west of the Mississippi River.

A later review of the official correspondence between Colonel Jefferson C. Davis in Jefferson City and General John C. Frémont, commander of troops of the western department, during the last days of the Battle of Lexington, indicates there was considerable confusion over what the true situation was and how the relief of Lexington was to be conducted.

Although a report by Colonel James Mulligan to General Frémont estimated that Confederate forces of 10,000 to 12,000 were heading toward Lexington from Warrensburg, Frémont dismissed its accuracy and believed that Confederate forces were never larger than 4,000 and were poorly armed. One report even estimated Confederate forces at 35,000. Another report conveyed a significant Union victory when Confederates were repulsed, with casualties as high as 1,400 Rebel soldiers. The Union reinforcements that finally did make it to Lexington were prevented from crossing the river by Rebel batteries. General Frémont disavowed one report of Lexington's surrender and continued to issue directions for the defense of Lexington several days after the garrison had fallen.

Union Casualties: 159 and more than 1,600 capured
Confederate Casualties: estimated at 100–200

Why It Matters: Lexington was an important port town along the Missouri River. Prior to the war, a steady stream of steamships disembarked settlers along its bustling riverfront of factories and warehouses. Pro-secessionist Missouri governor Claiborne Jackson had established Missouri's first military post at Lexington. By 1861, Lafayette County had a population over nineteen thousand, including six thousand enslaved persons. The capital, Lexington, was the fifth-largest community in Missouri, with a population over four thousand. This Confederate victory threatened the Union's ability to maintain control of key transportation locations and encouraged Southern sentiment and the support of Confederate recruiting in the Missouri River Valley. While Price's reputation as a bold battlefield commander was further enhanced, Major General Frémont dispatched a large Federal force, compelling Price to retreat to southwestern Missouri. For Missouri Civil War buffs seeking information regarding Lexington's numerous military actions, the Missouri State Historical Society website (www.shsmo.org) documents the occurrence of thirty-five military actions in Lafayette County between 1861 and 1865.

Tourism Notes: One hundred acres of the battlefield site are preserved. The Anderson House Mansion, now a Civil War museum, is believed to be the oldest building still standing that played an important role in a Civil War battle. Anderson House served as a field hospital for both sides and changed hands several times throughout the battle.

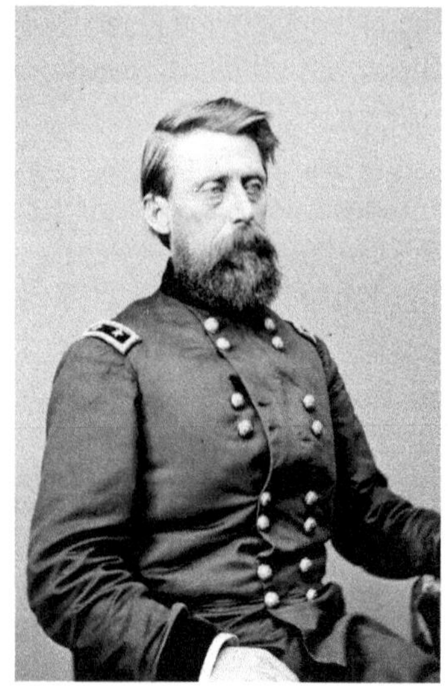

Jefferson C. Davis. *Courtesy of the Library of Congress.*

BIOGRAPHICAL SKETCH: Hamilton Rowan Gamble was appointed governor of Missouri after Union forces captured the state capital at Jefferson City and deposed Claiborne Jackson. He was the chief justice of the Missouri Supreme Court and wrote the dissenting opinion in *Dred Scott v. Emerson* against the overturning of the Dred Scott Decision in 1852. Hamilton Gamble was a practicing attorney in Franklin, Missouri, and the prosecuting attorney in Howard County. In opposition to the harsh treatment of pro-Southern sympathizers, Governor Gamble appealed to Lincoln to overturn General Frémont's declaration of martial law and the early slave emancipation proclamation in 1861. Although a slaveholder, Gamble often defended slaves in court. He died before the war was over and is buried at Bellefontaine Cemetery, St. Louis, Missouri.

BIOGRAPHICAL SKETCH: Union colonel Jefferson C. Davis assumed command of the 3rd Division of the Army of the Southwest and was involved in the fighting of Confederate forces as they withdrew toward Arkansas in late December. Davis later distinguished himself at the decisive Battle of Pea Ridge and was promoted to brigadier general. General Davis's leadership is recognized by many historians at many noteworthy battles or actions, including Sherman's Atlanta Campaign and March to the Sea, where he commanded a corps and was promoted to brevet major general. His reputation was clouded by the killing of Union general William "Bull" Nelson during an argument and the failure to assist a large contingent of freed slaves attempting to escape from Confederate capture while crossing Ebenezer Creek during Sherman's March to the Sea.

ACTION: Battle of Blue Mills Landing (Liberty), Clay County, September 17, 1861

In an early action for control of northeast Missouri, six hundred men under Union lieutenant colonel John Scott stationed at Cameron depart on September 15 for Liberty. On September 16, Missouri State Guard forces led by General David R. Atchison en route to reinforce General Sterling Price are preparing to cross the Missouri River. Union scouts discover Confederate pickets, and Lieutenant Colonel Scott launches an attack around 3:00 p.m. but is repulsed after an hour of intense fighting. Official correspondence of the commanders on both sides report an exaggeration of the size of each opponent's armies by as much as 25 to 50 percent, as well as wide discrepancies in the numbers of casualties inflicted.

Union Casualties: estimated at 50–100
Confederate Casualties: estimated 70–160

TOURISM NOTES: The Clay County Museum and Historical Society is located in the historic square, 14 North Main Street, Liberty, Missouri. Open Monday–Friday 1:00 p.m.–4:00 p.m. and Saturday 10:00 a.m.–4:00 p.m.

ACTION: Skirmish at Morristown, Cass County, September 17, 1861—*OR*, J.H. Lane, commanding, Kansas Brigade, September 27, 1861

Pro-Union Jayhawker Brigadier General James H. Lane leads approximately six hundred infantry and cavalry on a raid of a Rebel encampment at Morristown, five miles east of the Kansas border. The Confederate encampment was routed, abandoning a considerable amount of supplies and horses.

Union Casualties: 8
Confederate Casualties: 7

ACTION: Skirmishes at Hunter's Farm, near Norfolk, Mississippi County, and Elliott's Mills, September 22–27, 1861

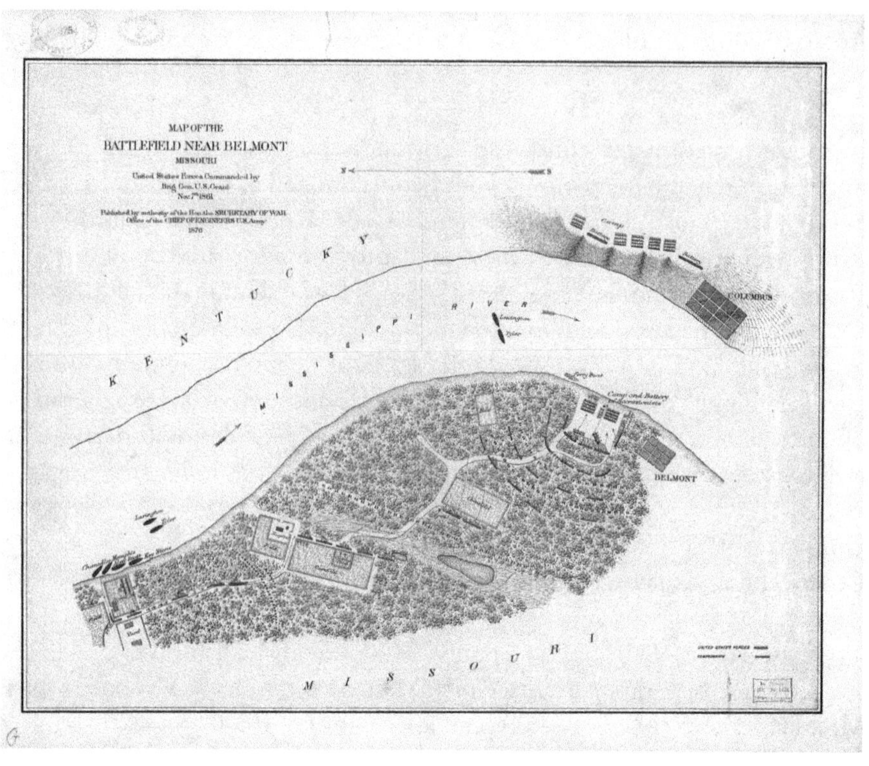

Map of the battlefield near Belmont, Missouri. *Courtesy of the Library of Congress.*

Federal forces pursue General Jefferson Thompson's Confederate forces operating in the vicinity of Belmont, Missouri.

Union Casualties: 2
Confederate Casualties and Losses: 15 or more

ACTION: Sacking and burning of Osceola, St. Clair County, September 23, 1861

Colonel James H. Lane's "Kansas Brigade" of Jayhawkers sacks and loots Missouri communities such as Butler, Harrisonville, Osceola and Clinton.

Osceola, a prosperous town along the Osage River, suffers tremendous looting and plundering, as well as the liberation of hundreds of slaves.

Before departing Osceola, Colonel Lane's drunken forces set nearly all of its eight hundred homes and buildings on fire. An atrocity Quantrill's guerrilla band later claims as one of the major justifications for the raid on Lawrence is the court-martial trial and execution of nine citizens of Osceola by Lane's Jayhawkers. Condemned by the governor of Kansas and the Federal commander at Fort Leavenworth, millions of dollars worth of property is stolen or destroyed. Osceola never regains its prominence.

Union Casualties: 9
Confederate Casualties: 25

BIOGRAPHICAL SKETCH: James H. Lane, a former congressman from Indiana, had voted for the Kansas-Nebraska Act and moved to Kansas in 1855. Lane had gained military experience during the Mexican-American War, commanding two Indiana regiments. One of the first senators elected after Kansas gained statehood, he was considered by many historians as the leader of the Jayhawkers, the most militant of the Free Soiler organizations. Lane returned to Kansas in 1861 to raise a Union regiment. Lane's brigade of 1,200 men were mostly raiders during the border conflict before the war and later filled the ranks of the 3rd and 4th Kansas Volunteer Infantry and 5th Kansas Cavalry. A fanatical abolitionist, Lane's forces entered Missouri and conducted operations with the intent of punishing all those not loyal to the Union and enforcing General John C. Frémont's emancipation edict.

ACTION: Operation near Charleston, Mississippi County, October 2, 1861—*OR*, Colonel R.J. Oglesby, 8th Illinois Infantry, October 2, 1861

A sizeable Union force of infantry, cavalry and artillery of 1,150 soldiers, under the command of Colonel Tuttle, 2nd Iowa, is dispatched from Bird's Point to intercept Rebel forces under the command of Confederate commander General Jeff Thompson.

ACTION: Operation near Charleston, Mississippi County, October 2, 1861—*OR*, Brigadier General U.S. Grant, commanding, District of Southeast Missouri, October 7, 1861

While Grant is confronted with the raiding nuisance of the elusive Confederate guerrilla leader Jefferson Thompson, he is provided intelligence on another enemy matter: the buildup of a large Confederate force at Columbus, Kentucky, estimated around forty-five thousand soldiers. Grant subsequently receives further intelligence of additional Confederate forces assembling at Union City, with possible intentions of attacking Paducah, Kentucky, within the next week to ten days.

Authors' Assessment: Grant's official reports may now be shedding some light on how his military thought process was evolving regarding how he would conduct future operations and the importance of judging Confederate intentions. For example, intelligence reports provide an indication that Confederate leaders were planning offensive operations or preparing to defend against a large Federal attack.

Tourism Notes: Across the Mississippi River from Missouri is a commemoration of Confederate general Leonidas Polk's occupation and operations at Columbus, Kentucky, which was also an important railroad spur of the Mobile and Ohio Railroad.

Action: Skirmish at Cameron, Clinton County, October 12, 1861—James Cavalry

Union Casualties: 5
Confederate Casualties: 8

Action: Skirmish at Wet Glaize (aka Dutch or Monday Hollow near Henrytown), Camden County, October 13, 1861

Union forces disperse Confederates raiding Federal communications facilities along the St. Louis–Springfield corridor.

ACTION: Skirmishes near Clintonville, Cedar County, Pomme de Terre, Hickory County, October 12–13, 1861—*OR*, Brigadier General Monroe M. Parsons, 6th Division MSG, Cedar Creek, October 14, 1861

Jayhawkers attempt to surprise and ambush Missouri State Guard forces camped on Smith's farm, near Clintonville and on Pomme de Terre. Missouri State Guard cavalry engage and drive off the pro-Union Jayhawkers, taking several prisoners.

Union Casualties: 6
Confederate Casualties and Losses: 5

ACTION: Operations in the vicinity of Ironton and Fredericktown, Iron County, and Madison County, October 12–25, 1861, and skirmishes at Fredericktown, Madison County, October 17–18, and Ironton, Iron County, October 21, 1861

Missouri, Illinois, Wisconsin and Indiana Union forces under Colonel J.B. Plummer and Colonel William Carlin skirmish and drive out General Jeff Thompson's Confederate forces.

Union Casualties: 66
Confederate Casualties: 200

TOURISM NOTES: Ironton, an important mining center during the war, was the site for one of Grant's headquarters. A memorial statue to General Ulysses S. Grant stands in Ironton near the Fort Davidson State Historic Site. A visitor center provides an electronic model of the Battle of Pilot Knob, with informative displays, weapons and artifacts.

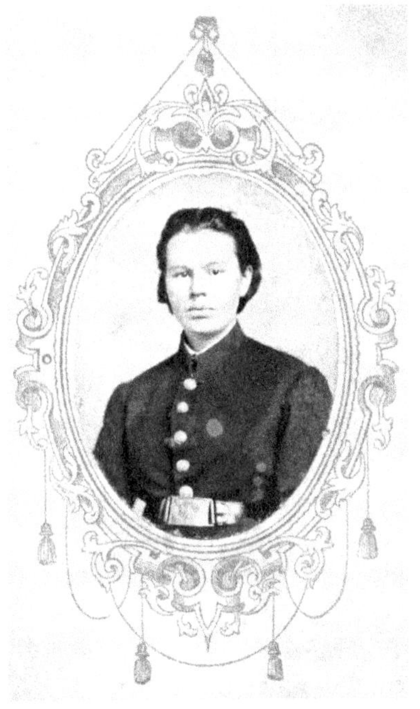

Frances Hook, also known as Private Frank Miller, Frank Henderson and Frank Fuller of Company G, 90th Illinois Infantry Regiment, 33rd Illinois Infantry Regiment and 11th Illinois Infantry Regiment. *Courtesy of the Library of Congress.*

Frances Hook—a female soldier disguised as a man and taking the names of Private Frank Miller, Frank Henderson or Frank Fuller—served with several Illinois infantry units during the Civil War. Frances was wounded at the Battle of Fredericktown, Missouri, later captured at Florence, Alabama, and imprisoned in Atlanta.

ACTION: Skirmish at Beckwith Farm near Bird's Point, October 13, 1861—Tuft's Cavalry

Union Casualties: 7
Confederate Casualties: 3

ACTION: Battle of Blackwell, Big River Bridge, near Vineland and Blackwell Station, Jefferson County, October 15, 1861

A Union contingent of forty soldiers guarding a wooden bridge of the Iron Mountain Railroad System is completely surprised by Confederate forces under General Jefferson "Swamp Fox" Thompson (he inherited his nickname due to his legendary elusive nature) in an early morning raid on the stone redoubt along the north side of the bridge. Thompson's 2nd and 3rd Regiment Dragoons, with an estimated four hundred men, kill several soldiers, wound Union captain Isaac Elliott and capture forty-five prisoners. A company of fifty Union soldiers downriver learns of the action and attacks Thompson's men in the act of dividing their spoils. Thompson's guerrilla band disperses the attacking Union forces and burns the Big River Bridge to discourage any Union pursuit.

Union Casualties and Losses: 39–50
Confederate Casualties: 9

WHY IT MATTERS: Throughout Missouri, a key part of Confederate strategy was to disrupt vital Union railroad operations and supply lines by burning wooden bridges, which often required several weeks or more to repair or rebuild. Governor Hamilton Gamble traveled to Washington to seek financial assistance from President Lincoln to raise Missouri State Militia cavalry units to deal with this threat by highly mobile Confederate cavalry and partisan operations. This was a particularly challenging task, as Missouri roads and waterways had many bridges to protect. In Jefferson County's case, there were thirteen railroad bridges to protect.

Tourism Notes: Local Civil War enthusiasts, led by author and reenactor John Hollingsworth, have placed a monument near the site on Wilsons Hollow Road.

Action: Skirmish at Linn Creek, Camden County, October 16, 1861—*OR*, Major Clark Wright, Frémont's Battalion of Missouri Cavalry, October 17, 1861

Soldiers foraging for corn while encamped make contact with a detachment of forty-five Rebels. Major Clark Wright sends out two detachments of fifteen men to cut off their retreat. A Lieutenant Kirby is instrumental in leading the action that drives the Rebel forces off, along with the release of two Union prisoners and the capture of Rebel supplies.

Union Casualties: 1
Confederate Casualties: 6

Action: Skirmish at Big Hurricane Creek, Bollinger County, October 19, 1861—8th Missouri

Union Casualties: 16
Confederate Casualties: 14

Action: Skirmish at Buffalo Mills, Dallas County, October 22, 1861

Confederate Casualties: 17

ACTION: Second Battle of Lexington, Lafayette County, October 16, 1861—*OR*, Major Frank J. Wright, commanding, 1st Squadron Prairie Scouts, October 24, 1861

Approximately 180 Union soldiers from 1st Missouri Cavalry and Irish Dragoons depart Jefferson City to conduct special scouting services. The Union force is ill-prepared for a hard journey and must stop in Georgetown to refit 232 horses and mules and remake ammunition rendered useless by rain. Two abandoned blacksmith shops are put into operation by soldiers who were experienced blacksmiths. While in Georgetown, an urgent request is sent out to relieve Lexington before the commander, Colonel White, and other prisoners can be executed by the occupying Rebel forces.

In a remarkable forced march of sixty miles, commenced the night before, Major Wright's cavalry force reaches Lexington the following morning, rapidly deploys and overwhelms Rebel pickets. Major Wright's men take possession of the town along with sixty prisoners, considerable weapons, horses and two steamboats. A third steamboat is seized the following morning and sent back to St. Louis with freed Union prisoners. Wright's force retains Lexington for thirty-six hours and evacuates toward Warrensburg before a sizeable Rebel force returns to retake the town.

WHY IT MATTERS: While the senior Union military commanders in Missouri were in desperate need for combat leaders prepared for the rigors of war, the engagement at Lexington provided reason to believe that Union volunteers under capable officers could rise to the hard challenges of fighting Rebel forces.

ACTION: Battle of Springfield, Greene County, aka Zagonyi's Charge, October 25, 1861

Under considerable pressure from Washington, Major General John C. Frémont, commander of the western department, departs St. Louis in early October to clear Confederate forces under Major General Sterling Price from southwestern Missouri. Frémont's force of nearly 20,000, including 5,000 cavalry under Major Frank White and Major Charles Zagonyi, arrive in southwestern Missouri and set up camp near the Pomme de Terre River. Major Zagonyi's forces, operating as advance guard, continue on to Springfield and attack a Confederate force of 1,000 to 1,500 under Colonel Julian Frazier in the midst of preparing an ambush. After the defeat of Rebel forces, Major Zagonyi continues into town to release Union prisoners and meets with Federal sympathizers. Fearing a large Confederate force counterattack, Zagonyi's cavalry in Springfield depart prior to nightfall. Several days later, General Frémont marches his entire force south to secure Springfield.

Union Casualties: 55
Confederate Casualties: 106

WHY IT MATTERS: Major General John C. Frémont was relieved in early November and replaced by Major General David Hunter. Although Union forces had regained control of an important city in southwest Missouri, Hunter withdrew east to supply bases in Sedalia and Rolla, ceding control of southwest Missouri back to the Confederacy in the late fall of 1861. This concession to Confederate control was short-lived. Recognizing the importance of diminishing Confederate operations in southwestern Missouri, the Union Army of the Southwest, under the command of Brigadier General Samuel Curtis, will mount a decisive campaign and engage the Confederate forces of Major Generals Earl van Dorn and Sterling Price just across the Missouri border at Pea Ridge, Arkansas, in March 1862.

TOURISM NOTES: Twelve markers depict both Major Charles Zagonyi's actions in 1861 and Brigadier General John Marmaduke's failed attack in 1863. More information is available at https://www.springfieldmo.org/listings/922/battle-of-springfield-tour.

ACTION: Skirmish at Spring Hill, Livingston County, October 27, 1861

Union forces engage the Confederate forces of General Sterling Price. A short skirmish ensues, but Confederate forces disengage and continue their withdrawal to southwestern Missouri.

ACTION: Callaway County becomes the "Kingdom of Callaway," October 1861

According to the Kingdom of Callaway Historical Society, a Federal force of six hundred Federal troops under the command of Brigadier General John B. Henderson assembled near the northeast border of Callaway County and Wellsville for the purpose of subduing strong Southern sympathizer sentiment in Callaway County. Jefferson F. Jones, a local leader and former state representative, musters a force of nearly six hundred men at Brown's Spring, north-central Callaway County, and prepares defensive positions awaiting the Federal invasion. Trees are cut down and painted black to deceive the Union forces; they would have to assault heavily fortified positions.

Union spies advise the Federal commander of the Callaway Guards' activities; General Henderson, concerned over possibly suffering heavy casualties, delays an attack to await reinforcements. An envoy is sent by Jefferson Jones to gain information about the Federal troops but also carries a letter stating that their intent is self-defense and noting that they would disband if the Federal invasion were called off and left Callaway's citizens in peace.

Remarkably, General Henderson agrees to such terms and negotiates a treaty on behalf of the Federal government that essentially recognizes Callaway County's independence. While the treaty is never adhered to in a meaningful way by the Federal government and raises the question of whether the Federal commander ever had such authority, Callaway County accomplishes what no other pro-Southern state does during the Civil War.

A widely held view of the hostile political climate confronting Union forces operating in areas of mid-Missouri with strong pro-Southern sentiments is reflected in the October 31, 1861 official report from Brigadier General Chester Harding, commander of the Missouri State Militia District Headquarters in Hermann, Missouri:

> *SIR: Having ascertained that a considerable force of rebels had encamped about 5 miles north of Fulton Callaway County that their number was increasing, and that they designed an attack upon some one of the important bridges on the Pacific Railroad. I deemed it my duty to cross the river and disperse them. Accordingly, 650 men, taken from Morton's Independent Ohio Regiment, and the Tenth Regiment Missouri Volunteers.*

At 11 p. m. on the 28th we marched, and reached Fulton 18 miles distant, at sunrise. I there learned that the rebels, anticipating an attack from the Federal forces, had made an arrangement with Brigadier-General Henderson by which they were allowed to disperse, and were exempted from arrest or punishment for their treasonable proceedings. General Prentiss and I had a consultation with the few leading Union men in Fulton, and decided to respect the agreement referred to, especially as I could not leave a garrison in the town to protect the loyal citizens from the vengeance which the secessionists would have taken had we interfered with the persons or property of their leaders....

That whole region is thoroughly disloyal. There is no faith to be placed in anything but the fears of the rebels. On our return a single individual rode up within 200 yards of our advance guard and fired at it, and this is an indication of the universal feeling there. There are not 200 Union men in the county of Callaway....

I am, sir, very respectfully, your obedient servant.

BIOGRAPHICAL SKETCH: Prior to the Civil War, John B. Henderson was a practicing lawyer and a two-term member of the Missouri State House of Representatives. A political appointee in 1861, he quickly rose to the rank of Union brigadier general, commanding state militia forces in northeast Missouri. Following the Kingdom of Callaway affair, a remarkable set of circumstances propelled Henderson to appointment in the United States Senate in 1862, filling the vacancy of the deposed and current senator, Trusten Polk, a former governor of Missouri and Southern supporter. Henderson, though a Democrat, was a staunch supporter of Lincoln.

Henderson played an instrumental role in the passage of legislation abolishing slavery. In late December 1863, two proposals were introduced in Congress by Representatives James Ashley and James Wilson. In early January 1865, Senator Henderson submitted a joint resolution for a Constitutional amendment abolishing slavery, a necessary requirement to ensure that the Emancipation Proclamation abolishing slavery was legal once President Lincoln's war powers were no longer in force. The masterful political maneuvering of Lincoln to ensure that this largely controversial measure became law might not have occurred after he had been assassinated.

Another interesting story in circulation recalls Henderson conferring with President Lincoln on April 14, 1865, to secure a pardon for a Missouri resident convicted of spying and sentenced to death. Such an executive order could have been Lincoln's last official act prior to departing for Ford's Theatre.

The Lincoln Presidential Library claims to have no such correspondence in its records. Critics also claim that such a pardon would have required some documentation in order for Secretary of War Edwin Stanton to overturn the execution, an order he had already refused orally. While the actual pardon is still in some dispute, the fact remains that convicted spy George E. Vaughn lived a long life in freedom and died in 1899.

ACTION: Secession convention at Neosho, Newton County, October 30–31, 1861

Dethroned Missouri governor Claiborne Jackson and the pro-Southern members of the Missouri legislature convene and make Neosho its provisional capital. Confederacy admits Missouri as the twelfth state.

ACTION: Expedition from Rolla, Phelps County, against Thomas Freeman's forces, November 1–9, 1861—*OR*, Colonel G.M. Dodge, 4th Iowa Infantry, commanding, Rolla, Missouri

Rolla, Missouri, is at the end of the southwest branch of the Pacific Rail Road from St. Louis and acts as a key supply center for south-central Missouri. President Abraham Lincoln recognizes its strategic importance, issues orders to hold Rolla by all means and directs the building of Fort Wyman in 1861 and Fort Dette later in 1863. Union soldiers under Colonel Grenville Dodge stationed at Rolla, Salem and Houston are the principle Union forces operating against guerrilla and Rebel marauders in the Current River watershed area.

Colonel Dodge must contend with a lawless land of bushwhackers, partisan rangers and any other sort of predator led by such partisan leaders as William Coleman and Thomas Freeman operating south of their Union outposts.

Colonel Dodge directs Colonel Nicholas Greusel and approximately five hundred infantry and cavalry to hunt down and drive Freeman and his Rebel forces from Texas County. Colonel Greusel's forces successfully force Freeman out of Texas County and confiscate Rebel supplies and contraband, including slaves from homesteaders suspected of supporting and harboring Rebel guerrilla forces.

BIOGRAPHICAL SKETCH: Grenville Dodge served in some of the war's most important battles and campaigns in the West, such as at Pea Ridge, Vicksburg and Corinth. While commanding a corps during the Atlanta Campaign, he bravely led a division against a desperate flank attack by Confederate general John B. Hood, suffering serious wounds.

He served in the critical position as General Ulysses S. Grant's intelligence chief in the West. His efforts improved on the previous inaccuracies that Allan Pinkerton provided McClellan of grossly exaggerating the size of General Robert E. Lee's army. Dodge used spies more effectively by leaving them out in the field for longer periods to observe and create more accurate accounts of enemy forces. Dodge utilized runaway slave information to verify other reports. He interviewed men in the Union army from the South familiar with the area where the army was operating. Eventually, his intelligence network numbered as many as one hundred agents spread throughout the South. At Dodge's headquarters in Corinth, Mississippi, his walls looked like a war room, organized with maps and precise orders of battle to give Union commanders a more accurate view of the enemy situation.

A trained engineer from Norwich University and a surveyor for the railroads prior to the Civil War, his most important contribution was serving as the Union Pacific's chief engineer during the construction of the Transcontinental Railroad after the Civil War. Grenville Dodge is pictured shaking hands with Samuel Montague in Andrew Russell's historic photograph of the joining of the Central Pacific and the Union Pacific at the Golden Spike ceremony on May 10, 1869.

ACTION: Operations launched from Bird's Point, Cape Girardeau and Ironton, Missouri, against Confederate general Jeff Thompson, November 2–12, 1861

ACTION: Expedition to Bloomfield, Stoddard County, November 1861

In early November 1861, Brigadier General Ulysses S. Grant directs Colonel R.J. Oglesby, commander of 8th Illinois Infantry, to lead an expedition into Stoddard County to eliminate Rebel forces commanded by General Jeff Thompson of the Missouri State Guard. About 2,200 Union soldiers of the 11th, 18th and 26th Illinois Infantry Regiments and forces from Cape Girardeau and Ironton converge on Bloomfield on November 8, 1861.

This Federal outpost near the Missouri boot heel will become the location for several military actions throughout much of the Civil War. The outpost is attacked and retaken thirteen times until finally burned down in 1864. Extensive casualties are suffered on both sides.

HISTORICAL NOTE: Bloomfield is where the military publication *Stars and Stripes* was first printed (it is still published by the Department of Defense for servicemen in Europe, the Middle East and East Asia). Several Union soldiers occupied the abandoned newspaper office of the *Bloomfield Herald and Design*, composed, printed and distributed the first issue to Union soldiers camped outside the town on November 9, 1861.

TOURISM NOTES: A 7,500-square-foot museum/library is located just south of Bloomfield next to the Missouri Veterans State Cemetery on State Highway 25. The museum displays *Stars and Stripes* newspapers published during all major conflicts from the Civil War to Operations Enduring and Iraqi Freedom. The library holds complete *Official Records* of the Civil War along with complete lists of Confederate soldiers and other historic records.

ACTION: Small skirmish in Renick, Randolph County, November 1, 1861

Union Casualties: 14

ACTION: Engagement at New (Little) Santa Fe, Jackson County, November 6, 1861—4th Missouri, 6th Kansas Cavalry, Kowald's Missouri Battery

Union Casualties: 8
Confederate Casualties: unknown

ACTION: Battle of Belmont, Mississippi County, November 7, 1861

In what is regarded by many historians as a test of his ability to conduct large-scale offensive operations, Brigadier General Ulysses S. Grant transported three thousand soldiers by steamship down the Mississippi River to surprise a Confederate stronghold at Fort Johnson, commanded by General Leonidas Polk. Simultaneously, Grant had sent a small diversionary force under Brigadier General Charles Smith to attack Paducah, Kentucky. At Belmost, Polk had anticipated Grant's actions and reinforced Fort Johnson with an additional two thousand soldiers. After landing three miles north of Belmont, Grant moved on Fort Johnson and successfully forced Polk's forces to retreat. Union forces conducted considerable looting and destruction, suggesting Grant may have lowered his guard, leaving him vulnerable to counterattack when Polk quickly returned with five Confederate regiments. This mistake forced Grant to reboard his forces on the Union naval steamship and gunboats and return to St. Louis.

Union Casualties and Losses: 498
Confederate Casualties and Losses: 966

WHY IT MATTERS: General Ulysses S. Grant's early experience with naval support became instrumental in recognizing the importance of coordinating closely with the Federal navy and naval flag officers like Andrew H. Foote regarding the strategic use of the Union naval flotilla along the Cumberland and Tennessee Rivers. The successful sieges and victories at Fort Henry, Fort Donelson and the Battle of Shiloh, as well as, most importantly, the strategically decisive campaign for Vicksburg, are a result of establishing this joint army and navy operating capability. After dismissing all of his top Federal army commanders, Lincoln brought his most successful battlefield commander, Major General Grant, east in 1864 to command the Northern armies against the Confederate army of General Robert E. Lee. Grant planned and commanded the final decisive campaigns to defeat the Confederate armies by organizing a joint army-navy coalition to surround, wear down and strangle Jefferson Davis's Southern armies. Essentially, Grant executed the final phase of General Winfield Scott's Grand Strategy, commonly known as the Anaconda Plan, dividing the South in half and blocking Rebel ports in order to slowly strangle the Confederacy's defense perimeter and ability to resupply and sustain its diminishing forces in the field.

ACTION: Engagement at Little Blue River, Jackson County, November 11, 26, 1861—7th Kansas Cavalry

Union Casualties: 16–41
Confederate Casualties: unknown

ACTION: Burning of Pleasant Hill, Cass County, November 18, 1861

Colonel C.R. Jennison orders his 7th Kansas Cavalry soldiers to plunder and destroy Pleasant Hill in retaliation for the burning of a Union wagon train near Pleasant Hill.

WHY IT MATTERS: In a correspondence to General George McClellan, General Henry Halleck wrote of how Jayhawker leaders Colonels Lane and Jennison had done as much damage to pro-Union Missouri sentiment as twenty thousand Rebel soldiers could have.

ACTION: Skirmish at Palmyra, Marion County, November 18, 1861—3rd Missouri Cavalry Detachment

Confederate Casualties: 8

ACTION: Raid on Warsaw, Benton County, November 21, 1861

Confederate forces destroy Federal stores in Warsaw, Missouri.

Action: Skirmish at Lancaster, Schuyler County, November 24, 1861—21st Missouri

Union Casualties: 3
Confederate Casualties: 3

Action: Skirmish at Black Walnut Creek, near Sedalia, Pettis County, November 29, 1861—4th Missouri Cavalry

Union Casualties: 15
Confederate Casualties: 17

Action: Skirmish at Dunksburg, Johnson County, December 4, 1861

A Rebel raiding party is repulsed by an armed force of local townspeople.

Action: Skirmish at Salem, Dent County, December 8, 1861—Bowen's Battalion Cavalry

Union Casualties: 12
Confederate Casualties: unknown

Action: Union forces scout through Saline County, December 3–12, 1861

Union Casualties: 16

ACTION: Skirmish at Bertrand, Mississippi County, December 11, 1861—2nd Illinois Cavalry

Union Casualties: 1
Confederate Casualties: unknown

ACTION: Events leading up to the Burning of Platte City, Platte County, December 16, 1861

Union troops track down bushwhacker guerrilla leader Silas Gordon for his role in the Platte Railroad Bridge Tragedy. Gordon's band had killed two Federal soldiers in a skirmish at Bee Creek in November and captured thirty to forty men during a raid on Weston, Missouri, in early December. Union general David Hunter orders Platte City leaders to deliver Gordon or the city would be burned. Silas Gordon manages to evade capture during Colonel James Morgan's 18th Missouri Infantry raid on Platte City. Two Confederate soldiers captured in the raid are taken to Bee Creek and executed in retaliation for the two Federal soldiers killed earlier.

ACTION: Skirmish at Milford on Blackwater River (near present-day Valley City), Johnson County, December 19, 1861

Union general John Pope, in command of the District of Central Missouri, sends two brigades of approximately 4,000 Union soldiers from Sedalia to drive out Rebel leaders Colonel Franklin Robertson, Colonel J.J. Clarkson and Colonel Ebenezer Magoffin recruiting in and around Warrensburg, Grand Pass and parts of west-central Missouri. After Colonel Robertson's regiment of 750 men elects its officers at Grand Pass, the Rebel force moves south on December 16, links up with Colonel Magoffin and sets up camp at Milford on the Blackwater River. Colonel Jefferson C. Davis's brigade, 1st Iowa Cavalry, 4th U.S. Cavalry and the 2nd Missouri Cavalry, "Merrill's Horse," seize control of the Blackwater Bridge and then surround and capture the exaggerated in size Confederate force of 1,300 regulars and militia camped at Milford. While estimates of captured Rebels by General Pope exceeded the amount sent to St. Louis by several hundred, many

Confederate officers were among those captured. Most likely those captured were placed in Alton Prison.

Union Casualties: 10
Confederate Casualties and Losses: estimated at 684

WHY IT MATTERS: Confederate recruiting was set back by the loss of fresh recruits and by the capture of recruiters who were suspected Southern sympathizers in the region. The capture of a sizeable contingent of Confederate soldiers takes out of potential service a Missouri State Guard regiment that might have been used against forces of General Samuel Curtis during his successful Pea Ridge Campaign in early 1862. General John Pope's victory and the capture of several thousand Rebel soldiers at Island No. 10 gained the attention of President Lincoln, who brought Pope east and placed him in command of the Union Army of Virginia during the conduct of the disastrous battle of Second Manassas.

AUTHORS' ASSESSMENT: Criticism by many Civil War historians over the poor leadership qualities of Northern army officers who gained appointments through political influence should not diminish their important role as hometown recruiters during the early stages of the conflict. Quite often the major task facing army commanders, particularly in the West, was timely communication and accurate intelligence so a more accurate assessment of the enemy situation could be derived. General Ulysses S. Grant recognized his shortcomings in tactical proficiency early in his Missouri service yet displayed an instinctual confidence in his leadership ability to adapt quickly and rise to the challenge of command. This skill of adaptation to changing situations, particularly when preparing for and conducting offensive operations, seemed to elude his predecessors, such as McClellan, Burnside and Hooker.

ACTION: Skirmish at Hudson, Bates County, December 21, 1861—7th Missouri Cavalry Detachment

Union Casualties: 5
Confederate Casualties: 10

ACTION: Skirmish at Wadesburg, Cass County, December 24, 1861—Missouri Home Guards

Union Casualties: 2
Confederate Casualties: unknown

ACTION: Skirmish at Hallsville, Boone County, December 27, 1861

3rd Missouri Cavalry scouts and engages Confederate troops.

ACTION: Raid at Mount Zion Church, Boone County, December 28, 1861

Union forces under Brigadier General Benjamin Prentiss attack and disperse Confederate recruits near Hallsville. The original church is burned down during the Civil War.

Union Casualties: 68
Confederate Casualties and Losses: 175

BIOGRAPHICAL SKETCH: General Benjamin Prentiss is best known for commanding a division at a decisive point of the Confederate attack on General Ulysses S. Grant's Army of the Tennessee during the first day of the Battle of Shiloh in 1862. The engagement was so intense that it was described as sounding like a "Hornets' Nest," due to the sound of so many bullets whizzing through the air. Although he held Confederate forces at bay long enough to provide Grant enough time to consolidate his beleaguered forces, Prentiss eventually surrendered the remainder of his division, approximately 2,200 soldiers. He was later released during a prisoner exchange and was promoted to major general.

General Prentiss continued to provide important leadership in another key engagement in the West. His successful defense of the Federal fortifications at Helena, Arkansas, in July 1863, from the Confederate forces of Generals Sterling Price, James Fagan and John Marmaduke ensured that Federals would retain control of eastern Arkansas and prevent the Confederate relief of Grant's siege on Vicksburg from Rebel forces in the west. General Prentiss's defense at Helena against Confederate forces nearly twice the size of Union forces is especially noteworthy after having to send the bulk of his army to reinforce Grant's operations around Vicksburg. At the Battle of Helena, the Confederates suffered more than 1,600 casualties to Union casualties of just 239, but more importantly, they were unable to prevent the fall of Vicksburg.

Tourism Notes: The rebuilt church is located five miles southeast from Hallsville in Boone County, on Route OO (Mount Zion and Flynn Roads). Many Confederate dead are buried at the church cemetery.

1861 in Retrospect

The violent struggle that began along the Kansas-Missouri border spread quickly throughout Missouri in 1861. By the end of the year, Missouri had already endured more than 120 battles and skirmishes, more than any other state. By the end of 1862, the total number of engagements had more than doubled.

Tourism Note: The Civil War Museum in St. Louis at Jefferson Barracks has an excellent timeline video display of Missouri's military engagements.

Actions in 1862

The general report of Brigadier General John C. Schofield, U.S. Army, of operations in Missouri and northwestern Arkansas, April 10–November 20, 1862, is thirteen pages and summarizes the general nature of Union forces' operations against Confederate forces over an eight-month period. Schofield commanded the Army of the Frontier, with three divisions under the command of Generals James Blunt, Francis Herron and Joseph Totten. General Henry Halleck ordered the Union commander of the Department of the Missouri to raise, organize and discipline a state militia as authorized by the president of the United States. Halleck also commented favorably on Federal progress with news of the Union victory at the Battle of Fayetteville, Arkansas.

Historical Overview: Just a few miles south of the Missouri border, a decisive Union victory of Major General Samuel R. Curtis at the Battle of Pea Ridge, Arkansas, in March 1862 and other military actions in the Trans-Mississippi Region forced Confederate leaders to send recruiters into northern Missouri the following summer to replenish depleted forces. Guerilla leader William Quantrill emerges as a formidable leader of a guerilla band raiding along the Missouri-Kansas border and aiding the recruiting effort in the Missouri Valley region, often using coercive methods. Deprivations on both sides increased as revenge became further fuel to continue the war as much as the original cause of states' rights, preserving the Union and slavery. Confederate president Jefferson Davis was not a believer in the

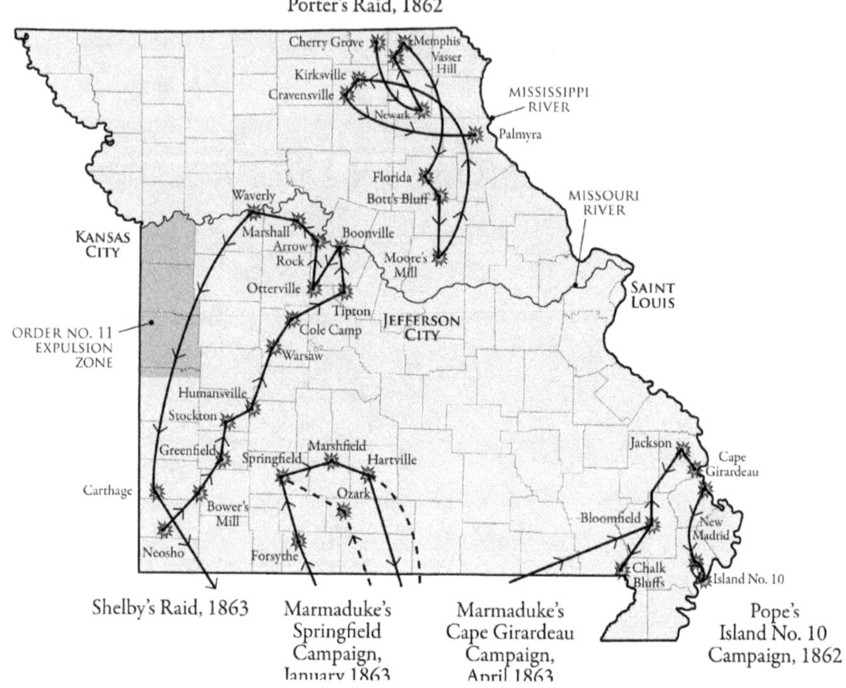

Raids involving Shelby, Porter, Marmaduke and Pope. *Courtesy of Danielle Kilmer.*

strategic value of guerrilla warfare and urged western commanders to not employ such operations. Nevertheless, the Confederate Congress approved the Partisan Ranger Act in April 1862, authorizing the formation of such bands.

Action: Sacking of Dayton and Rose Hill, Cass County, January 1, 1862

Colonel Charles R. "Doc" Jennison orders the 7th Kansas Cavalry "Jayhawkers" under Lieutenant Colonel Daniel R. Anthony to drive out Missouri State Guard forces recruiting in Dayton. Most Rebel forces had vacated the town, but Jennison's Jayhawkers send an intimidating message to pro-Southern sympathizers by burning nearly every home in the towns of Dayton and Rose Hill, enhancing the Jayhawkers' ruthless reputation.

BIOGRAPHICAL SKETCH: Charles Jennison moved to the Kansas towns of Osawatomie and then Mound City from Wisconsin and became a close friend of the staunch abolitionist James Montgomery. Both men were strong supporters of John Brown during the Bleeding Kansas period. Jennison became one of the more despised and lawless Jayhawkers, with a propensity for plunder and personal gain. Commissioned a colonel in the Kansas militia by Governor Charles Robinson, Jennison organized the 7th Kansas Cavalry, which became known as "Jennison's Jayhawkers." Jennison and his Red Legs' raiding of western Missouri left many pro-Southern towns smoldering with only the chimneys still standing, earning this geographical area the title of "Jennison's Smokestacks." Jennison's abolitionist beliefs attracted the attention of Horace Greeley's *New York Daily Tribune*. Overlooked for promotion to brigadier general, Jennison resigned and became a Red Leg raider and looter. After the Lawrence Massacre, he was called back into service by Governor Thomas Carney and raised the 15th Kansas Cavalry. Plundering during the pursuit of General Sterling Price's army in 1864 resulted in a court-martial and his dishonorable discharge shortly after the end of the war.

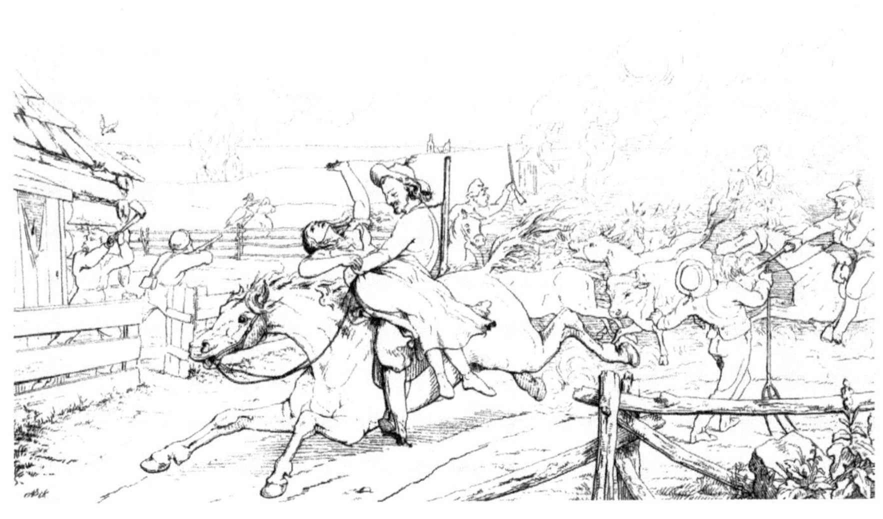

Antislavery guerrillas under Charles Jennison attacking civilians in Missouri. *Courtesy of the Library of Congress.*

Daniel R. Anthony was an avid abolitionist during Kansas's fight for statehood. His convictions and opinions became influential while serving as postmaster, mayor and a newspaper publisher in Leavenworth, Kansas.

Action: Skirmish at Calhoun, Henry County, January 4, 1862

Union Casualties: 10
Confederate Casualties: 30

Action: Skirmish at Charleston, Mississippi County, January 8, 1862—10th Iowa

Union Casualties: 24

Action: Attack at Roan's Tan Yard, aka Silver or Sugar Creek, Randolph County, January 8, 1862

A Confederate force under the command of Colonel John Poindexter is camped on Silver Creek, about eight miles east of Roanoke, Missouri. Companies of the 1st and 2nd Missouri Cavalry (Merrill's Horse), 4th Ohio Cavalry and 1st Iowa Cavalry conducting operations in northeast Missouri locate, attack and, after a brief battle, capture and disperse the Confederate forces, who suffer considerable losses estimated at 60 wagons of supplies and 160 horses.

Union Casualties: 25
Confederate Casualties and Losses: 148

Action: Jayhawker raid on Columbus, Johnson County, January 9, 1862—7th Kansas Cavalry

Union Casualties: 5
Confederate Casualties: unknown

Action: Skirmish at Knob Noster, Johnson County, January 22, 1862—2nd Missouri Cavalry

Union Casualties: 1
Confederate Casualties: unknown

Action: Expedition to Blue Springs, Jackson County, January 29, 1962—February 3, 1862

Operating in severe conditions of cold and snow, Captain William Oliver's 7th Missouri Volunteer Infantry skirmish with William Quantrill's guerrilla band and capture a considerable amount of guerrilla supplies and contraband. The report is interesting regarding Captain Oliver's description of his own troops suffering from a shortage of essential items like boots and foodstuffs like sugar, relying mostly on what his soldiers can forage for subsistence. Captain Oliver's report also highlights injuries suffered from operating in harsh conditions that placed many of his officers in hospitals or unable to conduct their duties for some time.

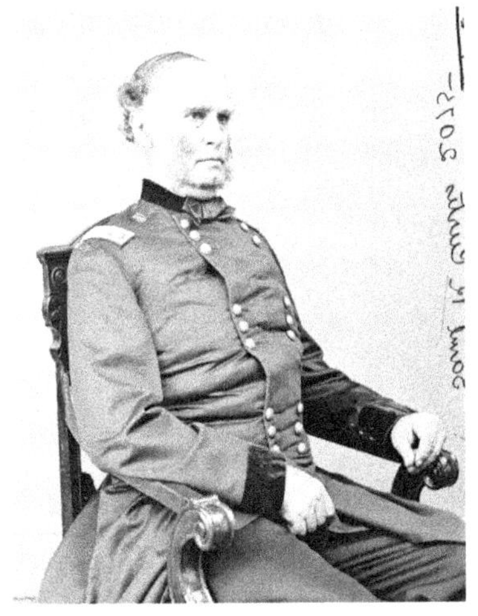

Samuel R. Curtis. *Courtesy of the Library of Congress.*

Union Casualties: 3
Confederate Casualties: 7

ACTION: General Samuel Curtis's Pea Ridge and Arkansas Campaign, January–July, 1862

Brigadier General Samuel R. Curtis and his Army of the Southwest, with more than ten thousand Union soldiers (including two divisions of German immigrants) and fifty artillery pieces, drives Confederate forces into northwestern Arkansas. Confederate major general Earl van Dorn, current commander of the Trans-Mississippi District with more than sixteen thousand Rebel soldiers, conducts a counteroffensive that culminates in a pitched battle across the border in Benton County, Arkansas, near the town of Leetown just south of the Missouri-Arkansas border.

ACTION: Scouting expedition to Lebanon, Laclede County, January 22, 1862

Lieutenant Colonel Clark Wright reports back to headquarters in Rolla that he occupied Lebanon and sent out several scouting parties to report on enemy strength and locations in southwest Missouri, particularly Springfield.

ACTION: Skirmishes at Bolivar, Polk County, and Marshfield, Webster County, February 9, 1862

Confederate Casualties and Losses: 10

ACTION: Skirmish at Springfield, Greene County, February 12, 1862—*OR*, Brigadier General Samuel Curtis, commanding, Southwest District of Missouri, February 13, 1862

General Samuel Curtis's forces defeats a Confederate cavalry regiment on the outskirts of Springfield and regains control of Springfield.

Confederate Casualties: 6

ACTION: Skirmishes at Crane Creek, Flat Creek, Potts Hill or Big Sugar Creek, McDonald County, along the border with Arkansas, February 15, 16 and 17, 1862—*OR*, Brigadier General Samuel Curtis, February 15, 18, 1862, and OR, Lieutenant Colonel Clark Wright, Wright's Battalion Missouri Cavalry, February 17, 1862

In order to determine the level of Confederate resistance, Union leaders report of conducting several skirmishes against the Confederate rear guard of General Sterling Price.

Union Casualties: 36
Confederate Casualties: unknown

ACTION: Skirmish at Independence, Jackson County, February 22, 1862

William Quantrill and a small detachment of his band ride into town unaware of the presence of Union forces. The 2nd Ohio Cavalry prevails and forces Quantrill's guerrilla band out of town.

Union Casualties: 4
Confederate Casualties: varies between 2 and 9

ACTION: Skirmish at Keetesville (Keytesville), Chariton County, February 25, 1862—*OR*, Colonel Clark Wright, 6th Missouri Cavalry, February 27, 1862

The camp of 6th Missouri Cavalry Union forces under Captain Samuel Montgomery is attacked by a substantial force estimated at five hundred Rebel soldiers of Colonel Young's Texas Rangers Brigade under the command of a Major Ross. Although many of Captain Montgomery's force are caught sleeping, they repulse the Confederate charge three times before withdrawing into Keetesville. The Texas Rangers break off the attack to gather horses and other abandoned supplies. Colonel Wright describes Keetesville as a center of strong Southern support that communicated intelligence on their location to the Rebel forces, as well as denied this information to Captain Montgomery.

Union Casualties: 3
Confederate Casualties: 10

TOURISM NOTES: The Town of Keytesville established a monument to Sterling Price in 1915. The General Sterling Price Museum was erected in 1964 and features an 1860s parlor setting, an array of artifacts, memorabilia and other period collections. It is open from May 15 to October 15, Monday–Friday 2:00 p.m.–5:00 p.m.

ACTION: General John Pope's (Union commander at the Battle of Second Manassas) southeast Missouri campaign, February 28–April 8, 1862

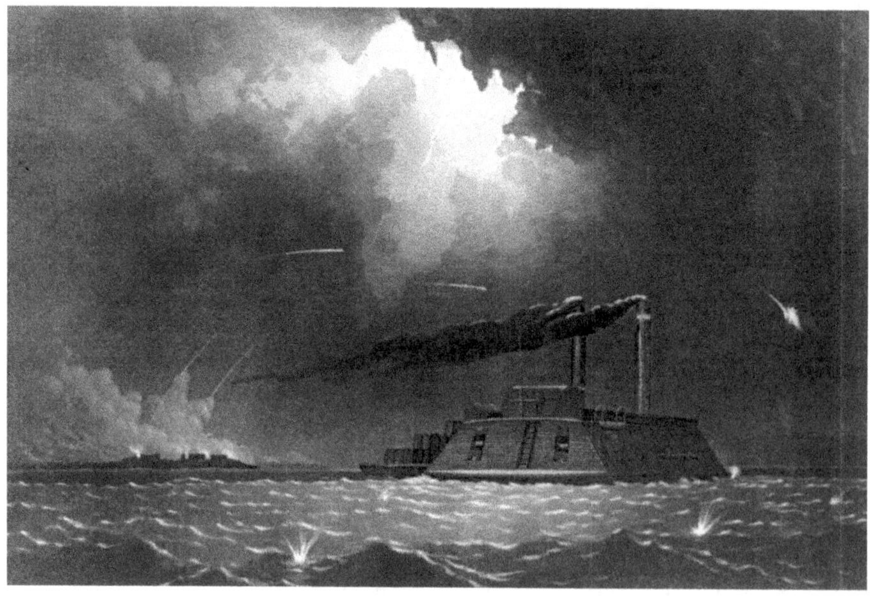

Ironclad under artillery bombardment from Island No. 10 in Mississippi River, Missouri, April 6, 1862. *Courtesy of the Library of Congress.*

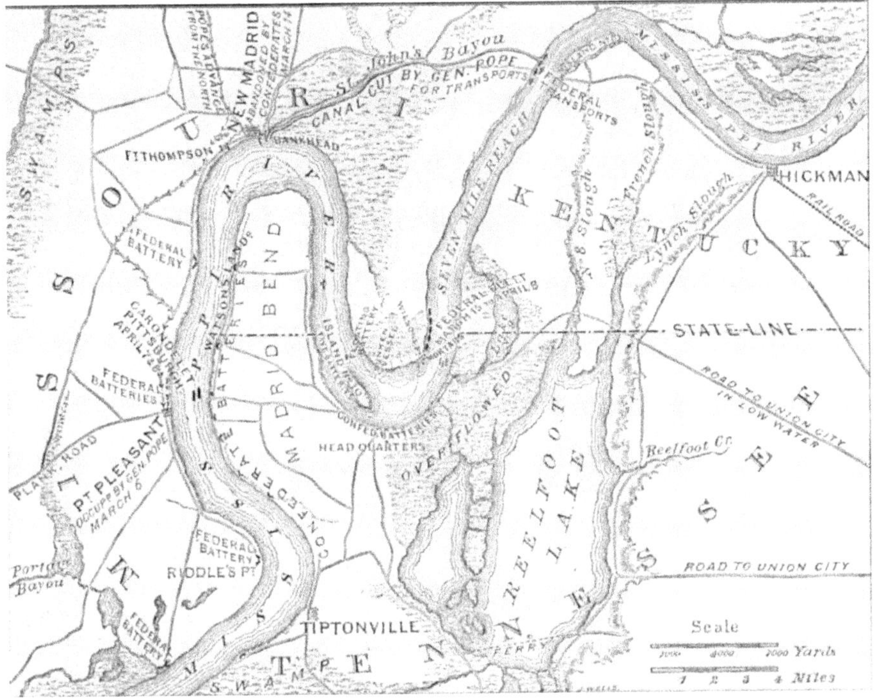

Military and Naval Operations About Island Number Ten. Courtesy of the State Historical Society of Missouri.

ACTION: Fall of New Madrid and Siege of Island No. 10, February 28–April 8, 1862

Confederate control of an island at a double bend in the Mississippi River makes Union attempts to pass it perilous. Confederates guarding the island garrison are restricted to one supply road toward the eastern shore of the Mississippi River. General John Pope begins his campaign overland and commences to siege New Madrid. Brigadier General John McCown abandons the fort and its supplies after one day of heavy bombardment. A flotilla of Union gunboats bombards Island No. 10 for three weeks. The possible escape of Confederate forces is thwarted when two Union gunboats, USS *Carondelet* and USS *Pittsburg,* slip past the fort and cut off any possible withdrawal and rescue by Southern vessels. Confederate leadership, believing their situation hopeless, surrender to Union naval flag officer Andrew Foote.

Union Casualties and Losses: 78
Confederate Casualties and Losses: 30 killed, approximately 7,000 Rebel soldiers taken prisoner

Why It Matters: Capture of Mississippi River stronghold enabled Union leadership to gain strategic control of the Mississippi River down to Fort Pillow just north of Memphis. New Orleans succumbed to Union naval forces under Admiral David Farragut three weeks later. The Confederacy was now dangerously close to being divided in half and cut off from the key transportation center of gravity, the Mississippi River.

Action: Major General Henry Halleck issues "No Quarter" directive, March 1862

As commander of the Department of the Missouri, General Halleck is confronted with constant sabotaging of bridges, railroad lines and depots that often caused the deaths of Union soldiers and innocent civilians. The directive simply states that any guerrilla caught in the act of such destruction would be summarily executed on the spot without due process. A more formal directive, General Order No. 100, was signed by President Lincoln on April 23, 1863. General Order No. 100 spelled out specific instructions regarding how soldiers should conduct themselves in wartime.

Action: Skirmish at Fox Creek, St. Louis County, March 7, 1862—4th Missouri Cavalry

Union Casualties: 5
Confederate Casualties: unknown

Action: Battle of Pea Ridge (aka Elkhorn Tavern), Benton County, Arkansas, March 7–8, 1862

Despite a strained relationship with his subordinate commander, Union general Franz Sigel, Major General Samuel Curtis's outnumbered Union forces conduct a dogged defense in the hilly terrain of northeastern Arkansas to defend against cautious Confederate attacks. At the end of the first day, Curtis's army is cut off from its supply lines in Missouri, and a tenuous stalemate arises as both armies seek cover for a chilly evening. Miscommunication regarding the relocation of Confederate artillery supply trains and superior positioning of Union artillery enable Federal forces to obtain a decisive firepower advantage on Confederate forces near Elkhorn Tavern. Union infantry take advantage of the artillery superiority to gain an advantageous position to aggressively attack Confederate forces. By late morning, the Confederate position is untenable, and its commander, General Van Dorn, must order a retreat that causes his Rebel soldiers to become detached from supply lines and leads to the eventual mass desertion of thousands of Missouri State Guard back to Missouri. Three seasoned Confederate generals, McCullouch, McIntosh and Slack, are killed, along with the mortal wounding and capture of many high-ranking Confederate officers.

Union Casualties and Losses: 1,384
Confederate Casualties and Losses: 2,000

Why It Matters: Arkansas's Confederate forces never regained enough strength until late in the war to threaten Union control of Missouri. The remainder of Van Dorn's army is sent east of the Mississippi River to reinforce the Army of the Tennessee, leaving Arkansas defenseless. Curtis continued his operations in Arkansas and is denied the capture of Little Rock but successfully seizes an important supply base at Helena, Arkansas, in July.

Tourism Notes: Pea Ridge is a National Military Park administered by the National Park Service. It's considered one of the best-preserved Civil War battlefields, including the well-reconstructed Elkhorn Tavern, where much of the heaviest fighting took place. The 4,300-acre park is near Garfield, Arkansas, just across the Missouri border on Highway 62. Visit the website at www.nps.gov.

ACTION: Skirmish at Mountain Grove and Mountain Grove Seminary, Texas County, March 9, 1862—*OR* Captain Josephus G. Rich, Phelps Missouri Infantry, March 12, 1862

Approximately sixty Missouri Home Guard, supported by fifty cavalry from Lebanon, attack and capture a Rebel force of thirty-five to forty men, including their officers, Colonel Campbell and Captain Holt.

Union Casualties: 12
Confederate Casualties and Losses: 35–40

ACTION: Skirmish near Lexington, Lafayette County, March 10, 1862

Commander reports fierce hand-to-hand fighting to subdue guerrilla band.

Casualties: 5
Confederate Casualties: 12

ACTION: Skirmish near Marshall, Saline County, March 15–16, 1862—*OR*, Captain Anson Moore, March 16, 1862; OR, Captain John B Kaiser, March 23, 1862

A Missouri State Militia force led by Lieutenant Jesse Turley surprises and routs a Rebel camp of fifty soldiers three miles from Marshall. Besides capturing considerable horse and other war materiel, twelve Union Missouri State Militia soldiers are recaptured. Turley's forces are reinforced in anticipation of a large Rebel force's counterattack.

Reinforcements under Captain John B. Kaiser, Boonville Missouri Cavalry Militia, arrive in Marshall later that morning and rout another secession camp, reclaiming supplies captured earlier.

Confederate Casualties: 8

ACTION: Skirmish at Liberty, Clay County, March 18, 1862

William Quantrill's band of forty guerrillas raids a small Union garrison in Liberty. The garrison holds out for nearly three hours before surrendering. Quantrill pardons the Union soldiers and departs soon after.

Union Casualties and Losses: 10
Confederate Casualties: unknown

ACTION: Skirmish at Leesville, Henry County, March 19, 1862—Iowa 1st Cavalry

Union Casualties: 4
Confederate Casualties: unknown

ACTION: Skirmish at New (Little) Santa Fe, Jackson County, March 22, 1862

Guerrilla Captain William Quantrill's band escapes an ambush by the 2nd Kansas Cavalry.

Union Casualties: 2
Confederate Casualties: 7

ACTION: Skirmish at Carthage, Jasper County, March 23, 1862—6th Kansas Cavalry

Union Casualties: 1
Confederate Casualties: unknown

Action: Raid on Warrensburg, Johnson County, March 26–27, 1862

William Quantrill and an estimated two hundred guerrillas are repulsed after several charges of the Union garrison of sixty soldiers assigned to the 7th Missouri Cavalry under the command of Major Emory Foster.

Union Casualties: 3
Confederate Casualties: estimated at 26

Action: Skirmish at Humansville, Polk County, March 26, 1862—8th Missouri Militia Cavalry

Union Casualties: 6
Confederate Casualties: 15

Action: Skirmish at Sni-A-Bar, Lafayette County, April 1, 1862

The 1st Missouri State Cavalry and Boonville State Militia Cavalry surprise and disperse William Quantrill's guerrillas.

Union Casualties: 2

Action: Skirmish at Walkersville, Salt River Township, Shelby County, April 2, 1862

According to the history of Monroe and Shelby Counties, while transporting a wagonload of supplies from Shelbina to Shelbyville, Colonel Henry S. Lipscomb and fourteen men from the 11th Missouri State Militia are ambushed near Walkersville on the Salt River by Tom Stacy and sixteen bushwhackers. Two militia, prominent citizens, are killed. After the Union militiamen arrive in Shelbyville and relate their story, three of the attacking party are hunted down and killed. This report may vary somewhat from the *Official Records*.

Union Casualties: 2
Confederate Casualties: 3

ACTION: Skirmish at Medicine Creek, Livingston County, April 8, 1862

Eight Missouri State Militiamen guard a railroad bridge east of Chillicothe, over Medicine Creek. While tending a fire outside the blockhouse, a party of nine to ten Confederate bushwhackers ambush them. A short engagement ensues in which the Union guards are able to find cover and return fire, forcing the attackers to retreat. The local Missouri State Militia commander, a Colonel King, sends out a scouting party but does not find the attackers.

Union Casualties: 4
Confederate Casualties: unknown

ACTION: Skirmish at Jackson, Cape Girardeau County, April 9, 1862—3rd State Militia Cavalry

Union Casualties: 1
Confederate Casualties: unknown

ACTION: Skirmish at Little Blue River, Jackson County, April 12, 1862

Confederate Casualties: 5

ACTION: Skirmish at New (Little) Santa Fe, Jackson County, April 14, 1862

1st Missouri Cavalry routs Quantrill's band, with eight casualties and five captured.

Action: Skirmish at Diamond Grove, Newton County, Missouri, April 14, 1862—6th Kansas Cavalry

Union Casualties: 1
Confederate Casualties: unknown

Action: Skirmish at Montevallo, Vernon County, April 14, 1862—1st Iowa Cavalry and 2nd Battalion State Militia

Union Casualties: 8
Confederate Casualties: 12

Action: Skirmish at Turnback Creek, Greene County, April 26, 1862—5th Kansas Cavalry

Union Casualties: 1
Confederate Casualties: unknown

Action: Skirmish at Neosho, Newton County, April 26, 1862—1st Missouri Cavalry

Union Casualties: 6
Confederate Casualties and Losses: 92

Action: Skirmish at Licking, Texas County, May 4, 1862—8th State Militia Cavalry

Union Casualties: 3
Confederate Casualties: unknown

Actions in 1862

Action: Skirmish at Bloomfield, Stoddard County, May 10, 1862—1st Wisconsin Cavalry

Confederate Casualties: 1

Action: Skirmish at Chalk Bluff, Dunklin County, May 15, 1862—1st Wisconsin Cavalry

Union Casualties: 4
Confederate Casualties: unknown

Action: Skirmish at Butler, Bates County, May 15, 1862—1st Iowa Cavalry

Union Casualties: 9
Confederate Casualties: 28

Action: Lincoln signs the Homestead Act of 1862, May 20, 1862

With profound national and regional repercussions for aiding the Union effort, Abraham Lincoln signs into law an act authorizing any citizen who had not taken up arms against the Federal government to apply for ownership of 160 acres of Federal land. After five years, and having shown proof of building a dwelling and growing crops, the farmer could file a deed of title for ownership free and clear. Union soldiers can deduct time served from the five-year requirement.

Action: Skirmishes at Florida, Monroe County, May 22 and 31, 1862—3rd Iowa Cavalry

Union Casualties: 2
Confederate Casualties: unknown

ACTION: Operations and Skirmishes around Miami and Waverly, Lafayette County, May 25–28—Missouri 7th Cavalry

Union Casualties: 2
Confederate Casualties: unknown

ACTION: Skirmish at or near Licking, Texas County, May 26, 1862

A Confederate force at Crow's Station attacks and partially destroys a Union wagon train heading toward their location.

ACTION: Skirmish at Monagan Springs near Osceola, St. Clair County, May 27, 1862—1st Iowa Cavalry

Union Casualties: 10
Confederate Casualties: unknown

ACTION: Skirmish at Neosho, Newton County, May 31, 1862—10th Illinois and 14th Missouri (Militia) Cavalry

Union Casualties: 5
Confederate Casualties: unknown

ACTION: Raid at Pink Hill, Jackson County, June 11, 1862

Quantrill's guerrillas continue harassing Union forces in eastern Jackson County and attack a Union mail escort.

Union Casualties: 5
Confederate Casualties: unknown

ACTION: Skirmish at Warrensburg, Johnson County, June 17, 1862—7th State Militia Cavalry

Union Casualties: 4, 2 found later horribly mutilated
Confederate Casualties: estimated at 8–9

ACTION: Raid on Sibley, Jackson County, June 22, 1862

Quantrill's guerrillas, operating along the Missouri River east of Kansas City, capture a naval vessel, the USS *Little Blue*. Quantrill's men leave behind forty sick and wounded Union veterans on board the vessel but loot and carry off a substantial amount of military supplies.

ACTION: Skirmish at Pineville (aka the Pineville Expedition), McDonald County, June 23, 1862

General Franz Sigel, operating in southwest Missouri near the Arkansas border in southwest Missouri, sends Union troops of the 2nd Wisconsin Cavalry to drive out Confederate forces under Major David Russell.

Confederate Casualties: unknown

ACTION: Skirmish at Raytown, Jackson County, June 23, 1862

Confederate forces skirmish and rout Federal forces of the 7th Missouri Cavalry.

Union Casualties: 2
Confederate Casualties: unknown

ACTION: Skirmish at Pleasant Hill, Cass County, July 8, 1862

A Union force attacks and successfully drives off an encampment of Quantrill's guerrillas.

ACTION: Skirmish at Lotspeich Farm, Sugar Creek near Wadesburg, Cass County, July 9, 1862—*OR*, Major James O. Cower, 1st Iowa Cavalry, July 13, 1862

A detachment of the 1st Iowa Cavalry commanded by Major James Gower learns of William Quantrill and a force estimated at 200 to 250 guerrilla raiders camped near the town of Wadesburg in Cass County. Major Gower sends a detachment of fewer than 100 men to conduct an early morning surprise attack on Quantrill's band. Quantrill's guerrillas repulse two Union cavalry charges. Federal forces break off the engagement and return to Clinton, Missouri. Union forces later attempt to attack Quantrill at the farm of a Mr. Hornsby, but the guerrilla band had already departed.

Union Casualties: 3
Confederate Casualties: 1 killed, several wounded

ACTION: Battle of the Ravines, near Pleasant Hill, Cass County, July 11, 1862

Major James Gower, 1st Iowa Cavalry, joins forces with sixty men of the 1st Missouri Cavalry of Warrensburg commanded by Captain M. Kehoe. Without coordinating with the Union force of a Major Gower, Captain Kehoe attacks Quantrill's guerrillas at Sear's House midmorning. Kehoe's men are repulsed and suffer heavy casualties.

The 1st Iowa Cavalry reengages Quantrill's forces east of Sear's House. Quantrill is positioned in the cliffs of the ravines along Big Creek Bluff. A determined Union attack against Confederate defensive positions inflicts heavy losses and routs them completely. Quantrill's forces scatter into small squads fleeing in several directions.

Union Casualties: 29
Confederate Casualties: 43–48

TOURISM NOTES: Pleasant Hill Cemetery is an important Missouri Civil War historic site. Mass graves contain thirty Union soldiers from the 1st Iowa Cavalry, 7th Missouri Cavalry and 6th Kansas Cavalry who fell at the Battle of the Ravines and Pouncy Smith Farm. Other notables include Confederate colonel Hiram Bledsoe and Caroline Abbott Stanley, Civil War author of the novel *Order No. 11*.

ACTION: The Militia Act of 1862, July 17, 1862

The Militia Act is enacted by Congress to allow African Americans to participate as soldiers and war laborers.

ACTION: Skirmish at Greenville, Dade County, July 20, 1862

Confederate forces arrive in Greenville, learn of a Union encampment nearby and surprise and disperse Federal forces of 12th Missouri State Cavalry from the area.

Union Casualties: 9
Confederate Casualties: unknown

ACTION: General John M. Schofield's counter-guerrilla campaign in Missouri, July 20–September 20, 1862

Union Casualties and Losses: 580
Confederate Casualties and Losses: 2,866

ACTION: Skirmish on Blackwater River near Columbus, Johnson County, July 23, 1862—7th Missouri Cavalry

Union Casualties: 2
Confederate Casualties: unknown

ACTION: Skirmish at Mountain Store and Big Piney, Pulaski County, July 25–26, 1862—3rd Missouri Cavalry and 2nd Missouri Artillery

Confederate Casualties: 5

ACTION: Skirmish at Greenville, Dade County, July 26, 1862—3rd and 12th Missouri Militia Cavalry

Union Casualties: 7
Confederate Casualties: unknown

ACTION: Skirmish at Ozark, Taney County, August 2, 1862—14th Missouri State Militia

Union Casualties: 2
Confederate Casualties: 10

ACTION: Skirmish at Clear Creek, near Taberville, St. Clair County, August 2, 1862—1st Iowa Cavalry

Union Casualties: 19
Confederate Casualties: 11

ACTION: Skirmish at Chariton Bridge, Chariton County, August 3, 1862—6th Missouri Cavalry

Union Casualties: 2
Confederate Casualties: 25

ACTION: Skirmish near Cravensville, Daviess County, August 5, 1862

A company from Colonel James McFerran's Missouri State Militia under the command of Captains Aaron Vickers and John Goodbrake clashes with the Rebel forces of Captain Jesse Clark south of Cravensville and five miles northwest of Gallatin, Missouri. Although Confederate forces outnumber a Union company of only thirty-five soldiers, their use of newer repeating-fire .52-caliber Sharp's carbines drives off the Rebel forces. Two captured Rebels are executed by firing squad for violation of previous parole orders.

Union Casualties: 5
Confederate Casualties and Losses: 16, along with the capture of horses and guns.

ACTION: Skirmish near Montevallo, Vernon County, Missouri, August 7, 1862

Montevallo, a known bushwhacker stronghold, is attacked by the 6th Missouri Cavalry. The 6th Missouri experienced one of the highest casualty rates of Union regiments during the war with 315 killed (279 by disease).

Union Casualties: 4
Confederate Casualties: 22

CAMPAIGN: Colonel Joseph Porter's north Missouri raid, July 1862–January 1863

HISTORICAL OVERVIEW: Colonel Joseph Porter hailed from the small northeastern Missouri town of Newark. His pro-Southern sentiments met with mixed responses in a sharply divided northeast Missouri. His brother was also a Confederate officer and trusted subordinate. Union colonel John McNeil was his chief adversary and regarded Porter as a traitor and bushwhacker. Porter demonstrated natural leadership ability against the Home Guard in Athens and Lexington, serving under the command of General John Marmaduke in 1861. After the Confederate defeat at Pea Ridge, General Sterling Price tasked Porter with returning to the region near his home in Missouri to raise recruits and establish weapons caches and a network of pro-Southern informants. By this time in the war, operations behind Union lines were considered illegal guerrilla operations, and those captured would be shot. Many historical accounts are taken from Joseph Mudd's recollection, *With Porter in North Missouri*, published in 1909.

ACTION: Skirmish at Cherry Grove, Schuyler County, July 1, 1862

By June, Colonel Joseph Porter has established a presence in northeastern Missouri raiding and recruiting in Marion, Knox, Lewis, Scotland and Schuyler Counties. Union forces of the 11th and 12th State Militia Cavalry under Colonel Henry Lipscomb attack and rout Porter's forces, driving them southward. After suffering some losses, Porter regroups with approximately seventy-five recruits near his home of Newark and continues recruiting and guerrilla operations.

Union Casualties: 3
Confederate Casualties: unknown

ACTION: Skirmish at Newark, Knox County, July 7, 1862—2nd State Militia Cavalry

Union Casualties: 2
Confederate Casualties: unknown

Action: Skirmish at Black Run River, Reynolds County, July 8, 1862—5th Kansas Cavalry

Union Casualties: 4
Confederate Casualties: unknown

Action: Militia Act of 1862, July 17, 1862

This act authorizes President Lincoln to call militia into Federal service, set quotas and enforce quotas on states. On August 15, 1861, the War Department had initiated the draft to fill unfilled quotas by volunteers. This controversial act caused violence throughout cities in the Northeast, primarily in New York City. The Draft Riots resulted as citizens protested loopholes that enabled sons of wealthier families to avoid Federal service.

Action: Raid on Memphis, Scotland County, July 18, 862

Colonel Joseph Porter, accused of wearing a Union uniform and accompanied by 125 or more Rebel soldiers, seizes the Federal arsenal at Memphis with little resistance. A noted bushwhacker gang led by Tom Stacy joins Porter. Circumstances muddled the responsibility for the mysterious death of a local doctor and distinguished citizen, and all males are rounded up, although Union militiamen are later paroled and released.

Union Casualties and Losses: 48
Confederate Casualties: 23

ACTION: Ambush at Vassar Hill (Oak Ridge), Scotland County, July 18, 1862

Ten miles southwest of Memphis along the south fork of the Middle Fabius River, Colonel Joseph Porter's Rebel force, estimated to be about several hundred men strong, ambushes the advance guard of a three-hundred-man detachment of 11th Missouri Cavalry under Major John Clopper. Most of the advance guard are killed or wounded. Major Clopper is reported to have conducted as many as six to seven mounted charges against Porter's men. After several hours and heavy Union casualties, one hundred men of the 11th Missouri State Militia Cavalry dismount to return effective fire and prevent any further carnage to Union forces. It is disputed which side was in possession of the field at the end of the action.

Union Casualties: 83
Confederate Casualties: estimated at 19

ACTION: Skirmish at Florida, Monroe County, July 22, 1862

A sixty-man Iowa Volunteer cavalry detachment under Major Henry Caldwell engages Colonel Joseph Porter and about three hundred Rebels for one hour before withdrawing to the Federal post in Paris, Missouri.

Union Casualties: 24–26
Confederate Casualties: unknown

WHY IT MATTERS: Brigadier General John Schofield ordered all able-bodied Missouri men to enroll and report for duty. Schofield later acknowledged that while the Union army mustered a considerable number of Missouri men, many went into hiding to avoid service or were successfully recruited to the Confederate cause.

ACTION: Skirmish on Boles' Farm, Monroe County, July 23, 1862—3rd Iowa Cavalry

Union Casualties: 10
Confederate Casualties: unknown

ACTION: Attack at Bott's Bluff, Monroe County, July 24, 1862

Near Bott's Farm, Major Caldwell's 3rd Iowa Volunteer Cavalry attacks through dense brush and drives Porter's larger force, estimated at four hundred men, south into central Missouri.

Union Casualties: 11–15
Confederate Casualties: unknown

ACTION: Colonel Odon Guitar's counter-guerrilla operations and the Battle of Moore's Mill, Callaway County, July 27–30, 1862

Confederate partisan Colonel Joseph Porter's force of Rebel recruits moves south through Callaway County to undertake guerrilla operations against Union guerrilla hunter Colonel Odon Guitar and the 9th Missouri State Militia Cavalry. Guitar, responsible for guerrilla hunter activities in northern Missouri, learns of Porter's activities and marches east from Columbia toward Fulton, where he joined forces with Merrill's Horse Brigade under the command of Lieutenant Colonel William Schaffer. Porter, with a force of 260 men, including guerrillas under Captain Alvin Cobb and 65 Blackfoot Rangers, leaves a conspicuous trail in the hopes of drawing Guitar's forces into an ambush in eastern Callaway County. On July 28, Guitar's force of about 700 soldiers is engaged by Porter's forces positioned near Auxvasse Creek. Several hours of intense action follows, highlighted by decisive action when an artillery battery was overtaken by Porter's Rebel forces during their surprise attack on Union positions. Guitar's Union forces counterattack and recapture the artillery battery. Running low on ammunition and having suffered heavy casualties, the Rebel force retreats.

Union Casualties: vary, but as high as 75
Confederate Casualties and Losses: estimated as high as 180

TOURISM NOTES: Several panels located at the site off Route JJ, south of the town of Calwood, Missouri, provide a historic overview of the battle.

In the fall of 2013, 151 years after the actual battle, local Callaway County Civil War historians, university archaeological students and the Missouri Civil War Heritage Foundation, in cooperation with the National Park Service, excavated the site. The discovery of nearly two hundred battlefield artifacts provided a unique insight into how the battle transpired and verified many of the earlier historical accounts of the battle. The artifacts are now on display at the Callaway Historical Society in downtown Fulton, Missouri. Callaway is one of the more historically interesting and distinguished counties of Missouri, and visitors can visit an informative museum at the Callaway Historical Society, open Tuesdays through Friday and every third Saturday.

In 2014, a memorial was erected at an unmarked grave site of twenty-four Rebel soldiers killed at the Battle of Moore's Mill on Route Z, one mile west of Calwood, after verification by sonar scanning equipment.

HISTORICAL TRIVIA: How many University of Missouri alumni do you think know that a large bust of Colonel Odon Guitar, one of the first trustees for the University of Missouri, resides in the front offices of the University of Missouri alumni center?

ACTION: Skirmish at Bollinger Mills, Cape Girardeau County, July 28, 1862—13th Missouri

Confederate Casualties: 10

ACTION: Capture of eight Rebel soldiers outside Richmond, Ray County, July 30, 1862

ACTION: Skirmish at Ozark, Christian County, August 1, 1862—*OR*, Colonel Robert R. Lawther, Missouri Partisan Rangers, August 1862

Colonel Robert Lawther and fifty-five Missouri Partisan Rangers march fifty miles to Ozark, reconnoiter and attack a much larger force of the

14th Missouri Cavalry militia. Fighting soon erupts in the town around the courthouse and adjoining buildings. Lawther reports of Union soldiers holed up in the buildings. After recognizing that his soldiers are outnumbered eight to one, Lawther orders his rangers to break off the attack. Lawther's reports of heavy Union casualties conflicts with other partisan reports.

Union force commander Captain Milton Burch gives a different account of the affair. While Lawther's rangers did commence a violent attack, Union soldiers had been warned of the approaching Rebel force and saddled horses, ready to answer the attack. Burch reports that his men were not hiding out in the buildings but rather rose up from their campsite and returned deadly fire, causing the Rebel forces to disperse in several directions.

Union Casualties: 2
Confederate Casualties: 1 initially but 9 from a later report

Action: Skirmish in northeastern Lafayette County, August 1, 1862

Missouri Union cavalry capture and execute twelve guerrillas.

Action: Raid on Newark, Knox County, July 31, 1862

Colonel Joseph Porter manages to recover most of his force after the retreat from Moore's Mill and marches back north to Newark, Missouri. Porter surprises the Federal garrison of seventy-five militia that took refuge in a brick schoolhouse. The militiamen surrender once faced with an ultimatum that the schoolhouse would be set on fire. Union soldiers are paroled, but Union-sympathizing store owners are not so fortunate and suffer considerable looting and destruction to their businesses.

Union Casualties and Losses: 68
Confederate Casualties: 73

Why It Matters: High casualties from poor and chaotic leadership during the advance became a source of growing discord in Porter's recruits. Elements of Porter's force credited with recruiting success at Paris and Clanton managed to rebuild his forces to an estimated two thousand men, but many were unruly and poorly equipped and trained. As greater Union forces amassed in pursuit, Porter contemplated if it was time to take his embattled force south to Arkansas, where they could be better trained and supplied.

Action: Battle of Kirksville, Adair County, August 6, 1862

Colonel Joseph Porter's brigade of approximately 1,500 mostly unarmed or poorly armed recruits is invited to rendezvous near Kirksville in northern Missouri by Confederate captain Tice Cain, a local farmer, to join forces with 500 new recruits. A Union force of 1,000 soldiers under Colonel John McNeil's 2nd Missouri Cavalry pursues the resilient guerrilla leader as he destroys bridges and other crossing sites. As McNeil's cavalry forces accompanied by Merrill's Battalion close in, Porter decides to make a stand and directs his soldiers to occupy and conceal themselves in homes, stores and the county courthouse and among crops in the fields. A Federal artillery battery engages Porter's men in the town square, while two Union columns, Merrill's Horse on the right and 3rd Iowa on the left, drive Porter's remaining forces west of the town. Heavy fighting takes place for more than three hours until a large contingent of Rebel soldiers is subdued and surrenders.

Union Casualties: 88
Confederate Casualties and Losses: 368

Confederate dead were initially buried in several mass graves at Forest-Llewellyn Cemetery. Colonel McNeill was later criticized for his controversial directive to court-martial and execute captured Confederate soldiers for violating previous parole agreements.

Why It Matters: The decisive defeat of Colonel Joseph Porter at Kirksville was a serious blow to Confederate recruiting and ensured Union control in northeastern Missouri.

Tourism Notes: A memorial placard on the courthouse square, approximate site of Union artillery, commemorates the battle. The Truman State University Library contains letters written by the Ziegler brothers that give accounts of their service for the Union army in Arkansas.

ACTION: Union forces' pursuit of Colonel Joseph Porter, August 1862

ACTION: Skirmishes near Cravensville, at Painter Creek, at Walnut Creek, and at Sears' Ford on the Chariton River, Adair and Macon Counties, August 5–9, 1862—*OR*, Colonel James McFerran, 1st Missouri Cavalry (Militia), Headquarters Breckenridge, August 16, 1862

Union lieutenant colonel Alexander Woolfolk's force of 400 men fight a six-hour engagement against Porter's Rebel band estimated at 1,500 soldiers on Panther Creek, near the Hannibal and Saint Joseph Railroad crossing site over the Chariton River.

Union Casualties: 12
Confederate Casualties: 70

Colonel James McFerran and 160 men of the Missouri 5th Cavalry and the 1st Regiment of Missouri State Cavalry join Colonel Woolfolk's forces and attack Porter's Rebel soldiers who were completing preparations to ambush Federal forces along Walnut Creek. After a short engagement, Porter retreats, but his rear guard is soon engaged at Sears' Ford. Union forces, exhausted and unable to move their artillery and ammunition supply wagons, withdraw to Laclede, Missouri. The pursuit of Porter is abandoned, and Colonel McFerran joins forces with General Benjamin Loan to track down Confederate colonel John Poindexter, who is recruiting in north-central Missouri.

Union Casualties: 15
Confederate Casualties and Losses: unknown, estimated as high as several hundred

WHY IT MATTERS: Unrelenting Union pursuit degraded the loyalty and support of Colonel Porter's recruits as Rebel desertions increased and as Union forces enjoyed increasing success in northeast Missouri.

TOURISM NOTES: In the southwest portion of Macon on Coates Street is the Woodlawn Cemetery, where a large rock marks the massacre of eleven captured Confederate soldiers on September 26, 1862. Union general Lewis Merrill ordered the execution by the 23rd Missouri Infantry after it was discovered that the captured Rebels had taken an oath of loyalty and were paroled but had again taken up arms for the Rebel cause. All citizens sympathetic to the Southern cause were made to watch the executions. After General Merrill departed, one injured man was spared after a woman threw her body over him before he could be finished off. This interesting tale can be found at the Macon County Historical Society website (http://www.maconcountyhistoricalsociety.com/civil-war.html).

ACTION: Raid on Palmyra, Marion County, August 12, 1862

Colonel Joseph Porter, with a remaining force of four hundred Rebels desperately living off what they foraged, captures a small garrison of twenty men in Palmyra after a two-hour engagement. Porter frees Confederates held in a local jail but abandons Palmyra to Federal forces and returns to his home near Newark, Missouri. Andrew Alsman, a sixty-year-old carpenter, respected citizen and Union sympathizer, was taken hostage. The story goes that Porter released the hostage, but Alsman is later found by the townsfolk murdered under mysterious circumstances.

ACTION: Colonel Joseph Porter's retreat from Whaley's Mill to Arkansas

Porter's seriously depleted Rebel force is routed and pursued to Bragg's schoolhouse, where the men are forced to disperse to avoid further capture. After several days of evading Union forces, Porter abandons any further attempts to raise Confederate forces and manages to make his way south through Monroe, Audrain, Callaway and Boone Counties to the Missouri River and eventually to Pocahontas, Arkansas, with the remaining contingent of his recruits.

WHY IT MATTERS: To further degrade Confederate recruiting, General John C. Schofield, commanding officer of Union forces in Missouri, issued General Order No. 19, requiring all able-bodied men to report to their nearest military post. While Schofield's order created considerable controversy, some historians believe that more than fifty thousand men were recruited to outfit as many as sixty-nine Union regiments.

ACTION: Skirmish at Stockton, Cedar County, August 9, 1862—Colonel McNeil's command of Missouri State Militia

Confederate Casualties and Losses: 49

ACTION: Campaign and pursuit of Colonel John Poindexter in north-central Missouri, August 8–15, 1862

Colonel John Poindexter, an early rising leader in General Sterling Price's Missouri State Guard, had fought in the Battles of Carthage, Wilson's Creek, Lexington and Pea Ridge. Price believes that Poindexter's capable leadership and demonstrated skills of persuasion could be used for successful recruiting in the central and north-central region of Missouri. Confederate recruiting benefited from reaching out to Southern soldiers released from duty who, faced with conflict back home, became willing recruits for the unconventional guerrilla warfare conducted in Missouri.

ACTION: Raid at Compton's Ferry, Livingston County, August 11, 1862

Union guerrilla hunter Colonel Odon Guitar's brigade pursues and attacks Colonel John Poindexter's force of approximately 1,200 to 1,500 recruits while crossing the Grand River in north-central Missouri. Poindexter suffers significant losses and is forced to retreat to Chariton County.

Confederate Casualties and Losses: unknown

ACTION: Raid at Yellow Creek, Chariton County, August 13, 1862

Colonel Odon Guitar's combined forces with Union brigadier general Benjamin Loan rout and eliminates Colonel Poindexter's forces two days after Compton's Ferry. Poindexter is wounded and escapes but is later captured in September 1863. Since Poindexter is wearing civilian clothes, Union authorities have legal reason to execute him as a spy or guerrilla. Poindexter is granted a reprieve after swearing a loyalty oath and promising to not reengage in guerrilla warfare.

WHY IT MATTERS: Colonel Poindexter's defeat and capture along with the Union army's successes against Colonel Joseph Porter's guerrilla operations in northern Missouri further impeded Confederate recruiting and guerrilla operations in north-central Missouri.

ACTION: Battle of Independence, Jackson County, August 11, 1862

Approximately 700 to 800 Confederate forces under Colonel John T. Hughes and guerrilla leader William Quantrill attack a Union army camp of over 300 soldiers under the command of Lieutenant Colonel James Buel in Independence. Many Union soldiers are caught and killed asleep in their tents, while the rest manage to break free to conduct a desperate defense. Despite the losses of Confederate leader Colonel Hughes and several other Confederate officers, Union forces are unable to break free and surrender soon after barricading themselves in the town's bank building. Quantrill lieutenant and guerrilla leader George Todd frees prisoners at the town jail except for City Marshal James Knowles and a captured 2nd Missouri State Militia leader, Captain Aaron Thomas. Both are executed for their roles in an earlier ambush of George Todd's band that killed several of his men. The remaining 150 or so Union prisoners are paroled.

Union Casualties and Losses: estimated at 230
Confederate Casualties: 32, including 3 colonels, buried together at Woodlawn Cemetery in Independence

WHY IT MATTERS: A Federal investigation conducted during court-martial proceedings against the two Union leaders, Lieutenant Colonel James Buel and Captain Breckenridge, was an indication that Union leadership was still not quite up to the task of training and leading soldiers to fight the bands of such ruthless adversaries as guerrilla leaders William Quantrill and George Todd.

Tourism Notes: The restored historic 1859 Independence Jail, located in the town square, the site of George Todd's two murders, tells the story of famous prisoners, deprivations against civilians and how the population lived and survived during this tumultuous period.

Action: Skirmish at Mussel Shoals, Grand River, August 13, 1862—9th Missouri Militia Cavalry

Union Casualties and Losses: 100
Confederate Casualties: unknown

Action: Skirmish near Barry Section, Barry County, August 14, 1862—5th Missouri State Militia Cavalry, Andrews' Company Enrolled Militia

Union Casualties: 9
Confederate Casualties: unknown

Action: Battle of Lone Jack, Jackson County, August 15–16, 1862

After having suffered severe losses from engagements in Arkansas, Missouri State Guard officers, Captain Joseph Shelby, Colonel Vern Cockrell, Colonel John T. Coffee, Colonel John Poindexter, Upton Hays, John Charles Tracy, John T. Hughes and DeWitt C. Hunter are directed to return and conduct recruiting operations in Missouri. The recent fall of Independence, Missouri, and the extensive recruiting efforts force General Schofield to direct General James Totten, commander of the 2nd Division of the Army of the Frontier, to take action against this Confederate plan.

One of the largest engagements in Jackson County, west-central Missouri, takes place at Lone Jack, Missouri. Initially, a Lexington militia force of 740 soldiers, under the command of Major Emory Foster attacks and disperses 800 to 1,600 Rebels under Colonel John T. Coffee camped outside Lone Jack. The following morning, approximately 3,000 Rebel soldiers under the command of Colonel Vern Cockrell silently take up positions west of Lone Jack with the intent to launch a surprise flank attack after Colonel Upton Hays engages Union forces. Hays's attack is delayed, allowing Foster's militia time to improve its defensive positions. During the attack, as the Union right flank is in danger of breaking, a Union cannon concealed in an Osage orange grove repulses the attacking Confederate forces. A battle of charges, retreats and counterattacks ensues for five hours. Confederate forces under Colonel Coffee return to reinforce the Confederate effort, while serious wounds to the Federal commander, Major Foster, compel Union forces to retreat. Union reinforcements from Generals James Blunt and Fitz Warren arrive two days later, forcing Confederate forces to relinquish their hold on Lone Jack.

Future James and Younger Gang outlaw Cole Younger is recognized for his display of bravery while personally resupplying Confederate forces along the front lines throughout the battle.

Union Casualties: 160
Confederate Casualties: 59–94 killed, wounded unknown

WHY IT MATTERS: The reputation of Quantrill's guerrillas' past treatment of captured Union soldiers instilled a resolve to make a determined stance by the outnumbered Federal forces. Missouri's Union militia forces demonstrated more seasoning and will to fight as they stood their ground against often better-led Confederate units.

BIOGRAPHICAL SKETCH: Considerable atrocities to dead and wounded were observed by Union soldier, University of Missouri graduate and future secretary of war and senator Stephen Elkins during the engagement. Elkins's father and brother, who fought for the Confederacy, had been influential in sparing Elkins from execution months earlier when he was taken prisoner by Quantrill's guerrillas. Missouri's battlefields became symbolic of a conflict in which families often served on opposite sides.

TOURISM NOTES: The Lone Jack Civil War Battlefield, Museum and Soldier's Cemetery is one of the oldest historic Civil War sites preserved in Missouri. A variety of artifacts is on display, including photos of those who fought and several dioramas depicting the circumstances surrounding major events, like the Lawrence Massacre, General Order No. 11 and the Battle of Westport. Located at 301 South Bynum Road, Lone Jack, Missouri, visitor hours (March–October) are Wednesday–Saturday 10:00 a.m.–4:00 p.m. and Sunday 1:00 p.m.–4:00 p.m.; it is open on weekends November through February.

Historical Situation: In July 1862, in the aftermath of the Peninsula Campaign, President Abraham Lincoln summoned Major General Henry W. Halleck to Washington, D.C., to serve as the general in chief of Union forces. Major General Samuel R. Curtis, the victor at the Battle of Pea Ridge, took command and reorganized the Department of the Missouri. Curtis created the Army of the Frontier under the command of Brigadier General John C. Schofield in October 1862 with a force of twenty thousand men responsible for operations against Confederate forces between Springfield and Fayetteville. The Army of Southeastern Missouri was created in November 1862 under the command of Brigadier General John W. Davidson with a force of approximately ten thousand men organized into two divisions commanded by Brigadier General William P. Benton and Colonel Chester P. Harding and the 4th Missouri Cavalry under Colonel George E. Waring.

A rebuilding of the Confederate army in Arkansas was undertaken by Major General Thomas Hindman in order to continue the defense of the state after the Confederate defeat at Pea Ridge. Major General Theophilus Holmes replaced Hindman, who took over Confederate forces in northwestern Arkansas and conducted operations during the late summer and early fall, raiding Union outposts such as Bloomfield, Greenville and Patterson.

Action: Skirmish at Union Mills, Marion or Ralls County, August 20, 1862—13th Illinois Cavalry, 1st Missouri Cavalry

Union Casualties: 7
Confederate Casualties: unknown

Action: Skirmish at Crooked Creek near Dallas (later renamed Marble Hill), Bollinger County, Missouri, August 24, 1862—*OR*, Major Bazel F. Lazear, 12th Missouri Cavalry (Militia), Greenville, August 29, 1862

An estimated Rebel force of several hundred men under Colonel William L. Jeffers surprises the Union soldiers of the 12th Missouri Cavalry along Crooked Creek. Heavy Rebel fire forces Major Lazear's militia to retreat until defensive positions are established along a picket fence. Major Lazear gathers up his forces the next day to counterattack, but the Rebel force has hastily abandoned its camp and supplies.

Union Casualties and Losses: 11
Confederate Casualties: widely vary between 6 and 40

Action: Skirmish at Coon Creek near Lamar, Barton County, August 24, 1862—2nd and 6th Kansas Cavalry

Union Casualties: 30
Confederate Casualties: unknown

Action: Skirmish at Bloomfield, Stoddard County, August 24, 1862—13th Illinois Cavalry

Confederate Casualties: 20

Action: Skirmish in Howard County, August 28, 1862—4th Missouri State Militia Cavalry

Union Casualties and Losses: 11
Confederate Casualties: unknown

ACTION: Skirmish at Ashley, Pike County, August 28, 1862—Pierce's Company State Militia

Union Casualties: 6
Confederate Casualties: unknown

ACTION: Skirmish near Iberia, Miller County, August 29, 1862—Missouri Enrolled Militia

Union Casualties: 7
Confederate Casualties: unknown

ACTION: Skirmish at California House, Moniteau County, August 29, 1862—13th Missouri State Militia Cavalry

Union Casualties: 4
Confederate Casualties: unknown

ACTION: Skirmish at Roanoke, Howard County, September 6, 1862—2nd Merrill Horse Cavalry

Union Casualties: 1

ACTION: Skirmish at Bloomfield, Stoddard County, September 11, 1862—13th Illinois Cavalry, 1st Wisconsin Cavalry

Union Casualties: 8
Confederate Casualties: unknown

ACTION: Skirmish at Newtonia, Newton County, September 13, 1862

In an effort to maintain a foothold in Missouri and hopefully redeem Confederate losses in early 1862 at the Battle of Pea Ridge, General Sterling Price's cavalry commander, Colonel Joseph Shelby, establishes the Camp Coffey training camp south of the Union garrison at Newtonia with 1,500 Missouri Rebel cavalrymen. The Union garrison, consisting of the 6th Missouri State Cavalry, is driven away to Mount Vernon and occupied by Rebel forces. Colonel Upton Hays, commander of the 6th Missouri Cavalry, CSA, is killed. Colonel Douglas Cooper moves the 31st Texas Cavalry and the 1st Cherokee Battalion to join forces with Shelby and occupies Newtonia two weeks later.

Union Casualties: 14
Confederate Casualties: unknown (other than death of Colonel Hays)

ACTION: Skirmish at Bragg's Farm, near Whaley's Mill, September 13, 1862—*OR*, Brigadier General John McNeil, Headquarters McNeil's column on the march, September 14, 1862

2nd Missouri State Militia Cavalry pursues and disperses Colonel Joseph Porter's force of four hundred to five hundred Rebel soldiers, capturing a considerable amount of horses and provisions.

Union Casualties: 3
Confederate Casualties and Losses: estimated over 22

ACTION: Skirmish at Strother's Fork of Black River, Iron County, September 13, 1862—*OR*, Colonel Samuel H. Melcher, Washington County (Missouri) Militia, Potosi, Missouri, September 15, 1862

Schofield's Hussars State Militia, 1st Missouri Militia Infantry, Washington County Enrolled Militia, commanded by Captains Craig and Breckenridge, attack and disperse a Rebel camp, taking several prisoners, horses and other provisions and freeing three Union prisoners.

Union Casualties: 2
Confederate Casualties and Losses: 12

ACTION: Skirmish at Mount Vernon, Lawrence County, September 19, 1862—*OR*, Brigadier General Egbert B. Brown, Headquarters 4th Brigade, Mount Vernon, September 19, 1862

Captain John Long's Rebel force of seventy engages Union militia forces of the 14th State Militia Cavalry and Weer's Battalion Enrolled Militia, anticipating a Rebel approach on Mount Vernon. The Rebel force retreats but is attacked later by Union militia cavalry attempting to cut off escape.

Union Casualties: 1
Confederate Casualties and Losses: estimated over 5

ACTION: Skirmish at Hickory Grove, Warren County, September 19, 1862—6th Kansas Cavalry

Union Casualties: 3
Confederate Casualties: unknown

ACTION: Skirmish at Shirley's Ford, Spring River, Jasper County, September 20, 1862—2nd and 3rd Kansas Indian Home Guard

Union Casualties: 29
Confederate Casualties: unknown

ACTION: Lincoln suspends writ of habeas corpus, September 24, 1862

Proclamation is issued by the president suspending habeas corpus against all Rebels, insurgents and persons who resisted the draft and were guilty of disloyalty. Lincoln uses his war powers to create the facility for administration of an Arbitrary Arrest Program, placing military commanders in the unfamiliar role of law enforcement.

Action: Skirmish near Cambridge, Saline County, September 26, 1862—9th Missouri State Militia Cavalry

Union Casualties: 5
Confederate Casualties: unknown

Action: Battle of Newtonia, Newton County, September 30, 1862

Approximately 6,000 Union soldiers from Fort Scott, Baxter Springs, Springfield and Mount Vernon converge on Newtonia to deal with a considerable Confederate force in and near Newtonia. A daylong battle begins during the early morning when approximately 1,500 soldiers from the Army of the Frontier of Union brigadier general James Blunt attack Confederate forces commanded by Colonel Douglas Cooper and Colonel Joseph Shelby. Rebel reinforcements bolster defending Confederate forces and force a withdrawal of engaged Union forces. Later, Union reinforcements arrive and threaten the Confederate right flank until the arrival of additional Confederate forces finally stops the Union advance and forces a retirement as darkness emerged. Union forces attempt an orderly withdrawal, but fear over the size of the pursuing Confederate forces turns into a rout of Blunt's forces throughout the night until Union forces reach safety in Sarcoxie, ten miles away.

Union Casualties: estimated as high as 245
Confederate Casualties: estimated at possibly 100

Why It Matters: Though a Confederate victory, control of the region of southwest Missouri eluded the South due to the continued presence of a large Union army. The Confederate leaders conducted bold, audacious raids in 1863 and 1864, but most military engagements consisted of Rebel partisan bands raiding and looting supplies from Union sympathizers for the duration of the war. The Battle of Newtonia witnessed Native Americans participating in a significant role for both sides.

Tourism Notes: The Ritchie Mansion in Newtonia, Union headquarters and site of both battles, tells the story of Confederate spy Myra Belle Shirley, later known as outlaw "Belle Starr," including her imprisonment and escape. Several websites highlight Newton County's violent Civil War history (www.newtoncountymotourism.org/map.php is a good place to start).

Action: Battle of Granby, Newton County, October 4, 1862—*OR*, Lieutenant Colonel M.W. Buster, Indian Battalion, Camp White Rock, Prairie, Mississippi County, October 7, 1862

The Federal army gains control over lead mines, but the mines' smelter is destroyed in the fighting.

Why It Matters: A large discovery of lead in 1850 led to the Granby Stampede, which spawned a boomtown of eight thousand people at its peak. By 1859, 25 million tons of lead had been stripped out of the mines, making it the largest mining and smelting operation in Missouri and a critical resource for both sides to control.

Action: Skirmishes at Liberty and Sibley's Landing, Jackson County, October 6, 1862—*OR*, Captain Daniel H. David, 5th Missouri Cavalry (Militia), Camp Thomas, Independence, Missouri, October 8, 1862

Captain Daniel H. David and four companies of the 5th Missouri State Militia Cavalry engage approximately 130 members of William Quantrill's and Colonel Child's guerrilla bands near a landmark known as Big Hill. A forty-five-minute engagement at close quarters forces Rebel guerrillas off Big Hill, and they quickly scatter from the site. Reinforcements under Captain Vanzant join Captain David, who continues the next day with some success; weary from traveling in thick brush, however, the pursuit is called off.

Union Casualties: Several
Confederate Casualties: Several, including capture of Colonel Child

Action: Raid on Concordia, Lafayette County, October 5, 1862, July 13, 1863

Bushwhackers plunder the town and murder several citizens.

Action: Skirmish near New Franklin, Howard County, October 7, 1862

Lieutenant Joseph Street, commanding a company of the 9th Cavalry Missouri State Militia, attacks and disperses a force of seventy-five Rebels camped outside New Franklin.

Confederate Casualties: estimated over 3

Action: Skirmish at Hazel Bottom, Barry County, October 14, 1862—Kansas 2nd Cavalry

Union Casualties: 3
Confederate Casualties: unknown

Action: Skirmish at Portland, Callaway County, October 16, 1862—1st Battalion State Militia Cavalry (Krekel's)

Action: Palmyra Massacre, Marion County, October 18, 1862

Ten Confederate prisoners of war are executed after Confederate forces fail to comply with Colonel John McNeil's ultimatum to return an abducted local Union supporter, and suspected Union spy, Andrew Alsman.

WHY IT MATTERS: Colonel McNeil's actions were reported by the news media and widely criticized. After the war, Colonel McNeil admitted that the unintended consequence of this event was an increase in Confederate army enlistments.

TOURISM NOTES: A granite monument was erected in memory of the executed Rebel soldiers, along with the placement of several informative panels to explain the massacre at Palmyra.

ACTION: Skirmish at Marshfield, Webster County, October 20, 1862—10th Illinois Cavalry

Union Casualties: 2
Confederate Casualties: unknown

ACTION: Skirmish at Van Buren, Carter County, October 22, 1862—12th Missouri State Militia Cavalry

Union Casualties: 1
Confederate Casualties: unknown

ACTION: Raid at Dayton, Cass County, October 23, 1862

William Quantrill and his band attack a Federal wagon train.

Union Casualties: 20
Confederate Casualties: unknown

ACTION: Skirmish at Grand Prairie, St. Louis County, October 24, 1862

Union Casualties: 3
Confederate Casualties: 28

Action: Skirmish at Clarkton, Dunklin County, Missouri, October 23 and 28, 1862—2nd Illinois Artillery, 72nd Infantry, 2nd Illinois Cavalry

Union Casualties: unknown
Confederate Casualties: 12

Action: Battle of Island Mound, Bates County, October 26–28, 1862

Escaped slaves from Missouri, Arkansas and Indian Territory are mustered into the Kansas militia's 1st Kansas Colored Volunteers under Captain James Williams. The regiment, as part of two battalions of 240 men commanded by Captain's Richard Ward and Henry Seaman as well as the 5th Kansas Cavalry, is ordered to break up a guerrilla force situated on Hog Island in the Osage River, nine miles east of the Kansas-Missouri border. On October 27, cavalry scouts (consisting of Native and African Americans) identify a combined force of approximately 350 Confederate guerrillas under Bill Truman and Dick Hancock along with Missouri State Guard recruits commanded by Colonel Jeremiah Cockrell. The Union force sends for assistance as they fortified the Toothman Homestead using fence rails to create breastworks, but by October 29, Kansas militia rations are running low. Skirmishing breaks out when guerrilla forces set the prairie around the Union camp on fire. This action is followed by the attack of a guerrilla force that divides the Kansas militia. A melee follows in which Kansas Colored militia caught in the path of the charging Confederate cavalry bravely stand their ground and form a line to return fire. Although significant Kansas militia casualties are incurred, the African American soldiers remain steadfast until Union reinforcements engage the guerrillas and force their withdrawal.

Union Casualties: 18
Confederate Casualties: 30–40

Why It Matters: This event is considered one of the earliest engagements of an African American regiment during the war. The 1st Kansas Colored Volunteers earned the nickname of "First to Fight, First to Fall" as the first all–African American unit to fight as free men before President Abraham Lincoln's Emancipation Proclamation, when the mustering of colored troops into United States Federal service occurred. A *New York Times* reporter witnessed the engagement and described how the fierce fighting of the black troops reflected a measure of cold resolve not to be forced back into slavery or endure their almost certain execution if captured. This event clearly demonstrated that African American soldiers could hold their own in a desperate pitched engagement. In December 1864, the Kansas militia was designated a Federal unit of the United States Colored Troops.

TOURISM NOTES: In 2012, Missouri's Department of Natural Resources designated forty acres 6 miles southwest of Butler on the Toothman Homestead as a State Historic Site. Several interpretive panels describe the Battle of Island Mound. From Highway 49/71, take Exit 131 and travel west on MO52 3.5 miles to Highway K, south 1.5 miles to NW 10002 Road and west for 0.8 miles to find the battle site on the left.

ACTION: Skirmish at Lamar, Barton County, November 5, 1862

Missouri Militia Cavalry fights off William Quantrill's guerrilla band during a raid and sets fire to the town.

Union Casualties: 4
Confederate Casualties: unknown

ACTION: Skirmish at Harrisonville, Cass County, November 3, 1862—5th and 6th Missouri Cavalry

Union Casualties: 13
Confederate Casualties: 26

TOURISM NOTES: The City of Harrisonville has created three large Civil War murals located on buildings just off the courthouse square. Burnt District interpretive panels and monuments are located at the Cass County Justice Center, 2501 West Wall.

ACTION: Battle of Clark's Mill at Big Beaver Creek, Douglas County, November 7, 1862

A Union force commanded by Captain Hiram Barstow moving southeast from Clark's Mill briefly skirmishes with a large Confederate force of approximately one thousand Rebels before falling back to Clark's Mill. Captain Barstow's force suffers heavy casualties during a desperate five-hour fight and eventually complies with Confederate demands to surrender. The Confederate commander later paroles the Union troops and burns the blockhouse at Clark's Mill before departing.

Union Casualties and Losses: 113
Confederate Casualties: unknown

WHY IT MATTERS: While some Confederate forces remained to maintain a tiny toehold in southwest Missouri, most returned to the Arkansas Boston Mountains.

ACTION: Skirmish at Beaver Creek, Texas County, November 24, 1862—99th Illinois Infantry, 21st Iowa, 3rd Missouri Cavalry

Union Casualties: 16
Confederate Casualties: 25

ACTION: Skirmish at Carthage, Jasper County, November 27, 1862—2nd Kansas Cavalry

Union Casualties: 1
Confederate Casualties: unknown

Action: George Todd's raid on New (Little) Santa Fe, Jackson County, late fall/early winter of 1862

Following the successful Union army Prairie Grove Campaign in Arkansas, many of Quantrill's guerrillas eventually return to Jackson County and commence guerrilla operations against Union forces and sympathizers. About 30 guerrillas under George Todd engage 62 Jayhawkers utilizing the preferred guerrilla tactic of surprise ambushes on enemy forces at close range, where the use of revolvers is most effective and lethal. Jayhawkers fight a desperate engagement until they are reinforced by a larger force of 150 Jayhawkers.

Action: George Todd's guerrilla campaign, Jackson County, Kansas-Missouri border, December 3–18, 1862

George Todd's guerrilla band conducts a campaign of terrible retribution and deprivations on suspected pro-Union supporters, at times raiding three settlements per day.

Action: Curtis's winter campaign, November 1862–February 1863

General Samuel Curtis's responsibility is essentially to ensure the strategic defense of Missouri, while General Henry Halleck oversees the Union strategy to take control of the Mississippi River. Curtis, concerned over seemingly uncontested Confederate raiding into Missouri, directs Brigadier General Frederick Steele's Union forces at Helena, Arkansas, be moved to reinforce the garrison at the important Federal railhead in Pilot Knob. After complaints from Federal military and political leaders over General Curtis's unexpected change of direction in strategy against the Arkansas capital in Little Rock, General Halleck countermands General Curtis's order and directs the Federal forces of Brigadier General Frederick Steele to return to Helena.

General Curtis then directs the Army of Southeastern Missouri to undertake a winter campaign through southeastern Missouri into Arkansas. Halleck raises concerns over the necessity of such a move but tends to defer to his commanders in the field. Over the objections of Curtis's senior commanders, the campaign proceeds. The campaign is an arduous trial of transporting and securing supply trains from the base in Pilot Knob over the difficult terrain of the Ozark Hills through Wayne, Reynolds, Carter and Oregon Counties, often moving at times over roads made impassable after heavy rains. One story mentions that a bridge built over the Black River at Carter's Ford was dismantled to build canoes to rescue soldiers after a deluge of nine inches. The shortage of food also results in Union forces arbitrarily replenishing shortages from the local population. Finally, in February, with the entire Army of Southeastern Missouri of ten thousand men at West Plains, the only military action is a surprise raid by Colonel George E. Waring's 4th Missouri Cavalry on Confederate forces at Batesville that results in the capture of forty prisoners, including three officers.

WHY IT MATTERS: This campaign is an example of the senior Federal army leadership's strategic shortcomings in the early years. John F. Bradbury pointed out in his study of this campaign in the *Missouri Historical Review* that the North still lacked a general who could envision and direct the overall strategic effort against the Confederate defense perimeter. Any belief by Missouri's Federal commanders that southern Missouri guerrilla operations were crippled was negated when Generals Marmaduke and Shelby conducted bold raids into Missouri during the first half of 1863.

Actions in 1863

In the spring of 1863, the guerrillas returned to Missouri from Texas stronger, more numerous and exceedingly dangerous. They had gotten their baptism by fire during their operations in 1862 and had learned how to fight," wrote Donald Gilmore in his balanced and well-researched book, *Civil War on the Missouri-Kansas Border*. Gilmore described how the guerrilla bands had mastered silence and stealth in their operations by covering their tracks, leaving little trace of their presence and size. Locals became important sources for providing information of Federal forces operating in the area. Like the Indians of the frontier when outnumbered, their superior knowledge of trails and roads enabled guerrilla bands to often gain the element of surprise just prior to an attack. Before Union reinforcements could respond, the guerrillas disappeared into the dense foliage in the country. Their preferred tactic was the ambush, especially effective when the element of surprise was achieved, delivering devastating firepower at close range. If Union soldiers panicked and fled, they often were tracked down and killed. Guerrilla attacks on fortified locations were usually much less successful and led to higher casualties. Success was enhanced when guerrillas could fight in familiar terrain that concealed their movement. The guerrillas' most important center of gravity was the freedom of action mobility provided, as was clearly demonstrated at the devastating massacres on Union troops at Lawrence, Baxter Springs and Centralia in 1864.

Federal forces enjoyed resounding victories at Shiloh in 1862 and Vicksburg in 1863, but the situation changed when Federal forces were pulled east from Missouri after the Confederate victory at Chickamauga, Tennessee, and during the Siege of Chattanooga. Missouri now had to rely primarily on state militia units conducting garrison duty to deal with the constant harassment and raiding by southern guerrilla and partisan bands. Large-scale operations such as Confederate raids on Springfield and Cape Girardeau were repulsed in the winter and spring of 1863, an indication that such actions may have been bold and audacious but were not sustainable and usually failed to achieve meaningful strategic goals of occupying key terrain and capturing and holding Union supply points.

Confederate guerrilla captain William Quantrill, commanding a large guerrilla force of more than 400 of some of the most ruthless and violent bushwhackers, raided and burned nearly all of Lawrence to the ground, murdering an estimated 150 male inhabitants. Deprivations at Lawrence provide further justification among combatants for adopting an unofficial policy of "No quarter asked, No quarter given" toward captives and often innocent civilians. The reputations of Quantrill associates such as William "Bloody Bill" Anderson, Archie Clement, the Todd brothers, John Thrailkill and the James and Younger brothers became legendary. After the war, stories filled volumes of fiction and pseudo-nonfiction literature describing deprivations of blood-thirsty revenge against Union troops and Northern supporters, overshadowing the equally heinous acts by pro-Union and Federal forces.

The Union commander on the Kansas-Missouri border, General Thomas Ewing, unable to deny the support of guerrilla bands by pro-Southern sympathizers, conducted his own version of nineteenth-century ethnic cleansing when he issued General Order No. 11, a directive forcing the evacuation in fifteen days of an estimated fifteen thousand to twenty thousand suspected Southern sympathizers from four western Missouri counties. Jayhawker bands were known to have assisted in the removal of these largely innocent settlers. Decisive Union victories at Vicksburg and Gettysburg provided Northern leadership cause to believe that the Union would ultimately prevail.

TOURISM NOTES: General Ewing wrote the historic General Order No. 11 in the Pacific House Hotel in the River Market Area, Fourth and Delaware, Kansas City, Missouri. There is some question of whether it was signed at the Pacific House Hotel or possibly another location, such as Westport.

ACTION: Operations against Brigadier General John Marmaduke in Missouri, December 31, 1862–January 25, 1863

General John Marmaduke's division, 1st Corps, Trans-Mississippi Department of the Confederacy, undertakes a bold campaign to threaten Union supply lines between Springfield and Rolla and draw the Union Army of the Frontier out of Arkansas. Marmaduke, with approximately 1,900 men (although Union estimates were considerably higher), departs Arkansas into southwestern Missouri, attacking small Union garrisons at Fort Lawrene and in Forsythe and Ozark, Missouri.

ACTION: Second Battle of Springfield, Greene County, January 7–8, 1863

Confederate Brigadier General John Marmaduke's forces learn of the weakly defended supply depot at Springfield while moving north through Forsyth. In order to prevent Union reinforcements, Marmaduke's forces drive off the Union forces at Ozark. Colonel Emmett MacDonald destroys Union Fort Lawrence at Lawrence Mill on Beaver Creek southwest of Ava, Missouri. Colonel Joseph Porter's Confederate brigade is directed to move on Springfield instead of its securing its original objective of Hartville. Although forewarned of a sizeable Confederate force en route to take Springfield, Brigadier General Egbert Brown's Union forces of the 18th Iowa Infantry; 3rd, 4th and 14th Missouri State Militia Cavalry; and 74th Enrolled Militia, along with citizens and convalescents, choose to remain and defend from four earthen forts and a two-story blockaded college academy building used as a prison.

General Brown orders several buildings burned to obfuscate Confederate forces approaching from the south and west. After heavy fighting, Confederate forces occupy the brick academy and push Union forces back, but an attack on Fort No. 4 is repulsed. After taking heavy casualties and unable to continue pressing the Union position as the sun was setting, Marmaduke withdraws down the Ozark Road.

Union Casualties and Losses: estimated at 146–231
Confederate Casualties and Losses: estimated at 150–290

TOURISM NOTES: Springfield has created an informative website on Ozark Civil War history (http://www.ozarkscivilwar.org). The website has links to many of the other major engagements in southwest Missouri, such as Carthage, Dug Springs, Wilson's Creek, Zagonyi's Charge, Pea Ridge, Prairie Grove, Hartville, Mine Creek, Newtonia and Price's Missouri raid. A walking tour of twelve interpretive panels of the Battle of Springfield, beginning at Park Central Square, is available at www.springfield1863.org.

ACTION: Battle of Hartville and the death of Confederate colonel Joseph Porter, Wright County, January 9–11, 1863

After Marmaduke's forces are repulsed at Springfield, he learns of Union forces approaching and reorganizes for a confrontation. Colonel Samuel Merrill and 750 men from of the 99th Illinois Infantry, 21st Iowa Infantry, 3rd Iowa Cavalry and 3rd Missouri Cavalry depart Houston, Missouri, and, after reconnoitering Marmaduke's forces, take up defensive positions in Hartville.

After an intense four-hour battle, Union forces repulse several Confederate attacks. Union forces withdraw first, but Marmaduke's Confederate forces soon withdraw back to Arkansas. Reports indicate that Colonel Joseph Porter is mortally wounded by artillery fragments during a cavalry charge. Porter manages to return with the army to Camp Salado and Batesville, Arkansas, where he dies from his wounds.

The location of his grave remains unknown, but oral word passed down over time suggests that he is buried on the farm of cousin Ezekiel Porter, just north of Hartville, now known as Porter's Cemetery, near Competition, Missouri.

Union Casualties: 78
Confederate Casualties: 111

Actions in 1863

Action: Skirmish at Columbia, Boone County, January 21, 1863—61st Enrolled Militia

Union Casualties: 2
Confederate Casualties: unknown

Action: Raid on Granby, Newton County, March 3, 1863—8th Missouri Militia Cavalry

Union Casualties: 4
Confederate Casualties: unknown

Action: Skirmish at Blue Springs near Independence, Jackson County, March 22, 1863—1st and 5th Missouri Militia Cavalry

Union Casualties: 14
Confederate Casualties: unknown

Action: Battle of Fort Benton (Patterson, Missouri), Wayne County, April 20, 1863—3rd Missouri Militia Cavalry

Union Casualties and Losses: 60
Confederate Casualties: unknown

Campaign: General John Marmaduke's Cape Girardeau campaign, mid-April to early May 1863

Brigadier General John Marmaduke, commanding a division of approximately five thousand Rebel soldiers, advances north into Missouri from northeast Arkansas seeking desperately needed supplies for his poorly armed and equipped troops. Marmaduke directs one brigade column under Colonel George Carter and Colonel Colton Green to capture the Federal garrison at Bloomfield, Missouri. A second column, led by Colonel

Joseph Shelby with his Iron Brigade, and another brigade commanded by Colonel John Burbridge, accompanied by the support of eight to ten artillery pieces, are sent north to intercept and capture Union brigadier general John McNeil traveling to Union headquarters near Pilot Knob. The Mingo Swamps in Stoddard County delay Confederate forces en route to Bloomfield and provide McNeil time to retreat northeast to the Union fortifications at Cape Girardeau.

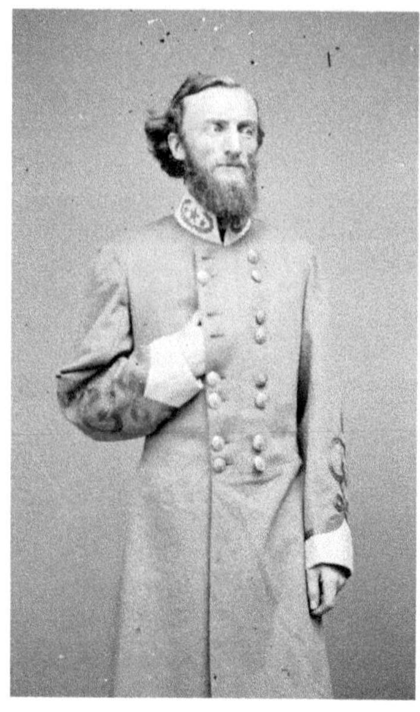

John S. Marmaduke. *Courtesy of the Library of Congress.*

ACTION: Battle of Cape Girardeau, Cape Girardeau County, April 25–26, 1863

Disobeying orders, Colonel Carter pursues General McNeil to Cape Girardeau and demands the garrison's surrender. McNeil believes the defensive positions of the fortress to be impregnable and refuses to surrender; instead, he prepares for a powerful Confederate siege. McNeil and his force of four thousand men withstand an attack on the morning of April 26 by Marmaduke's division. The attack, essentially an artillery duel, lasts four to five hours and inflicts considerable casualties on Confederate forces. Marmaduke, stymied by the formidable nature of the forts on the western side, withdraws his forces to Arkansas. Confederate reports of casualty figures appear to have been exaggerated but were estimated at one hundred killed and three hundred wounded.

Union Casualties: 12
Confederate Casualties and Losses: 335–400

HISTORICAL NOTE: In 1861, Brigadier General Ulysses S. Grant had approved the construction of a large mutually supporting fortress (Forts A,

B, C and D) at strategic locations to protect Cape Girardeau from attacks by land and Confederate river gunboats. Fort B was located on high ground currently occupied by Southeast Missouri State University.

Biographical Sketch: John Marmaduke, who began the war as a second lieutenant, was promoted to the rank of major general in the Confederate cavalry by the war's conclusion. John Marmaduke participated and distinguished himself in more than a dozen major engagements both in and away (Shiloh and the Louisiana Red River Campaign) from Missouri. John Marmaduke later served a term as governor of Missouri in the 1880s.

Why It Matters: While historically considered a tactical draw, strategically it was a Union victory because of the decision made by Marmaduke to withdraw in order to avoid the unnecessary expenditure of lives to overcome such defenses. Confederate forces were increasingly unable to hold territory in Missouri for any length of time and were forced to withdraw to Arkansas. While raids may have been instrumental in gaining new recruits, Confederate leaders had to deal with the relentless demands of feeding and equipping them and their horses.

Action: Battle of Chalk Bluff and St. Francis River, Butler County, May 1–2, 1863

Chalk Bluff is General John Marmaduke's last engagement of his second expedition into Missouri. Marmaduke's forces have to cross the St. Francis River on the Missouri-Arkansas border in order to safely return to their home base in Helena. The St. Francis River has steep chalky white banks, making a hasty river crossing by cavalry a treacherous and risky task. The 2nd Division of the Army of the Frontier, under the command of Brigadier General William Vandever, is delayed by Marmaduke's rear guard to provide time to build a bridge over the St. Francis River and safely cross into Arkansas. The crossing will remain a key terrain feature to the end of the war, as both sides considered it an important transportation hub to raid and control.

Union Casualties and Losses: 120
Confederate Casualties and Losses: 210

WHY IT MATTERS: General Marmaduke's crossing worked, saving his force, but it came at a high cost in casualties and concluded his Spring Offensive with little success.

TOURISM NOTES: A small portion of the battle site is preserved as the Chalk Bluff Battlefield Park and is listed in the National Register of Historic Places. A hiking trail crosses the battlefield where informative historic markers and panels are provided to explain the battle in more detail.

ACTION: Raid on Plattsburg, Clinton County, May 21, 1863

Elements of Captain William Quantrill's guerrilla band raid and capture Federal troops garrisoned near the county courthouse.

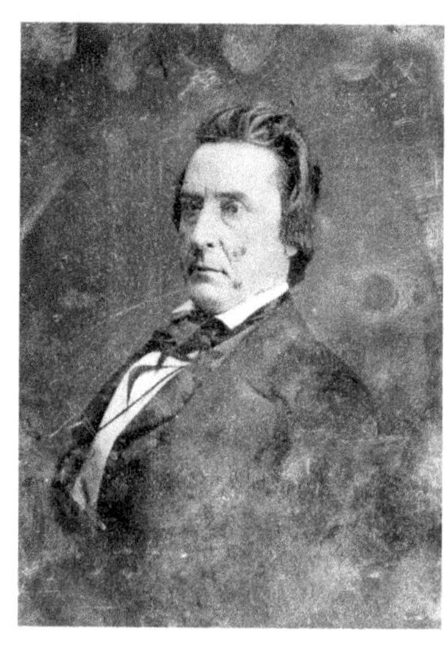

David Rice Atchison. *Courtesy of the Library of Congress.*

BIOGRAPHICAL SKETCH: A statue of David R. Atchison was erected outside the Clinton County Courthouse in Plattsburg, recognizing his unofficial role as president of the United States for one day. An important lawyer, judge and politician, in 1843 he became the first senator from western Missouri at the age of thirty-six. He rose to be the U.S. Senate's president pro tem two years later. During his twelve years of service, Atchison played an influential role in major political decisions leading up to the secessionist crises and the American Civil War. He graduated from Transylvania University in Lexington, Kentucky, with the future president of the Confederacy, Jefferson Davis. His staunch antislavery stance positioned him as a rival and, later, bitter enemy of another important Missouri senator, Thomas Hart Benton, although both were Democrats.

Their rivalry and views on territorial expansion influenced Congress to repeal provisions of the Missouri Compromise of 1820 banning slavery and support Atchison's proposal to Senator Stephen Douglas of introducing the

Kansas-Nebraska Act in 1853, recommending statehood by the process of popular sovereignty. Atchison embroiled himself into further controversy as an abolitionist by helping found the town of Atchison, Kansas, as a proslavery settlement named after him.

As events would indicate, Free Soilers, a name given to antislavery political activists, would control the Kansas territorial legislature. Atchison incited proslavery Missourians by calling for the violent overthrow and killing of abolitionists in the territory. The term "Border Ruffians" was coined after a mob of five thousand armed proslavery Missourians was recruited at Atchison, Kansas, to seize polling places in Kansas at gunpoint, casting thousands of fraudulent votes on election day, March 30, 1855. A proslavery legislature was elected and upheld by the Federal government. Territorial Governor Andrew Reeder objected and was fired by President Franklin Pierce.

Raids and ambushes would become the order of the day as the territory earned the title of "Bleeding Kansas." Abolitionist fanatics like John Brown came west and committed acts of murder while organizing resistance against proslavery supporters.

ACTION: Skirmish and burning of Nevada City (Nevada), Vernon County, May 1863

Guerrilla leader Captain William Marchbanks's bushwhacker force attacks Federal militiaman, forcing them to take refuge in the building of the town jail. Militia successfully hold out in the town jail until the bushwhackers depart. Two days later, the townspeople are given only twenty minutes to vacate their homes before Nevada City is burned down by a suspected company of state militia.

WHY IT MATTERS: Considered the bushwhacker capital, Nevada is an example of a community near the Kansas-Missouri border that truly experienced the horrors of war, as half of the local population, including nearly all adult males, eventually fled Nevada.

TOURISM NOTES: Several Civil War historic sites can be visited in Nevada, Missouri. The Burning of Nevada interpretive panel resides on the west side of the Vernon County Courthouse. The Bushwhacker Museum provides an interesting history of Vernon County, particularly during the Missouri conflict, and is housed in a thirteen-thousand-square-foot building. One block from the courthouse square sits the restored Vernon County Jail. The Vernon County Jail, dating back to 1860, was one of two buildings not destroyed at the time of the burning of the town and has been restored. A monument to the Battle of Dry Wood Creek sits out front. Vernon County claims to have mustered more men into the Confederate army than any other Missouri county. Notorious outlaws Frank and Jesse James were suspected of hiding out in Vernon County. Frank lived in Nevada for several years after Jesse's death. The home is still standing. Take either of two Nevada exits off I-49 or enter off Highway 54 west from Fort Scott, Kansas, or east from El Dorado into town.

ACTION: Skirmish at Westport, Jackson County, June 17, 1863—9th Kansas

Union Casualties: 20
Confederate Casualties: unknown

ACTION: Fall of Vicksburg, July 4, 1863

General Ulysses S. Grant's Vicksburg Campaign and the capture of New Orleans in 1862 complete the return of control of the Mississippi River to the Union. Nearly half of the Confederacy lies west of the Mississippi River, and General Kirby Smith's Confederate Trans-Mississippi Department is now an isolated region.

ACTION: Skirmish at New Madrid, New Madrid County, August 7, 1863—24th Missouri Infantry

Union Casualties and Losses: 10
Confederate Casualties: unknown

Action: Burning of Pleasant Hill, Cass County, August 10–12, 1863

Cole Younger's guerrilla band conducts a three-day spree of destruction and burning of Pleasant Hill. Cass County earns the historical designation of the "Burnt District."

Action: Raid on Pineville, McDonald County, August 12, 1863

A skirmish between the forces of the 6th Missouri Militia Cavalry rout the Confederate forces of Captain John T. Coffee, resulting in the burning of the county courthouse and the destruction of most county records.

Historical Situation: Beginning in August 1863, the Union commander in the West, Brigadier General John Ewing, issued a series of general orders. The first, General Order No. 9, confiscated the slaves of homesteaders considered disloyal. These freed slaves could then enlist in the Federal army, providing an opportunity to fight against their old masters.

Action: Lawrence Massacre, Douglas County, Kansas, August 21, 1863

Guerrilla attrocities reach their zenith when Confederate partisan leader Captain William Quantrill organizes a force of 400 to 450 guerrillas near Warrensburg, Missouri, and attacks Lawrence, Kansas. During a ten-hour rampage, his men kill 150 civilians, primarily men and boys, and destroy 185 homes and buildings.

For official accounts of Quantrill's raid on Lawrence, Kansas, refer to the Report of Quantrill's Raid, Brigadier General Thomas Ewing Jr., commander of the District of the Border, August 31, 1863, and the Report of Quantrill's Raid, Major General John C. Schofield, September 14, 1863.

Why It Matters: Union commanders in Missouri believed that Confederate combatants in the area were actively supported by homesteaders in rural portions of four Missouri counties on the Kansas border south of the Missouri River: Bates, Cass, Vernon and Jackson. Federal forces were determined to put a stop to guerrilla raiding by any means necessary, even if it meant dispossessing civilian homesteaders.

ACTION: General Thomas Ewing issues General Order No. 11, August 25, 1863

Ewing orders the eviction of homesteaders (estimates as high as fifteen thousand to twenty thousand) and Missouri citizens from four Missouri counties along the Kansas-Missouri border. This act continues to encourage a climate of Confederate partisan reprisals. Jennison's Kansas Jayhawkers help evict and then burn the homes of suspected Southern sympathizers and guerrilla supporters, further enraging an already bitter populace. Senator Thomas Hart Benton becomes an outspoken opponent of this policy and considers it the Union's policy of ethnic cleansing.

TOURISM NOTES: A large metal plaque resides on the Bates County Courthouse grounds in Butler, describing the depopulating of Bates County regardless of loyalties and the destruction of nearly every structure by Union soldiers, forever changing the county.

Two excellent books provide comprehensive guides for tourists in Missouri. Gregory Wolk's *Friend and Foe Alike* provides a comprehensive guide of tour stops throughout Missouri. The north-central section ranges from Weston and Kansas City along the western border to Lexington and provides the location for thirty-two historical tour stops. Tour stop no. 119 at the corner of Fourth and Delaware features an interpretive panel of General Order No. 11 providing a historical account of the Pacific House Hotel, where General Ewing wrote the order, and the sobering events that followed for homesteaders affected by its onerous requirements. Additionally, the Civil War Round Table of Western Missouri has assembled a book, *Civil War Monuments and Memorials in Western Missouri*, that contains excellent pictures and locations of eighty-two historical Civil War sites in Missouri.

The blog *Trans-Mississippi Musings* provides an excellent overview of the Pacific House Hotel's history (transmississippimusings.com/pages/posts/the-pacific-house-and-order-number-11-historical-marker-18.php).

ACTION: Attack on the escort of Major General James Blunt at Baxter Springs, Kansas, October 6, 1863

During the Union army's pursuit of Quantrill's guerrillas after the Lawrence Massacre, a detachment of Quantrill's band captures a Union force away from Fort Scott, Kansas, near the Kansas-Missouri border and proceeds to rob and murder a large contingent of the Union soldiers.

Union Casualties and Losses: 77
Confederate Casualties: unknown

WHY IT MATTERS: Such attrocities increased the Union army's efforts to hunt down Quantrill and his guerrillas. Several of his lieutenants, including George Todd, William "Bloody Bill" Anderson and Archie Clement, anxious to spread their form of terror, broke off from Quantrill and journeyed into central Missouri, beginning a new phase of deadly raids on Union supply trains and rural population centers for a year or so before Union forces finally prevailed against these murderous bands.

ACTION: Depopulation of Butler, Bates County, September 1863

One month after General Ewing's Order No. 11, Union forces considered to be part of Jayhawker leader Colonel Charles Jennison's regiment plunder and destroy the city. No structures are left standing—a thriving community of six thousand three years before is now a smoldering ghost town.

CAMPAIGN: General Joseph Shelby's Missouri raid, September 22–October 26, 1863

Shelby's distinguished Iron Brigade travels 1,600 miles with eight hundred men, twelve wagons and two cannons, destroying ten Federal outposts and capturing forty colors, four hundred wagons and six thousand horses and mules while inflicting six hundred to one thousand casualties and paroling another six hundred. Casualties among Shelby's brigade were just one officer lost, but more than 15 percent of his troops did not return. In December 1863, Joseph Shelby, recognized for his gallant leadership, is promoted to brigadier general.

Biographical Sketch: Joseph Shelby was a slaveholder and wealthy hemp rope manufacturer in Waverly, Missouri. He was involved in the Kansas-Missouri Border War and organized and commanded a Border Ruffian company that was involved in harassing abolitionists voting for the Kansas territory legislature. Shelby became a close friend of highly respected pro-Union Missouri politician Francis P. Blair from St. Louis but declined Blair's offer of a Union army officer commission. Shelby was not particularly a supporter of slavery, but he was an ardent states' rights advocate. He was a good friend of John Hunt Morgan and early in the conflict aided Morgan's Kentucky Raiders in obtaining firing caps. After observing the outbreak of violence in St. Louis, Shelby returned to Waverly and raised one hundred men for the Missouri State Guard.

He participated in nearly every major battle in Missouri under General Sterling Price and became one of the most audacious cavalry officers for the Confederacy. He served with distinction at Carthage, Wilson's Creek, Lexington, Pea Ridge and Westport, as well as in the retreat from Westport. His famous Iron Brigade was formed after the Battle of Pea Ridge and took on a major role on the attack on Federal fortifications during the Battle of Helena, Arkansas, on July 4, 1863, where Shelby was wounded. During Price's raid in 1864, Shelby, now a general officer, along with Generals Marmaduke and Fagan formed the core of Price's cavalry army and were responsible for conducting numerous rear-guard actions, preventing the destruction of Price's army during the desperate retreat after the Battle of Westport.

Shelby's Iron Brigade was known to consist of veteran cavalrymen and known Rebel guerrillas. Toward the end of the conflict, word traveled that many guerrillas would be tried as criminals regardless of whether they surrendered their arms. After the surrender of the Confederate army, General Shelby and his remaining forces escaped from Missouri to Mexico and unsuccessfully offered their services first to Juarez and later to Emperor Maximilian I. Shelby and his men have been referred to by some as "the Undefeated." While many historians today consider Nathan Bedford Forrest the finest and bravest of Confederate cavalry commanders, Union major general Alfred Pleasonton—former commander of the cavalry forces of the Army of the Potomac at Gettysburg and at the largest cavalry battle, Brandy Station—believed that Shelby was superior in many respects to Forrest. Many Civil War historians are expected to contest that.

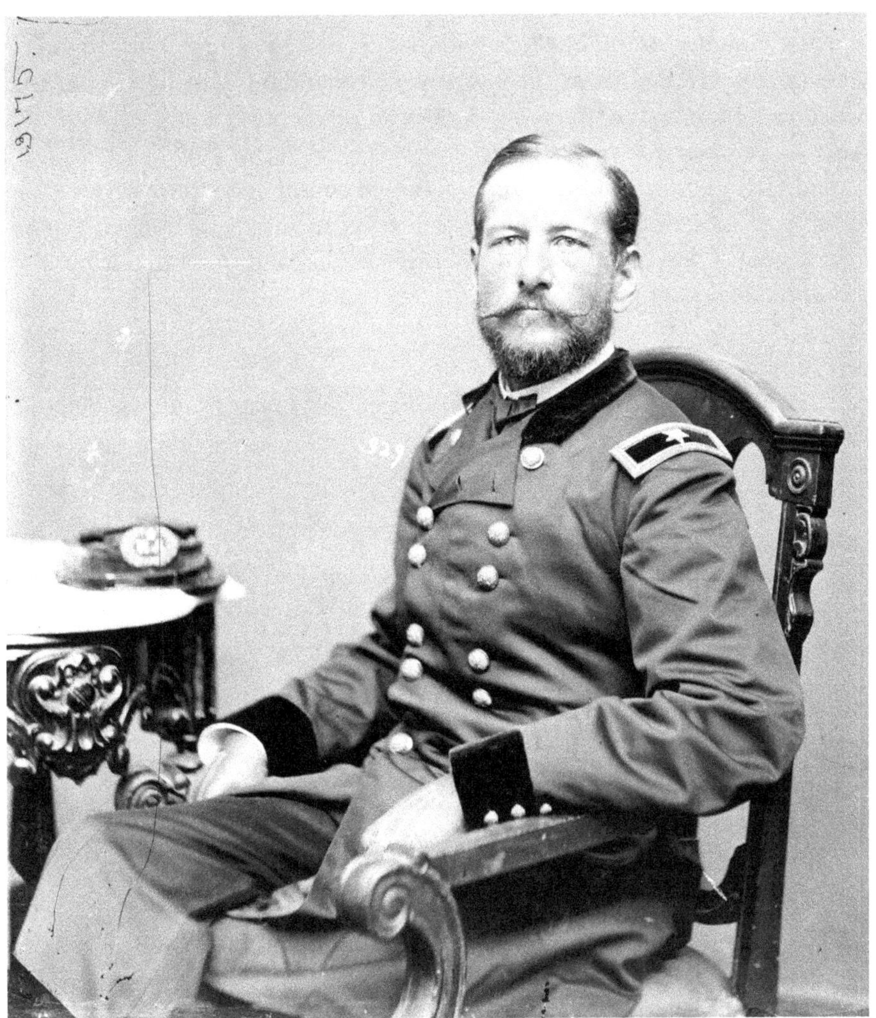

Alfred Pleasonton. *Courtesy of the Library of Congress.*

Joseph Shelby's adjutant (and chief of staff), John Newman Edward, became the future editor and founder of the *Kansas City Times*. A suspected white supremacist, Edward is credited with creating the legends of Jesse and Frank James and other bushwhackers turned bank robbers after the war.

ACTION: Colonel Joseph Shelby's raid into central Missouri—*OR*, Brigadier General Egbert B. Brown, U.S. Army, commanding, District of Central Missouri, Operations of October 6–26, 1863

A total of twenty-three official reports can be consulted in the *The War of the Rebellion: A Compilation of the Official Records* regarding the actions of Union forces against Joseph Shelby's Iron Brigade. Colonel Joseph Shelby also submitted his own official report.

ACTION: Colonel Joseph Shelby's Iron Brigade departs from Arkadelphia, Arkansas, September 22, 1863

ACTION: Skirmishes at Neosho, Newton County, at Bowers' Mill, Lawrence County, October 1863

ACTION: Skirmishes at Greenfield, Dade County, and Stockton, Cedar County, October 5, 1863

ACTION: Skirmish at Humansville, Polk County, October 6, 1863

ACTION: Skirmish near Warsaw, Benton County, October 7, 1863

ACTION: Skirmish near Cole Camp, Benton County, October 9, 1863

ACTION: Skirmishes in Tipton, Moniteau County, and Syracuse, Morgan County, October 9, 1863

The Confederate cavalry of Colonel Joseph Shelby surrounds the town of Tipton. The Confederates drive out a Union militia of one hundred local Union soldiers and capture the town. Shelby's forces destroy a nearby railroad bridge at La Mine Bridge before continuing operations toward Syracuse.

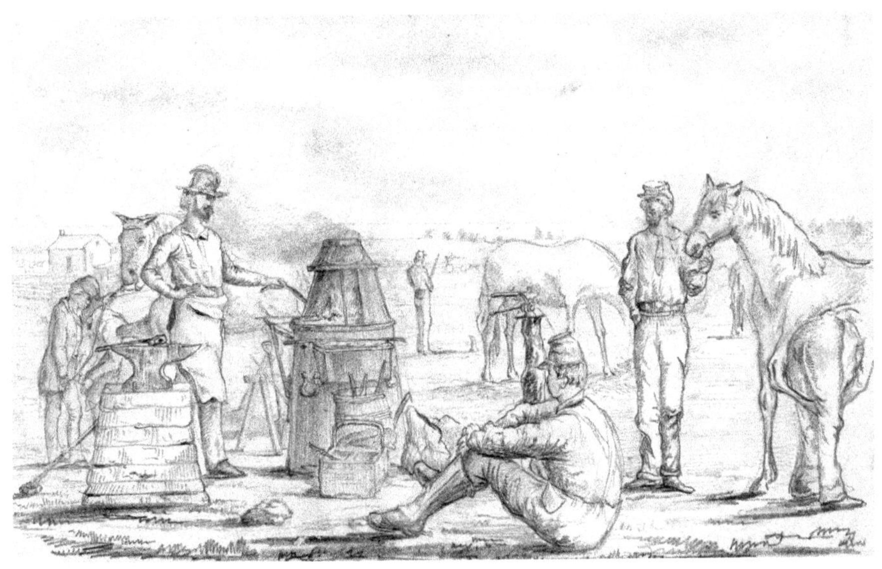

Blacksmithing in the army, near Tipton. *Courtesy of the Library of Congress.*

ACTION: Skirmish in Boonville, Cooper County, October 11, 1863

Colonel Joseph Shelby's Confederate cavalry force enters the town of Boonville. The town's few defenders quickly decide that they cannot protect the town and surrender to Shelby. Shelby departs in anticipation of the arrival of Federal reinforcements.

Action: Skirmish at Merrill's Crossing and Lamine Crossing, Otterville, Cooper County, October 12–13, 1863—Missouri Enrolled Militia, 1st Missouri Militia Battery; and 1st, 4th and 7th Missouri Militia Cavalry

Union Casualties: 16
Confederate Casualties: 123

Action: Skirmish in Arrow Rock, Saline County, October 13, 1863

On October 13, Brigadier General Egbert B. Brown, commanding a sizable Union cavalry force, follows Colonel Joseph Shelby and his Confederate cavalry force. The two sides engage in a brief skirmish at Arrow Rock. Federal forces almost surround Shelby's command, but Shelby's brigade slips through Union forces.

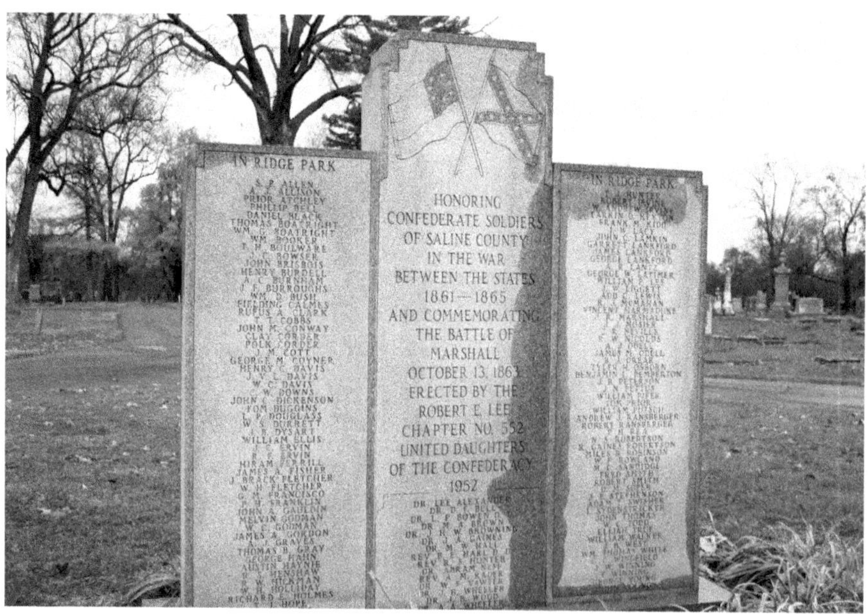

Confederate Memorial Ridge Park Cemetery, Marshall. *Courtesy of Brian Warren.*

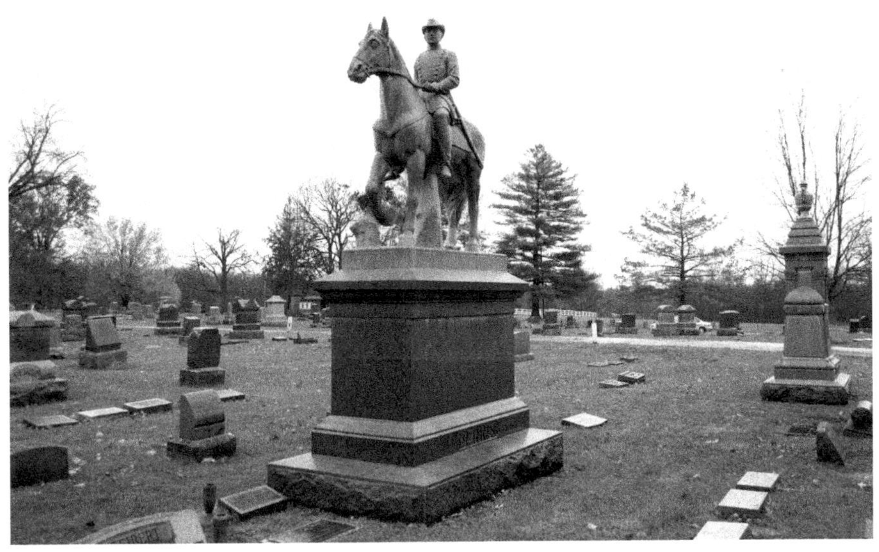

Mounted Soldier Ridge Park Cemetery, Marshall. *Courtesy of Brian Warren.*

ACTION: Battle of Marshall, Saline County, October 13, 1863—*OR*, Brigadier General Egbert Brown, commanding, Central District of Missouri, Jefferson City, October 13, 1863

Brown's forces decisively engage Shelby's cavalry forces, estimated at 2,000 Rebels, in Marshall, Missouri. A five-hour hard-fought battle ensues in which Shelby's raiders are defeated by General Egbert Brown's brigade of 1,600 soldiers. After capturing a substantial amount of Confederate weapons and supply trains, Union forces pursue scattered Confederate forces. Marshall is the high-water mark of Shelby's raid, and he is forced to return to Arkansas.

Union Casualties: 30
Confederate Casualties and Losses: estimated in excess of 176

TOURISM NOTES: A self-guided tour pamphlet of this battle can be downloaded from http://visitmarshallmo.com/pdf_files/battle%20of%20marshall%20pamphlet.pdf. An interpretive panel describing the raid and the Battle of Marshall is located at Indian Foothills Park east of town at 1510 East Eastwood Street overlooking railroad tracks and Salt Fork Creek.

ACTION: Skirmish at Scott's Ford, near Cuba, Crawford County, October 14, 1863

ACTION: Skirmish at Cross Timbers, Hickory County, October 16, 1863—18th Iowa

Confederate Casualties: 10

ACTION: Skirmishes at Johnstown, Deer Creek, Humansville, Polk County, October 16, 1863

ACTION: Skirmish in Cedar County, October 17, 1863

ACTION: Skirmish at Carthage, Jasper County, October 18, 1863

ACTION: Skirmish near Harrisonville, Cass County, October 24, 1863

ACTION: A Union patrol hunts down guerrilla leader Joe Cole, Portland, Callaway County, December 1, 1863

A known bushwhacker chief responsible for the deaths of several citizens and militiamen met his demise near Portland in a gunfight with a patrol of the 67th Enrolled Missouri Militia from Wellsville, commanded by Lieutenant A. Kempinski.

Actions in 1864

As the Civil War was entering its fourth year, the scale of physical destruction and human slaughter was far from over in the South and in Missouri. Union strategy called for establishing garrisons at county seats, where the main stone or brick buildings were sandbagged so a small group of sharpshooters could hold off raiding guerrilla bands. Fortified blockhouses were erected to protect rail line bridge crossings. Cavalry patrols were sent out daily between the garrisons. Communication was established to alert nearby garrisons in an attempt to corner or disrupt operations of roving guerrilla bands. Garrison commanders also had to deal with protecting provisions along supply routes that tied up Union forces engaged in escort duty. This became profoundly difficult, as guerrilla bands regularly cut telegraph lines and ambushed Union forces whenever the opportunity presented iteself. In a last desperate attempt to relieve the Union siege at Petersburg and Sherman's destruction of the South and possibly upset President Lincoln's reelection, the Confederacy authorized General Kirby Smith to conduct a raid through Missouri. The plan envisioned the ambitious tasks of seizing St. Louis and threatening Union supply operations in Kentucky and Tennessee. Confederate general Sterling Price's raid into Missouri with more than ten thousand Rebel soldiers is considered the longest cavalry raid, traveling 1,500 miles and fighting forty-three actions.

ACTION: Pursuit of Quantrill lieutenant Andrew Blunt in Jackson and Lafayette County, March–April 1864—*OR*, Brigadier General Egbert Brown to Colonel Robert Van Horn in Kansas City

Former Quantrill guerrillas Andrew Blunt and James Wilkerson and twenty followers are pursued and hunted down east of Kansas City. Blunt and nine of his companions are killed, and all are buried except Blunt, who is left to rot as a warning to any young guerrillas waiting to join up.

ACTION: Quantrill's guerrillas return from their winter sanctuary in Texas into Missouri and commenced raiding along Missouri border counties, May 1864

Quantrill's company of guerrillas return north to Missouri and attempt to draw Captain Philip Rohrer and his 7th Missouri Cavalry out of Carthage for a general engagement. Two days later, Quantrill's men attack a small garrison in Lamar, Missouri. Sergeant Jefferson Cavender's small garrison repulses two fierce guerrilla assaults. Union brigadier general Egbert Brown attempts to hunt down the elusive guerrilla bands with three thousand men from the 4th and 7th Missouri Cavalry, exhausting his forces. Egbert concluded the pursuit.

Confederate Casualties: 30

ACTION: Massacre at Lane's Prairie, Phelps County, May 26, 1864

A small detachment of 3rd Wisconsin Cavalry encounters a guerrilla party of twenty Rebels dressed in Federal uniforms. It is not clear whether the Wisconsin men are aware of their true identities and intent, but witnesses report that the cavalry soldiers are led into the nearby woods, where the guerrilla force opens fire. Some manage to escape, but Sergeant Legrand Carter and his men are found the next day by a party from Rolla, dead and stripped of their pants and boots.

Union Casualties: 5
Confederate Casualties: unknown

ACTION: Guerrillas commence raiding of Missouri steamboats, June–July 1864

Guerrilla bands attempting to seize riverboats cause General Samuel Curtis to forbid river traffic past Jefferson City by unarmed crews.

ACTION: Union forces conduct counter-guerrilla operations, June 1864

The local *Kansas City Journal* warns of increasingly larger guerrilla operations threatening the heavily populated Kansas City. Mobilization and arming of all able-bodied males commences to defend Kansas City. A large Union force from the 5th, 11th and 15th Missouri Cavalry under the command of Colonel Thomas Moonlight joins up with the 2nd Colorado Cavalry under Colonel J.H. Ford and commences pursuit of Quantrill's forces in eastern Jackson County toward Hickman Mills, Lone Jack and Sni River Hills. General Egbert Brown's forces conduct a determined pursuit of guerrilla bands, now led by Quantrill lieutenants Dick Yaeger, David Poole, Fletcher Taylor and George Todd. Brown's men cover 3,810 miles in nine days. Guerrilla leader Dick Yaeger is killed.

Union Casualties: 23
Confederate Casualties: 27

ACTION: Skirmish near Kingsville, Johnson County, June 12, 1864

The 1st Missouri Militia Cavalry detachment under the command of Sergeant J.V. Parman is ambushed by guerrillas under Anderson wearing blue uniforms. Only two Union soldiers manage to escape.

Union Casualties: 12

Action: Skirmish twelve miles south of Lexington, Lafayette County, June 14, 1864

The 1st Missouri State Militia Cavalry, escorting a wagon train, is badly mangled by William Anderson's band. The wagon train manages to return to its post but at a loss of considerable supplies and the killing of many U.S. Army mules.

Union Casualties: 10

Action: Skirmish at Columbia, Boone County, June 17, 1864—Missouri Enrolled Militia

Union Casualties: estimated at 2

Action: Counter-guerrilla operations intensify in Jackson and surrounding counties, July 1–20, 1864

In his largest operation to date, Brigadier General Egbert Brown conducts more than one hundred patrols, traveling over ten thousand miles and fighting twenty-eight actions. There are no prisoners taken during this campaign.

Union Casualties: 44
Confederate Casualties: estimated at 100

Action: Skirmish near Fayette, Howard County, July 1, 1864—9th Missouri Militia Cavalry

Union Casualties: 2
Confederate Casualties: unknown

Actions in 1864

Action: Skirmish at Platte City, Platte County, July 3, 1864—9th Missouri Militia Cavalry

Union Casualties: 2
Confederate Casualties: unknown

Action: Skirmish in Clay County, July 4, 1864—9th Missouri Militia Cavalry

Union Casualties: 4
Confederate Casualties: unknown

Action: Skirmish at Little Blue River, Jackson County, July 6, 1864

The 2nd Colorado Cavalry is engaged by George Todd's guerrilla band.

Union Casualties: 8
Confederate Casualties: unknown

Action: Skirmish at Richmond, Ray County, July 8, 1864—Enrolled Missouri Militia

Union Casualties: 2
Confederate Casualties: unknown

Action: Events leading up to raid on Plattsburg, July 1864

Confederate colonel John "Coon" Thornton recruits for several months in northwest Missouri and intends to join forces with General Sterling Price during his raid in 1864. Colonel Thornton arrives in Parkville and Platte City to gather Southern sympathizers and Confederate ex-patriots masquerading as Union garrison soldiers of the 82nd Enrolled Missouri Militia (aka the

Paw Paw militia). Thornton moves his force north to Camden Point, where it is surprised by Union cavalry and militia, routed and forced to retreat east toward Kingston in Caldwell County. By early July, two companies of the 89th Enrolled Missouri Militia (EMM) under the command of Captains John Turney and B.F. Poe are garrisoned at Plattsburg.

ACTION: Paw Paw Rebellion Skirmish at Camden Point, Platte County, July 13, 1864

A Confederate cavalry force of approximately two hundred to three hundred men under Colonel J.C. Thornton is ambushed while resting in a pasture outside Camden Point by more than seven hundred Federal forces of the 2nd Colorado and 15th Kansas Cavalry. Reportedly, four captured Rebels are executed. The town of Camden Point is later burned. One of the oldest Confederate memorials west of the Missouri River was placed at the Pleasant Grove Cemetery in 1871.

Union Casualties: 15
Confederate Casualties: 31

ACTION: Second Burning of Platte City, Platte County, July 13, 1864

Several dozen bushwhackers taking refuge in Platte City are captured and executed while Union forces set fire to Platte City, burning it for the second time.

TOURISM NOTES: A historical marker is located at the southbound I-29 rest stop, seven miles north of Platte City.

ACTION: Skirmish at Fredericksburg, near Excelsior Springs, Clay County, July 17, 1864, and August 12, 1864

The 2nd Colorado Cavalry, commanded by Captain Thomas Moses, is engaged by a large guerrilla force of two hundred to three hundred mostly raw recruits and disloyal Enrolled Missouri Militia disguised in blue uniforms on the O'Dell family homestead at the small hamlet of Fredericksburg. (Local historian Harry A. Soltysiak notes that two engagements occurred, but only one is recognized on local monuments.) The guerrilla forces are led by Colonel John Thrailkill, who had recently escaped from Alton Prison, and Quantrill guerrilla captain Charles Fletcher Taylor. Moses Colorado Cavalry troops initially hold their positions, but the guerrilla force is relentless in its attack and forces Union forces to disperse and retreat.

Union Casualties and Losses: 12
Confederate Casualties: estimated over 16

Tourism Notes: The area is now part of the Excelsior Springs Golf Course.

Action: Skirmish at Bloomfield, Stoddard County, July 14, 1864—2nd Missouri Militia Cavalry, Missouri Enrolled Militia

Union Casualties: 2
Confederate Casualties: unknown

Action: Skirmish at Ozark, Camden County, July 14–15, 1864—14th Kansas Cavalry

Union Casualties: 3
Confederate Casualties: unknown

Action: Skirmish at Webster, Washington County, July 19, 1864—Missouri Home Guard

Union Casualties: 1
Confederate Casualties: unknown

ACTION: Skirmish at Arrow Rock, Saline County, July 20, 1864—1st Missouri Militia Cavalry, Citizen Guard

Union Losses: 3
Confederate Casualties: unknown

ACTION: Skirmish at Plattsburg, Clinton County, July 21, 1864

Plattsburg is an engagement between elements of the 89th Enrolled Missouri Militia and guerrilla leader John Thrailkill's band of Confederate recruits. For several days, the garrison in Plattsburg has been aware of a sizeable Confederate force of approximately four hundred approaching from the east. An interesting tale of bravado is told locally concerning Thrailkill's Confederate force when it reaches the outskirts of Plattsburg. While a Union advanced guard awaits on the outskirts of town, a flag of truce from the guerilla force is observed by one of the garrison officers, Captain John Turney. Turney is subsequently approached by a Confederate courier and handed the following correspondence, which is promptly shown to the garrison commander:

> *COMMANDING OFFICER AT PLATTSBURG: JULY 21, 1864*
>
> *I hereby demand an immediate surrender of the town. We are not bushwhackers, but Confederate soldiers. Your men will be treated as prisoners of War.*
>
> *John Thrailkill, Major, commanding Confederate forces*
>
> *Maj. John Thrailkill, July 21, 1864*

The story continues with this succinct response by the garrison commander:

> *Sir: We are not here for the purpose of surrendering, but to defend the flag of our Country.*
>
> *B.F. Poe Captain, Commanding Post*

As Major Thrailkill deploys his men, Captain John Turney orders an attack but is killed in the initial exchange. Lieutenant George McCullough takes over for Captain Turney and orders the men to fall back, rejoin the garrison under Captain Poe and prepare to defend in Plattsburg. But Thrailkill soon learns of a Union Missouri State Militia cavalry unit approaching from Cameron, causing Thrailkill to call off the attack on Plattsburg.

Union Casualties: 2–5
Confederate Casualties: 2–4

ACTION: Skirmish at Carthage, Jasper County, July 21, 1864—Missouri Enrolled Militia

Union Casualties: 17
Confederate Casualties: unknown

ACTION: Skirmish near Camden Point, Platte County, July 22, 1864—2nd Colorado Cavalry, 9th Missouri Militia Cavalry

Union Casualties: 4
Confederate Casualties: unknown

ACTION: Skirmish at Elk Chute (Elkshute), Dunklin County, August 4, 1864—6th and 12th Missouri Cavalry, 2nd and 3rd Missouri Militia Cavalry

Union Casualties: 3
Confederate Casualties: unknown

ACTION: Skirmish at Cowskin, Barry County, August 5–7, 1864—8th Missouri Militia Cavalry

Union Casualties: 6
Confederate Casualties: unknown

ACTION: Operations in southwest Missouri and northwest Arkansas, August 15–24, 1864—1st and 2nd Arkansas Cavalry, 6th Missouri Cavalry

CAMPAIGN: Major General Sterling Price's Missouri raid, August 4–December 2

HISTORICAL SITUATION: On July 13, 1864, a little-known assistant commissary of subsistence for Department of Alabama, Mississippi and East Louisiana, Captain J. Henry Behan, wrote a letter to President Jefferson Davis urging Confederate leadership to take advantage of the scarcity of Union forces in the Trans-Mississippi Region. Captain Behan's bold plan called for sending three armies under Generals Magruder, Taylor and Price into Missouri to seize St. Louis, cross the Mississippi River into Kentucky and capture Louisville. The operation, if successful, would next attempt to seize Union supply stores in Nashville and Chattanooga. Should this plan succeed, it might cut off General William T. Sherman's supply lines and possibly create a situation where Sherman is confronted with General John Hood's army to his front and a Confederate army in his rear. Confederate president Jefferson Davis's military advisor General Braxton Bragg and Secretary of War James Seddon reviewed the plans, but Confederate leadership was by then too occupied with attempting to relieve the desperate sieges of Lee's army at Richmond and Petersburg and Hood's army at Atlanta to give the plan much attention.

While General Sterling Price enjoyed considerable respect as a veteran of the Mexican-American War, former governor of Missouri and the commander of important Confederate victories at Wilson's Creek and Lexington, he was now fifty-four years old, weighed three hundred pounds and could no longer walk erect. The Confederate commander of the Trans-Mississippi Region, General Kirby Smith, eventually decided to order a smaller invasion and reluctantly assigned General Price to command the newly formed Army of Missouri. Smith's misgivings were not enough to overcome the expected outcry if Price was not given command. Price, while still popular, soon discovered that he had overestimated pro-Southern sentiments in Missouri after residents had suffered from nearly four years of war.

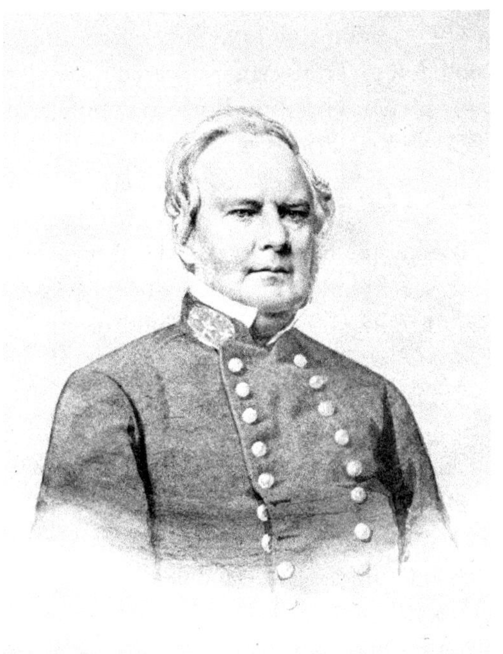

Left: Confederate general Sterling Price. *Courtesy of the Library of Congress.*

Below: *Price's Missouri Raid, August–October 1864. Courtesy of Danielle Kilmer.*

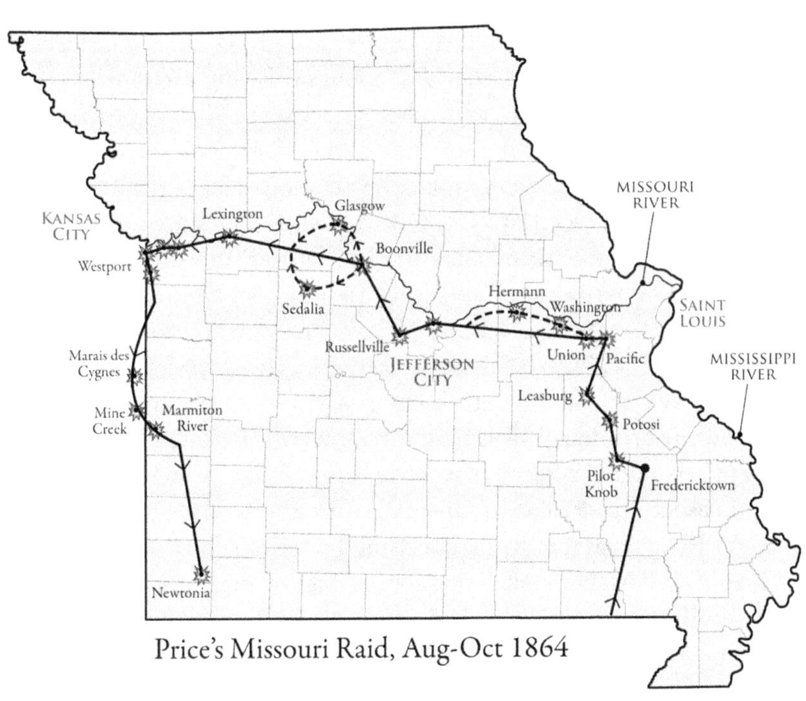

WHAT'S AT STAKE: In a late, desperate attempt to pull forces away from Sherman's Atlanta Campaign, Confederate Trans-Mississippi commander General Kirby Smith ordered Major General Sterling Price to conduct an ambitious raid with the Army of Missouri. Price's army, a large cavalry force of more than ten thousand men, was assigned the ambitious tasks of capturing St. Louis, seizing the state capital at Jefferson City, installing a pro-secessionist government and then crossing the Mississippi River into Illinois and threatening supply lines in Tennessee. Should Price's army be successful, it could possibly alter the outcome of the upcoming fall presidential elections.

ACTION: Battle of Pilot Knob, Fort Davidson, Iron County, September 27, 1864

General Sterling Price's Confederate Army of Missouri surrounds Union forces at Fort Davidson. Price's Confederate forces suffer heavy casualties after repeated repulses from attacks by the well-defended Federal forces of Brigadier General Thomas Ewing. Although the first attack fails, General Price still demands the surrender of Union forces. Ewing, outnumbered eight to one, suspects that next time Price would make better use of his artillery to bombard the fort before assaulting and considers the Confederate demand to surrender. But General Ewing recognizes that his African American soldiers were likely to be executed if captured, so he declines Price's offer. Under the cover of darkness, Federal forces muffle the sounds of cavalry and artillery, quietly evacuate over the drawbridge and march over a path between two Confederate camps. Despite the detonation of the fort's powder magazine after the Federal withdrawal, Price remains unaware of the departure until morning. In addition, Confederate couriers fail to get through to notify General Joseph Shelby, who was busy north of Potosi destroying rail lines to block the Federal forces' withdrawal.

General Price's inability to break camp and mount a pursuit until noon the next day ensures that Ewing's men have a sufficient head start to reach Leasburg on September 29 after a thirty-six-hour forced march of sixty-six miles. At Leasburg, Federal forces meet up with rations and entrenching tools destined for Rolla, feed their bellies and build a formidable earthwork fortress before Shelby and Marmaduke's divisions arrive the next morning.

Union Casualties and Losses: 184
Confederate Casualties and Losses: 1,500

WHY IT MATTERS: General Sterling Price's forces suffered heavy casualties on an objective of questionable strategic importance. Price, with only Brigadier General James Fagan's division, one-third of his forces, advanced to within forty miles of St. Louis but decided to turn away from the city, his primary objective, instead proceeding to Jefferson City and capturing the state capital. Price provided Union commanders time to assemble sufficient forces west of the Mississippi River and concentrate on Price's rear-guard and logistical trains.

ACTION: Raid on Potosi, Washington County, September 27, 1864

General Joseph Shelby and five hundred guerrillas chase a small detachment of the 50th Missouri Infantry Volunteers and more than one hundred citizens into the town courthouse. Threatening destruction of the building by artillery shells, the men surrender and are stripped of their belongings and taken off as prisoners of war. Several are surly and disrespectful to the Rebel force and are shot in front of the remaining prisoners without any legal recourse. After hoisting the Rebel flag, the rest of the town citizens' stores are plundered, and the Potosi leadworks and several trains at the depot are destroyed.

ACTION: Skirmishes at Mineral Point, Washington County, September 27, 1864

Mineral Point is alerted of approaching Rebel cavalry forces. A Union force of 1,500 to 2,000 men commanded by Colonel Mills and General A.J. Smith repulses a Rebel force estimated at 200 Rebel cavalry, inflicting heavy casualties.

General Joseph Shelby's cavalry force ambushes a Union wagon train two miles south of Mineral Point, scattering the Union guard and confiscating the wagon supplies, including the capture of twenty-three African American teamsters. Shelby's raiders burn bridges; tear up railroad tracks; destroy train depots, tanks and telegraph lines; and kill three African Americans before returning to Potosi for the night. The next morning, Shelby's men rejoin General Price at Fort Davidson.

Union Casualties: unknown
Confederate Casualties: 50

ACTION: Union retreat from Fort Davidson, September 28, 1864

ACTION: Skirmish at Huzzah and Red Haw and the Battle of Leasburg, Crawford County, Missouri, September 29–30, 1864

Union forces conduct a sixty-six-mile, thirty-nine-hour retreat fighting six rear-guard actions and arrive in Leasburg exhausted. They construct hasty defense fortifications along the railroad, burning barns and haystacks in order to make a determined stand against Price's army. Union forces reject the demand to surrender. Generals John Marmaduke and Joseph Shelby decide that further attacks are useless and rejoin Price's main body at Union, Missouri.

TOURISM NOTES: A historical waymarker of the engagement can be found in Leasburg on Second Street.

ACTION: Skirmish at Pacific (Franklin), Franklin County, October 1, 1864

According to local historian Scott Williams, an Arkansas Confederate brigade under Brigadier General William L. Cabell and dispatched by General Sterling Price cut the railroad lines east of town. Indiana and Illinois infantry units under Union commander Colonel Edward H. Wolff arrive by rail line and drive Cabell's cavalry and artillery units from the town.

Union Casualties: 7
Confederate Casualties: unknown

Action: Skirmish at Union (Vitt's Mill), Franklin County, October 1, 1864

Confederate forces of Marmaduke's brigade (divison) under Brigadier General John B. Clark Jr. drive off approximately two hundred Union militia forces at Vitt's Mill. Colonel Robert R. Lawther's regiment is dispatched at midnight north to Washington and takes possession of the town with no resistance. The following day, Confederate forces take possession of a Union supply train at Miller's Station (New Haven) and seize Hermann. The Confederate forces transport the captured supplies by train to Hermann for distribution. Confederate forces reportedly operate the flour mill at Vitt's Mill for several days before departing.

Union Casualties and Losses: 102
Confederate Casualties: unknown

Tourism Notes: An interpretive panel of the skirmish at Vitt's Mill is located at the corner of Main Street and Highway 47 in Union, Missouri.

Action: Skirmishes at or near Jefferson City, Cole County, October 6–8, 1864

Sterling Price turns northwest, occupies Hermann and commences to destroy railroad bridges along the Meramec, Moselle and Gasconade Rivers en route to the Osage River and to threaten the defenses of Jefferson City. A furious fight by Confederate general James Fagan's advance forces at Moreau Creek pushes Federal pickets back up on the city's defenses.

Major General William Rosecrans, commander of the Federal Department of the Missouri, calls out the state militia and instructs district commanders Generals John McNeil, Egbert B. Brown, Clinton Fisk and John Sanborn to send the bulk of their forces to reinforce Jefferson City. Faced with superior Union defenses, General Price has no choice but to bypass Jefferson City and continue westward. Price, though, is also burdened with protecting a supply wagon train of five hundred wagons now full from looting accompanied by a considerable herd of cattle.

Why It Matters: While General Sheridan had replaced former Union army cavalry commander General Alfred Pleasonton and transferred him to the Trans-Mississippi Region, Pleasonton was still considered a capable and experienced cavalry officer and commander. In Jefferson City, Pleasonton organized 4,100 horse soldiers into three cavalry brigades under Generals Sanborn, McNeil and Brown. This force constituted the bulk of the Union army sent to disrupt and delay General Sterling Price's force until a larger force could be assembled.

ACTION: Skirmish at Russellville, Cole County, October 9–11, 1864

Pleasonton's three brigades under the overall command of General Sanborn engage Confederate general Fagan's division acting as rear guard to Price's army. Price orders General Marmaduke's division to assist Fagan's delay of Federal forces. Sanborn temporarily halts at California, Missouri, for reinforcements and supplies. Along with receiving several days' rations, General Sanborn is reinforced by a 1,500-man brigade under Colonel E.C. Catherwood before departing on October 13 in pursuit of General Sterling Price.

ACTION: William "Bloody Bill" Anderson's guerrilla campaign in Missouri, July–October 1864

HISTORICAL SITUATION: After the massacre at Lawrence, Kansas, "Bloody Bill" Anderson and other Quantrill followers disagreed with Quantrill over future actions. Quantrill preferred to maintain a low profile and moved his band south to avoid engagements with Union forces hot on his trail. Anderson and several of Quantrill's other hardened lieutenants—Archie Clement, the Todd brothers, John Thrailkill and David Poole, among others—parted ways and headed into central Missouri to continue their looting rampage. Couriers were sent prior to General Sterling Price's raid into Missouri to direct these guerrilla bands to raid, capture and disrupt supply and troop transportation along the St. Louis/Hannibal/Macon/St. Joseph corridor.

BIOGRAPHICAL SKETCH: William "Bloody Bill" Anderson spent his youth in Huntsville, Missouri, until 1857, when his family moved to Agnes City, Kansas. Anderson attended school in Huntsville and was considered a quiet, well-behaved son. By 1860, his fortunes had changed for the worse after his mother was killed by lightning. Bill got in a scrape with local Kaw Indians and was later suspected of dealing in stolen horses along the Santa Fe Trail. In 1862, Bill's father was killed by Judge Baker, a friend of the family. The story goes that Bill and his brother sought revenge and engaged Judge Baker and another man in a brief gun battle, forcing Baker and the other man to seek safety in a nearby store. Anderson then set the store on fire, killing both men. Anderson then burned another man's home, stealing his horses before heading back into Missouri. Anderson and his brother linked up with a man named Jim Reed and commenced raiding in the area near the towns of Lexington and Warrensburg. Reed later married Belle Starr, suspected Southern spy, infamous horsethief, outlaw and socialite from Carthage, Missouri.

The Anderson boys soon made contact with William Quantrill and eventually joined his band around May 1863. Anderson was promoted to lieutenant under Quantrill and participated in the Lawrence Massacre. Anderson followers like Archie Clement, Frank and Jesse James and Cole Younger honed their guerrilla raiding skills riding with Quantrill and Anderson. Their reputations in Missouri as some of the most feared bushwhackers soon followed. After the Lawrence Massacre, Quantrill and Anderson headed south to Texas to avoid Union forces hot on their trail. Anderson and his band returned to Missouri with Quantrill, but constant pursuit by Union forces compelled Quantrill's guerrillas to eventually break up into smaller groups, with many heading east.

Anderson returned to his childhood home in Randolph County, where he continued to raid and loot Union sympathizers and troops. Anderson appeared to be quite literate and engaged in a war of letters with the Lexington town newspapers and the Union commander, Colonel James McFerran, over the nobleness of the guerrillas' cause.

Tourism Notes: Historic Huntsville and Randolph County have assembled an informative website and historic map detailing locations of numerous historic events and people who grew up in the area (https://sites.google.com/site/historichuntsvillemissouri/history-of-randolph-county-beginnings-and-the-civil-war).

ACTION: Bank robbery and murder of local man at Huntsville, Randolph County, July 14, 1864

ACTION: Raid on Renick, Randolph County, July 23, 1864

Anderson's band of sixty-five men rob stores, down telegraph lines and burn the railroad depot.

ACTION: Skirmish at Allen, an old stage stop one to two miles north of Moberly, Randolph County, July 23, 1864

Anderson's band attacks and forces the 17th Illinois Cavalry into the shelter of a nearby fort.

Union Casualties: 6
Confederate Casualties: 5

ACTION: Small skirmish at Huntsville, Randolph County, July 24, 1864

ACTION: Raid on the Salt River Bridge, Shelby County, July 26, 1864

Anderson's men burn a bridge over the Salt River and then withdraw south.

ACTION: Skirmish at Dripping Springs, Boone County, August 15–16, 1864

The *Columbia Missouri Statesman* reports that Anderson guerrilla captain Clifton Holtzclaw and an estimated force of one hundred guerrillas camped north of Columbia, Missouri, are engaged by a detachment of the 17th Illinois Cavalry and local militia under the command of Captain William Hebard. The next day, the undermanned Union forces are able to keep Holtzclaw's superior guerrilla force contained for several hours until additional Union forces of the 3rd Missouri Militia, 9th Missouri State Militia Cavalry and the 61st Enrolled Missouri Militia arrive to drive off the guerrilla band.

Union Casualties: 9
Confederate Casualties: in excess of 24

Tourism Notes: The Boone County Historical Society has an informative website (www.boonehistory.org). An eight-page downloadable Boone County battlefield brochure is also available (http://www.centraliabattlefield.com/uploads/4/8/4/7/48471379/battlefield_brochure_multi-page.pdf).

Action: Skirmish at Rawlings Lane, Howard County, August 28, 1864

While operating in Howard and Boone Counties, Anderson's band of bushwhackers sets an ambush for a forty-five-man Federal patrol under the command of Captain Joseph Park, 4th Missouri State Militia. Park's patrol is alerted and decides to seek Anderson's guerrilla force out along a road between New Franklin and Rocheport. Anderson's guerrillas use a common tactic of luring Federal patrols into a trap by sending a small force to act as bait and then drawing them into a much larger force situated just over a hill or hiding in the brush. Anderson's ruthless lieutenant, Archie Clement, prematurely orders his small picket to fire on Federal forces before they are drawn entirely into the ambush lane. The Union patrol responds with a disciplined fighting retreat to New Franklin, taking shelter in log buildings along the road until they are reinforced by a larger Federal force commanded by Major Reeves Leonard. Reports follow that Union soldiers captured were scalped or otherwise mutilated by Archie Clement, a known scalper and one of the more vicious Anderson followers.

Union Casualties: 8
Confederate Casualties: unknown

Tourism Notes: An interpretive panel, "The Affair at Rawlings Lane," is located on the grounds of Sunset Hills Cemetery, where eight soldiers of the 4th Missouri State Cavalry were killed. The cemetery is located at the west end of South Street. Exit 103 off I-70, take Highway B north two miles to South Street and then go west to the cemetery. The historic Walnut Grove Cemetery and interpretive panel can be located by traveling north into town along Main Street and then going east on Locust to 1106 Locust. The cemetery was believed to be an outpost that could watch for approaching enemy on the Old Rocheport Road. Many Civil War soldiers are buried at the cemetery.

ACTION: Skirmish at Lone Jack, Jackson County, September 1, 1864—7th Missouri Militia Cavalry

Union Casualties: 3
Confederate Casualties: unknown

ACTION: Skirmish near Roanoke, Howard County, September 10, 1864

The 6th Missouri Militia Cavalry skirmishes with the guerrilla band of Clifton Holtzclaw.

Union Casualties: 2
Confederate Casualties: 6

ACTION: Skirmish at Goslin's Lane near Rocheport, Boone County, September 23–24, 1864

As noted in an 1882 account in a history of Boone County, in this action a Federal wagon train of eighteen wagons being escorted by 70 soldiers of the 3rd Missouri State Militia under Captain McFadden en route to Rocheport from Sturgeon is ambushed by a guerrilla band of approximately 100 riders under John Thrailkill and George and Thomas Todd; 12 Federal troops and 3 African American teamsters are killed (supposedly executed) while the entire train of commissary stores, including eighteen thousand rounds of ammunition, is captured. A Federal force of 350 soldiers is dispatched to find Anderson's guerrilla band.

Union Casualties: 11 or 12, as well as 3 African American teamsters

TOURISM NOTES: An interpretive panel can be located by taking Exit 117 north off I-70 toward Harrisburg; go right onto MO-J for 6.3 miles, and the marker is located just past West Bradley Lane before a bend in the road. Rocheport is located at the Missouri River junction and I-70 mile marker 186, north at Exit 115. Rocheport hosts a station for hikers and bikers traveling along the historic Katy Trail. Meriwether Lewis and William Clark camped near there on their journey up the Missouri River in 1804.

ACTION: Skirmish at Fayette, Howard County, September 24, 1864

Guerrilla leaders William "Bloody Bill" Anderson and George Todd lead a force of 250 guerrillas on an ill-advised attack against heavily armed and well-defended Federal forces of the 9th Missouri State Cavalry in the nearby town of Fayette, Missouri. Several charges result in heavy losses. After the guerrillas retreat, it is reported to Anderson that the dead guerrillas were dragged through the streets and horses trampled over their corpses.

Union Casualties: 8
Confederate Casualties: 43

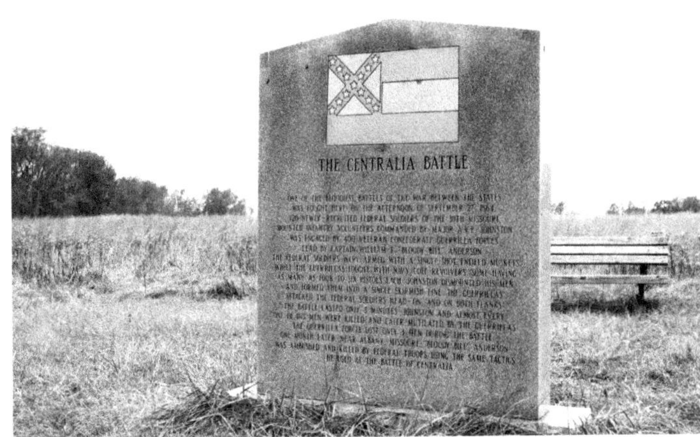

Confederate memorial, Battle of Centralia. *Courtesy of Brian Warren.*

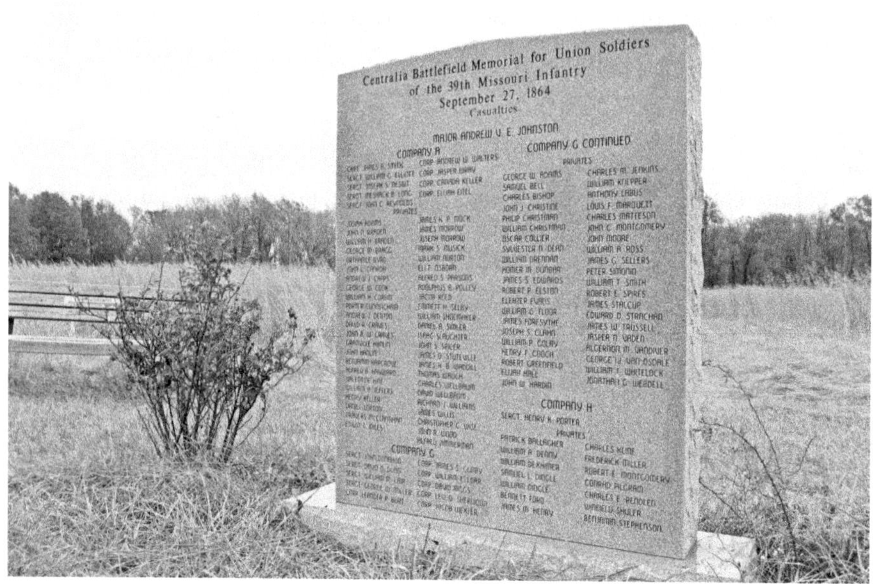

Union memorial, Battle of Centralia. *Courtesy of Brian Warren.*

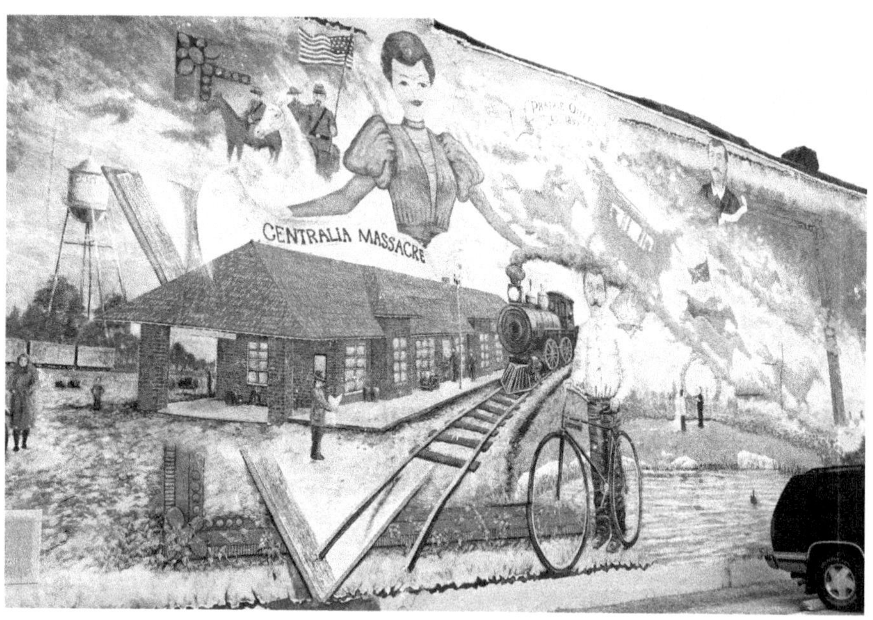

Mural of the Battle of Centralia, Centralia. *Courtesy of Brian Warren.*

TOURISM NOTES: An interpretive panel is located at the campus of Central Methodist University in front of the Student Center at 411 Central Methodist Square. The Old Trails Regional Partnership has provided downloadable routes for Civil War journeys through the Missouri heartland (http://www.oldtrails.net/routes/civil-war.html). In addition, the Boonslick Historical Society publishes a quarterly journal accessible on its website that covers many topics on the Civil War in Missouri.

ACTION: Massacre and Battle of Centralia, Audrain County, September 27, 1864

After a morning of looting in Centralia, "Bloody Bill" Anderson's men capture, murder and mutilate Union soldiers seized from a westbound train near the town depot. Alerted to the smoke and commotion in Centralia, the 39th Union Mounted Infantry, commanded by Major A.V. Johnston, immediately sets off from Paris to Centralia in time to find the bodies of twenty-two mutilated Union soldiers of the 1st Iowa Cavalry. Major Johnston receives but pays little heed to valuable information gathered from local townsfolk of a much larger guerrilla force of several hundred camped south of town. Regardess of the warning, Major Johnston leaves a contingent of Union soldiers to protect Centralia and immediately sets out in search of Anderson's guerrilla encampment.

Approximately three miles south, Johnston is lured into chasing a small raiding party into a field on the west side of the guerrilla encampment along Young's Creek. Spotting a guerrilla group of riders along the tree line next to Young's Creek, Major A.V. Johnston orders his force of about 120 soldiers to dismount, secure their horses and engage Anderson's guerrillas on foot. The Union force manages to only fire one volley before Anderson's band immediately counterattacks and swarms over the Union line, dispersing and nearly killing every Union soldier. Noted guerrilla outlaws Frank and Jesse James participate in this bloody massacre. It is later confirmed by Frank James that it was Jesse who committed the act of killing the Federal commander, Major Johnston.

Anderson, fresh from the slaughter in Centralia, meets up with Price on October 10. Some Confederate forces display Union scalps from their bridles. Another report claims that this is an embellishment by Yankee propaganda and that it is only the partisan gang of Captain John Pringle. Price is appalled but badly needs the guerrilla band's services and orders

Anderson and other guerrilla leaders to resume attacking and disrupting railroad lines in northern Missouri.

Union Casualties: estimated at 150 killed
Confederate Casualties: 3

WHAT IF: While traveling by stagecoach to Centralia the day of the massacre, Congressman John Rawlings was taken prisoner by Anderson's guerrillas. While Rawlings was questioned about his true identity with a gun pointed to his head, a train to Centralia carrying several Union soldiers was heard off in the distance, distracting his interrogators and allowing Rawlings to avoid probable execution. Rawlings was considered the father of the University of Missouri for ensuring that Columbia, Missouri, would be the site of the first university in the Louisiana Purchase after the Morrell Land Grant was enacted by Congress providing land for state universities.

TOURISM NOTES: The Centralia Battlefield Society has placed a panel in the town square describing the initial massacre and the route to the battle south of town. The site of the massacre of Union soldiers is marked on the south side of the railroad tracks in use today. The route to the subsequent battle site three and a half miles south is marked. Access to parking is on the east side of the battle site, with a clear path and bridge over Young's Creek to the open field where the massacre of Johnston's Union forces took place. Reenactments are often conducted on the anniversary, quite authentic and well attended.

ACTION: Skirmish at Leasburg, Crawford County, September 29–30, 1864—14th Iowa, 2nd Missouri Militia Cavalry, 2nd Missouri Light Artillery

ACTION: Skirmish in Concordia, Lafayette County, October 10, 1864

A guerrilla band led by Quantrill lieutenant David Poole attacks and inflicts heavy casualties on the local militia.

Tourism Notes: St. John's Cemetery contains the grave sites of several victims of bushwhacker raids. According to local history, the town was given its name by the postmaster at the war's conclusion as a sign of hope for reconciliation and concord between the North and South.

Action: Skirmish at Vollrath Farm near Boonville, Cooper County, October 11, 1864—*OR*, Lieutenant Colonel John F. McMahan, 6th Missouri State Militia Cavalry

General Sterling Price's army has been looting for two days when the 6th Missouri State Cavalry, under the command of Lieutenant Colonel John F. McMahan, and 8th Missouri State Cavalry, under Colonel Joseph J. Gravely, join forces and engage a much larger force of 1,500 Missouri State Guard commanded by Brigadier General John Marmaduke. Federal forces are thrown back by Generals Marmaduke and Fagan's rear-guard forces positioned in the heavily wooded Vollrath Farm. General Sterling Price's army, along with a large contingent of recruited young men, confiscate every available horse before departing Boonville the next day.

Union Casualties: 12
Confederate Casualties: 43

Why It Matters: Confederate forces were unable to seize control of a vital Missouri River port and establish defensive positions to delay Union forces concentrating from the East.

Tourism Notes: An interpretive panel, "Skirmish at Vollrath Farm," is located opposite of Walmart on Main Street adjacent to Boonslick Road.

Action: Battle of Petite (Tete) Saline Creek to Anderson's Branch near Boonville, Cooper County, October 13, 1864

A furious cavalry battle on Old Tipton Road (Route B, three-fourths of a mile south of I-70) begins at the Tete Saline (Wilkin's Bridge) Bridge and lasts for several hours. Confederate forces led by Howard County native

Colonel Sidney Jackman fend off repeated cavalry charges by 350 men of the 5th Missouri Militia Cavalry, commanded by Lieutenant Colonel Joseph Eppstein.

Union Casualties: 10
Confederate Casualties: reported as considerable but unknown

Tourism Notes: Readable images of local interpretive panels can be found at www.mocivilwar.org. The panel about the skirmishes at Vollrath Farm and Tete Saline Creek are located off I-70 Highway, Exit 103—go north on Route B about 1 mile to the stoplight and then go left a short distance on Logans Lake Road to the Boonslick Drive intersection. More Civil War information can be found at the Boonville Tourism Center, located next to the Old Train Depot on the north end of town on East Spring Street, three blocks west of Main Street.

Action: Raid on Danville, New Florence and High Hill, Montgomery County, October 14, 1864

"Bloody Bill" Anderson and Lieutenant Archie Clement take a platoon of men into Danville to avenge the alleged rape of two girls at the Danville Female Academy by Union forces. Thirty-five guerrillas silently ride into Danville along Boone Slick Road, attack the Union soldiers and spare the school but burn eighteen buildings in the business district and the railroad depots in nearby Florence and High Hill.

Union Casualties: 10 (2 soldiers and 3 civilians in Danville and 5 civilian prisoners in High Hill)

Tourism Notes: Nine miles west of Danville is the historic Crane's Store and Museum in Williamsburg, one mile north of Exit 161, I-70 Highway. An interpretive panel next to the store provides a historical overview of this early Missouri town. The general store, built in 1926, has retained its original charm. The museum and store display a wealth of artifacts and memorabilia dating as far back as the pre–Civil War Boone's Slick Trail days. Guerrillas often stopped to rest in this pro-Southern community. It was suspected that Anderson and his band stayed in Williamsburg prior to the raid on Danville. One of the three Berry brothers who are believed to have ridden with Anderson at Centralia returned to Williamsburg, where he ran a store until he died in the 1920s.

Action: Battle of Glasgow, Chariton and Howard Counties, October 15, 1864

Approximately 1,500 to 1,800 soldiers under Generals Joseph Shelby and John Clark advance on Colonel Chester Harding's outnumbered force of 800 Union soldiers at Glasgow. Colonel Harding's force retreats to Hereford Hill but surrenders by early afternoon. William Quantrill and what's left of his band participate in this rather one-sided Confederate victory.

An African American unit, the 62nd U.S. Colored Troops, having been organized in December 1863 and attached to the Department of St. Louis, participates in this action.

Union Casualties and Losses: 512
Confederate Casualties: 50

Tourism Notes: An interpretive panel can be found by traveling west on Market Street to a dead end overlooking the Missouri River.

Why It Matters: While Confederate forces captured considerable supplies, an unnecessary stay of three days delayed Price's operations toward Kansas City and provided Union forces time to close on Price's army.

Action: Skirmish at Sedalia, Pettis County, October 15, 1864

About 1,500 men of Shelby's Iron Brigade under General Jeff Thompson attack Sedalia and defeat forces commanded by Colonel John Crawford and Lieutenant Colonel John Parker positioned along two fortified redoubts before sacking the town. Thompson eventually halts the looting, abandons the town and rejoins Price.

Union Casualties: 24
Confederate Casualties: unknown

ACTION: Major and minor skirmishes at Lexington, Lafayette County, October 17, 19 and 21, 1864

Union forces under Major General William Rosecrans, commander of the Department of Missouri, and Major General Samuel Curtis, commander of the Department of Kansas, are directed to trap General Sterling Price's army in a pincer movement. Curtis's Kansas militia units, unwilling to enter Missouri, are eventually replaced by a force of 2,000 men under Major General James Blunt. Union forces are driven back by Price's main force of 8,500 cavalrymen and are pursued west along Independence Road until nightfall.

Union Casualties: unknown
Confederate Casualties: unknown

WHY IT MATTERS: While Federal forces were yet unable to concentrate sufficient forces to stop General Sterling Price's army, Union leadership was provided valuable time to gain more reliable information about the size and composition of Price's forces.

ACTION: Skirmish at Little Blue River, Jackson County, October 21, 1864

Major General James Blunt's forces establish strong defensive positions along the west bank. Sterling Price's main force engages a Union covering force commanded by Colonel Thomas Moonlight Blunt, responsible for protecting all possible fording sites. Blunt's forces contest Confederate attacks for five hours, but eventually the superior Confederate numbers force Union troops to withdraw farther west.

Union Casualties: 115
Confederate Casualties: unknown

ACTION: Battle of Independence, Jackson County, October 21–22, 1864

Union forces moving from the west under General James Blunt attempt a determined stand behind a rock wall against Sterling Price's army but are forced to retreat back west. Sterling Price's army's stay in Independence is short, as ten thousand Federal cavalry soldiers approach from the east under Union major general Alfred Pleasonton. Federal cavalry cross the Little Blue River and attack Price's rear guard, forcing Confederate forces west. Two Confederate brigades suffer heavy casualties in an attempt to stem the onslaught. Brigadier General John Marmaduke's division engages and halts the western attack of Federal forces.

Union Casualties: 83
Confederate Casualties: 140, including guerrilla leader George Todd

ACTION: Battle of Byram's Ford, aka Big Blue River, Jackson County, October 22–23, 1864

A sizeable Union force of more than twenty thousand soldiers from the east is bearing down on General Price's now outnumbered force, seeking a decisive engagement. Byram's Ford becomes a hotly contested geographic location when Price determines that Byram's Ford is essential to moving his five-hundred-wagon supply train, including five thousand cattle, over the Big Blue River, heavily defended by Union general Blunt's forces on the west bank. In an effort to disguise a flank attack on Blunt's defenses, General Joseph Shelby conducts a fierce frontal assault. Blunt's forces are forced to retire to Westport, enabling Price's supply train to cross over Byram's Ford and complete its movement southward toward New (Little) Santa Fe.

General Marmaduke's cavalry, now in possession of the west bank of the Big Blue River, is attacked at 8:00 a.m. the following morning by Major General Alfred Pleasonton's cavalry division marching from the east. General Marmaduke is forced to retire during a simultaneous attack from Union commanders Brigadier General Egbert B. Brown and Connell Edward Winslow and Lieutenant Colonel Frederick Benteen's (who later served with Custer at Little Big Horn) force on the west bank by late morning.

Union Casualties: unknown
Confederate Casualties: unknown

Why It Matters: General Sterling Price's now beleaguered force faced much greater Union forces to his front and rear, risking encirclement and certain destruction.

Action: Battle of Westport, Brush Creek, Jackson County, October 23, 1864

Major General Price's diminished force of 8,500 Rebels attempts to dislodge General Samuel Curtis's 22,000 Union soldiers occupying a defensive position in Westport. General James Blunt, anticipating such an assault, attacks first, sending Jennison's Jayhawkers and Ford's brigade south across icy Brush Creek to dislodge Shelby and Fagan's brigades' positions on high ground above Brush Creek. Union forces soon become engaged in desperate fighting with Shelby and Fagan's brigades for nearly four hours; Federal forces are repulsed twice. Seeking to avoid any more frontal assaults, General Samuel Curtis's scouts come across a local farmer who, unhappy over the Confederate abduction of his horse, leads Union troops to a gulch along the west flank of Shelby's forces on the high ground south of Brush Creek. Shelby and Fagan, running short of ammunition and suffering heavy casualties from Union artillery north of Brush Creek, begin a desperate withdrawal south toward the Wornall House. Further fighting turns into a desperate, heavily contested engagement as Confederate forces are made to retreat south along Wornall Road to Forest Hill (now Gregory Boulevard).

Union Casualties and Losses: 1,500
Confederate Casualties and Losses: 1,500

Why It Matters: This battle, referred to by some historians as the "Gettysburg of the West," essentially ended Price's raid through Missouri and forced Price's army into a long, desperate retreat to Arkansas. The Battle of Westport is often studied by career army officers attending senior command and staff education at Fort Leavenworth (called staff rides by army historians).

Tourism Notes: The Westport Historical Society and other historical groups have assembled a marvelous tour guide of the critical engagements of the battle around Westport and south Kansas City, including a set of panels (Eagle Scout Project located on the southern edge of Loose Park)

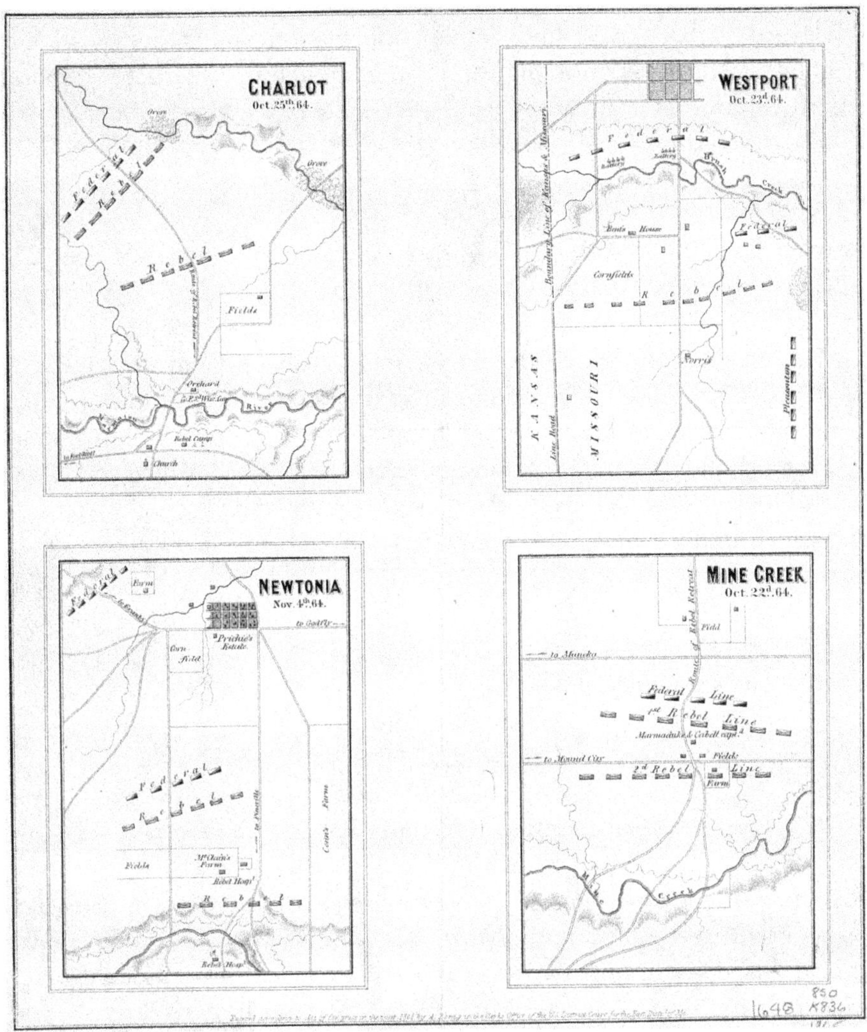

Battle maps of Price's raid. *Courtesy of the State Historical Society of Missouri.*

describing the scene of much of the contested fighting south of Brush Creek and Westport. Other historic sites include the old historic Wornall House, used as a hospital for both the North and South during the Battle of Westport. Located at 6115 Wornall Road, the landmark is a museum showing the daily life of a prosperous antebellum family. A large statue of General Joseph Shelby was erected where he was buried, along with many of his cavalry soldiers, at the Forest Hill Cemetery at Troost and Gregory

Boulevard. Tourists will find helpful information and a downloadable printable Battle of Westport map and tour guide at http://battleofwestport.org/Tours.htm

ACTION: Battle of Marais des Cygnes, Linn County, Kansas, October 25, 1864

In the first of several pitched battles pursuing Price's Confederate forces south, General Alfred Pleasonton forces an engagement at the Marais des Cygnes River in Linn County, Kansas. A determined Union assault is launched after an early morning artillery bombardment. General Price leaves General Fagan's cavalry as a covering force and successfully crosses his wagon supply trains over the high-water river. Confederate forces suffer minor losses.

Union Casualties: unknown
Confederate Casualties: unknown

ACTION: Battle of Mine Creek, Linn County, Kansas, October 25, 1864

On the same day, brigades of Pleasonton's division again overtake Confederate forces attempting to cross another body of water, Mine Creek. Difficulty in negotiating the ford compels General Price's forces to defend the north bank of Mine Creek. Federal forces recognize the Confederate predicament and conduct a ferocious mounted attack. Superior Union firepower quickly causes the disintegration and rout of the exhausted and demoralized Confederates. Price's Confederate forces suffer heavy and unsustainable losses, including the capture of six pieces of artillery, six hundred men and Generals John Marmaduke and William Cabell.

Union Casualties: 100
Confederate Casualties and Losses: 1,200

ACTION: Battle of Marmiton River (aka Shiloh Creek, Charlot's Farm), Vernon County, October 25, 1864

After several days of constant fighting, General Price gathers the remnants of his now seriously diminished (many disarmed) and exhausted force to make another stand against Brigadier General John McNeil's two brigades. After a two-hour pitched battle, McNeil, unaware of the extent of unarmed forces, does not pursue.

Union Casualties: unknown
Confederate Casualties: unknown

TOURISM NOTES: A Kansas City historian, author and blogger under the name of "Civil War Muse" has provided an informative overview of the battle on his blog (http://www.transmississippimusings.com/pages/posts/the-battle-of-marmaton-river-charlots-farm-71.php).

ACTION: Battle of Newtonia, Newton County, October 28, 1864

Sterling Price's army, exhausted and in full retreat, stops to rest two miles south of Newtonia, Missouri. General James Blunt's Union cavalry surprises the Confederates, who flee in great disorder until General Joseph Shelby courageously leads his Iron Brigade to the front, dismounts and engages the Union forces. This being one of many critical rear-guard actions after Westport against a much larger Union army in pursuit, Price's army most likely could not have made it back to safety in Arkansas. The Union forces of General Blunt are reinforced by General John Sanborn, but fierce Confederate resistance continues until nightfall, preventing the capture and destruction of the remnants of Price's army.

Union Casualties: 400
Confederate Casualties: 200

WHY IT MATTERS: General Price's army, with only half of his original force of twelve thousand remaining, made its way back to Arkansas and Indian Territory. General Price portrayed the accomplishments of his raid in a victorious light, reporting to General Kirby Smith of marching nearly

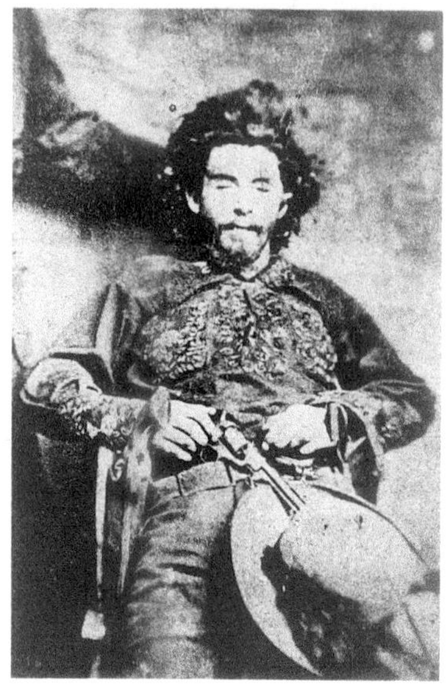

William "Bloody Bill" Anderson, dead. *Courtesy of the State Historical Society of Missouri.*

1,500 miles, fighting forty-three military actions, capturing and paroling more than three thousand Federal forces, capturing eighteen pieces of artillery and destroying nearly $10 million of Missouri property. But strategically, Price failed to achieve the critical military and political objectives of recruiting additional forces and politically challenging the legitimacy of the pro-Union government of Missouri. Ironically, Price's raid may have achieved the unintended consequence of clearing Missouri of most of its guerrilla forces, who were either killed or left Missouri with Price. It constituted the final major, concerted Confederate action in the Trans-Mississippi Theater.

In retrospect, widespread, uncontrolled brutality by maurauding guerrilla bands undermined popular Southern support. Missouri joined Kansas in reelecting the Republican slate, ensuring the passing of the Thirteenth Amendment, ending slavery. President Lincoln received 70 percent of the Missouri popular vote.

ACTION: William "Bloody Bill" Anderson's death, Battle of Albany, north of Orrick, Ray County, October 26, 1864

Anderson's violent ride through central Missouri ends after he was cornered near the railroad town of Orrick. Major Samuel Cox had been directed by Union headquarters to hunt Anderson down. Anderson is killed just as his victims are in Centralia, riding directly at three hundred men of the 51st and 33rd Mounted Missouri Infantry protected behind a tree line. Anderson's murderous reign ends with a fatal shot to the head. He is later decapitated, with his head put on display as a warning to all remaining guerrillas. A grave site and markers of his demise are located in Richmond, Ray County, and near Albany (now Orrick), Missouri.

Union Casualties: 4
Confederate Casualties: 7

WHY IT MATTERS: Misuse of guerrilla forces for indiscriminant raiding and looting would undermine Southern sentiment among the population, an important center of gravity for Price's raid. General Sterling Price possibly missed an opportunity to use the guerrilla forces in a more strategic manner—scouting, harassing and frustrating Federal forces' efforts to concentrate against his army. For all practical purposes, Anderson's demise is symbolic of the end of meaningful guerrilla raiding and terrorizing of the countryside. The message to guerilla forces was clearly one of "leave or die because Federal forces will hunt you down." It also implied that repatriation after the war might not be possible for guerillas suspected or known for committing atrocities, regardless of the validity of their motives.

In fact, Quantrill and Anderson's compatriots Archie Clement, Frank and Jesse James, Cole Younger and many others who survived the war were unable to assimilate into society, continuing to leave a bloody trail of bushwhacking, robbing and murdering.

TOURISM NOTES: A tiny cemetery is located on the battlefield, north of Orrick, just east of Route O. "Bloody Bill" Anderson is buried near Richmond at Pioneer (Morrison) Cemetery. Anderson's grave markers can be found in the southwest corner of the small cemetery located four blocks northwest of the town square at the corner of North Thornton and Crispin Street.

HISTORICAL TRIVIA: In 1865, Samuel Cox was a founding partner in the mercantile firm of Ballinger, Cox and Kemper in Gallatin, Missouri. The business relationship was short-lived, but Cox's partner, J.M. Kemper, was the father of William Thornton Kemper Sr., founder of the two largest bank holding companies headquartered in Missouri: Commerce Bancshares and UMB Financial. In 1869, the Daviess County Savings Association Bank was the site of the first suspected bank robbery (called the Gallatin Bank Robbery) of notorious outlaws Frank and Jesse James.

ACTION: Skirmish at Upshaw Farm, Barry County, Missouri, October 29, 1864—*OR*, Lieutenant Colonel Hugh Cameron, commanding officer, 2nd Arkansas Cavalry

The 2nd Arkansas Cavalry, a Federal force under the command of Lieutenant Colonel Hugh Cameron, skirmishes with a Confederate mounted force of approximately 450 new Southern recruits commanded by Colonel Eli Hodge, from Buck Prairie, Lawrence County, Missouri. Although Union forces are outnumbered nearly two to one, the poorly armed Confederate force is routed with a significant loss of soldiers, horses, armament and supplies. Of those captured are the commander, Colonel Hodge, and ten Confederate captains.

Union Casualties: 2
Confederate Casualties: 87

ACTION: Skirmish at Hermitage, Hickory County, November 2, 1864

Union Casualties: 6
Confederate Casualties: unknown

ACTION: Brown's Farm Massacre, northwest of Hatton, Callaway County, November 4, 1864

As noted in the *Fulton Gazette*, on April 27, 1864, seven Callaway County boys are executed at the farm of Hamilton Brown just south of the Callaway County–Audrain County border by 150 Federal soldiers of the 64th Enrolled Missouri Militia from Wellsville under the command of Major James C. Bay. Callaway County is one of the secession-sympathetic counties designated as part of "Little Dixie." Although not in uniform and unarmed, nearly 200 young men are recruited for Confederate service by William R. Terry and Frank F. Turley. The Rebel force is unable to cross the Missouri River north of Columbia to link up with the remnants of Price's army near Glasgow and turns back north to join up with Colonel Caleb Dorsey, a leader in Shelby's cavalry. The next morning, Major Bay's Wellsville militia raids the Rebel camp at Four Mile Creek, scattering most of the men. Most of the Rebel body manage to escape and ride on to link up with Colonel Dorsey in Audrain County. Some of the Rebels, local Callaway boys, are pursued to the horse lot of Brown's farm, ordered to dismount, disarmed and executed.

Final Actions and Aftermath

By June 1865 the loss of life, per capita and destruction of property in this region far exceeded that of Virginia's Shenandoah Valley, and those parts of Georgia and the Carolinas through which Major General William Tecumseh Sherman's armies marched.

—Edwin Cale Bears, chief historian, emeritus, National Park Service

Action: Skirmish near Columbia, Boone County, February 12, 1865—9th Missouri Militia Cavalry

Union Casualties: 2
Confederate Casualties: unknown

Tourism Notes: Tourists can visit the State Historical Society of Missouri and research library at 1020 Lowry Street on the campus of the University of Missouri, Ellis Library and Museum, open 8:00 a.m.–4:45 pm. Its collection consists of 460,000 pamphlets, books and other state publications; 500,000 manuscripts; 2,900 maps; 150,000 state archival records; and 57,000 reels of microfilm. The State Historical Society publishes the quarterly *Missouri Historical Review*, the only state history scholarly journal in print since 1906. Considerable historical information is provided at www.shsmo.org.

Action: Skirmish near Sturgeon, Audrain County, February 27, 1865—9th Missouri Militia Cavalry

Union Casualties: 2
Confederate Casualties: unknown

Action: Confederate Army of Robert E. Lee surrenders to General Ulysses S. Grant at Appomattox Court House, April 9, 1865

Action: President Abraham Lincoln assassinated by John Wilkes Booth, April 14, 1865

Action: Expedition from St. Louis to receive the surrender of Confederate general Jefferson Thompson, May 1865—17th Illinois Cavalry, accompanying Federal commissioners from department headquarters at Cape Girardeau to arrange terms of capitulation

Action: Major General Kirby Smith surrenders the remnants of the Trans-Mississippi Department, Galveston, Texas, May 26, 1865

Kirby Smith will flee oversees to avoid being tried for treason. In 1875, Smith becomes a professor at University of the South, Sewanee, Tennessee, where he remains until his death in 1893.

Action: Last recorded skirmishes in Missouri, Ray County, Chariton County and Switzler's Mills, involving local Union militias, May 27, 1865

Action: William Quantrill's death, June 6, 1865

Quantrill is finally tracked down by Union forces in Louisville, Kentucky, on May 10, 1865. His body is interred three times, with a final resting place at the Confederate Memorial State Park, Higginsville, Missouri.

TOURISM NOTES: The Confederate Memorial State Historical Site in Higginsville is the location of a Confederate Cemetery, chapel and former home for nearly 1,600 Confederate veterans and their families.

THE AFTERMATH

Both General Sterling Price and General Joseph Shelby refused to surrender and marched their remaining troops to Mexico to make an unsuccessful attempt to offer their soldiers services to Emperor Maximilian. Price contracted cholera or chronic diarrhea, returned to Missouri and died shortly thereafter. He is buried at St. Louis's historic Bellefontaine Cemetery. Sterling Price participated in fifteen notable battles, eleven of which he served as ranking commander. Having only won five of the battles and unable to establish a permanent presence in Missouri, his Civil War record was mixed at best. The United Daughters of the Confederacy erected a bronze statue to General Price at Price Park, Ash and Bridge Street in Keytesville, and maintain a museum in the town. "Old Pap," as his soldiers fondly referred to him, had experienced victory in the early stages of the war, but decisive losses at Pea Ridge and Westport left a shadow over his military career.

Joseph Shelby and approximately one thousand of his cavalrymen were immortalized as "the Undefeated" for not surrendering. He was a major cavalry commander in more than ten battles, and his brigade earned the title the "Iron Brigade." Shelby returned to Missouri from Mexico two years later and resumed farming. He was later appointed as U.S. marshal for the Western District of Missouri. He died in 1893.

The burial place of Missouri governor and governor-in-exile Claiborne Jackson is located at the Sappington Cemetery State Historical Site in Nelson, Missouri, five miles southwest of Arrow Rock on Route AA.

Also buried at the Sappington State Historical Site is Confederate general John S. Marmaduke. Marmaduke is recognized for the leadership he displayed while leading Confederate cavalry during three Missouri raids. Marmaduke was involved in nearly all the major actions in the Trans-Mississippi Region. After leading a regiment in the Battle of Shiloh in 1862, he returned to Arkansas and was promoted to brigadier general. He was a senior Confederate leader of cavalry forces in nearly every major action in Arkansas, such as the Battles of Prairie Grove, Fayetteville, Helena and

Poison Springs and the Red River Campaign, as well as the defense of Little Rock. Marmaduke's standing as a prominent citizen was revitalized after the war when he wrote for an agriculture journal, drawing attention to discriminatory pricing of farmers by the railroads. Public service began when the governor of Missouri appointed him to the first rail commission. After losing a bid for the Democratic nomination for governor in 1880, he was elected in 1884 and became the first ex-Confederate to be elected to a major political office in Missouri. He went on to quell the railroad strikes of 1885 and 1886, ultimately enacting legislation to regulate the railroad industry. Governor Marmaduke was active in providing adequate funding for Missouri public schools.

Although President Andrew Johnson declared an end to the insurrection on August 20, 1865, the healing from this awful conflagration was far from over. Massive dislocation caused by the destruction of the rural countryside and infrastructure set the conditions for a long, bitter and uneven recovery. While the Freedmen's Bureau was created to assist former slaves in transitioning to a different society, masses of African Americans wandered aimlessly or migrated to cities seeking some sense of order and opportunity. The army, sharply reduced to twenty thousand troops by Congress to police a population of 8 million, was grossly undermanned to administer the Reconstruction process, let alone curtail the resurgence of violence from embittered Southern soldiers returning home. Although much work remained to be done in the South, the United States Army was called away to conduct another police action against Indian tribes resisting white settlers migrating through their sacred hunting grounds.

A typical example of the bitter division after the war is illustrated on a historic interpretive panel on the lawn of the Callaway County Courthouse. After the war, law and order in Callaway County remained elusive, as in 1873 when Callaway County sheriff and former Missouri State Guard company commander George W. Law was gunned downed in Fulton by vigilantes while transporting a prisoner to a more secure location. The story goes that while lying mortally wounded, Law indicated that he recognized some of the vigilantes as having served with him during his service with Confederate forces at Vicksburg, where he lost an arm. Later, in 1875, in an effort to encourage reconciliation between the North and South, former Confederate president Jefferson Davis traveled to Fulton, Missouri, and gave a speech to an estimated ten thousand people.

Appendix I

Overview of Military Tactics and Strategy during the Civil War

Military tactics in the Civil War usually called for large forces positioning units during a general engagement or the rapid movement of mobile cavalry and guerrilla units—or both working in concert. In general engagements, command and control were essential features, and tactics at that time called for changing from column to line formation. Often the commander positioned himself at the front of the formation to facilitate command and control should an encounter with the enemy occur. The column formation provided for superior command and control and was used primarily for movement along a road or trail to a designated location.

For general engagements, just prior to battle leaders would march their troops into a line formation that afforded maximizing firepower to the front, often enhanced by the use of cannons if available. But it became difficult to control once the engagement began due to the great volume of noise, smoke and warfare's tendency toward chaos. Decisive firepower was the objective in an engagement, and when the firepower from an adversary became too strong, the weaker force was often confronted with the situation of either finding a weak point in the enemy's lines or withdrawing before incurring heavy casualties.

Because of their rapidly moving features, guerrilla and cavalry operations also made command and control more difficult for the leader once engaged with an enemy force. Ambush tactics were often used to surprise enemy units. Experienced leadership and superior knowledge of terrain often provided decided advantages over less experienced leadership.

But the conduct of battles is never neat and tidy, as the nineteenth-century military theorist Karl von Clausewitz wrote about in his thoughtful strategic work, *On War*. Written after serving as a Prussian staff officer during the Napoleonic Wars, he wrote of a prevailing uncertainty in wartime that creates a tension called friction (often mislabeled as the fog of war in discussions regarding current conflicts) that general officers must quickly learn to cope with. Clausewitz attempted to persuade political and military planners that in order to be successful, generals must learn to accept the constant uncertainty that is present throughout wartime. Clausewitz believed that it was essential that military leaders mastered the military profession by studying past conflicts in order to develop clarity for command in wartime.

The American Civil War has often been characterized as the first true "total war," a moniker that probably requires further characterization. The development of railroad transportation systems, motor-powered flotillas, mass production and the ability to produce weapon systems with interchangeable parts provided to both sides (but to a much greater extent the North) an ability to transport and equip much larger armies. The American Civil War witnessed the transportation of armies of thousands of men hundreds of miles in just a few days ready to conduct major battles. The telegraph provided the capability of rapidly communicating orders to commanders in the field. Its security and reliability was just as important to success on the battlefield as the guns that were used by the armies. Total war also adversely affected the civilian populations by placing on them the burden of supplying and caring for the dead and wounded, as battles occurred often where such facilities were nonexistent. Innovation and mechanization increased the lethality of weapons and weapons systems, causing unimaginable scenes of human and animal carnage. Photographers could now preserve these revolting scenes for sober reflection and timeless preservation.

Historically, these changes occur unevenly and were never more apparent than in Missouri. The transportation network was a combination of river waterways, primarily the Mississippi River and the Missouri River, augmented by a nascent but rapidly expanding railroad network that would soon connect supply depots to the armies they served. When the Civil War broke out, only one railroad line in Missouri reached the Kansas border, from Hannibal to St. Joseph. As the war progressed in Missouri, railroad lines extended farther west to support Union operations. Confederate forces did not have a reliable means of transportation other than by horse, mule and wagon. Union supply and communications support represented an important target for marauding Confederate and guerrilla bands. A heavy reliance on cavalry and mounted infantry characterized the vast majority of skirmishes, ambushes and other often brief but violent engagements in Missouri. State boundaries were of value in name only.

To replenish supplies and recruits, Confederate forces operating out of Arkansas, western and southern Missouri raided pro-Union sympathizers and Union supply depots on nearly a daily basis. Protection of railroads, telegraph lines and supply depots became a critical requirement for Federal leaders in order to conduct sustained operations against highly elusive Confederate and partisan forces. The large number of small guerrilla and Confederate cavalry units operating in Missouri forced Union leadership to establish garrisons in major towns of counties from which scouting parties would conduct reconnaissance operations.

RIVERINE STRATEGY AND CAMPAIGN

Union leadership entered into an army-navy-civilian coalition with the awarding of a contract to St. Louis River salvage expert James Eads to build shallow-draft ironclads that could operate on the western rivers. They were primarily built at Eads Union Marine Works, now a St. Louis suburb, Carondelet. The ironclads *Essex* and the *Benton* were the first to see military action.

The Department of the Missouri headquarters at St. Louis served as the equipping, training and launching base for the Army of the Tennessee under Major General Henry Halleck and Brigadier General Ulysses Grant. Operations along the Tennessee and Cumberland Rivers could only be accomplish when accompanied by the newly created gunboat flotilla under the command of naval officer Andrew H. Foote.

These important victories, along with decisive Union victories against Confederate forces at Battle of Pea Ridge and Battle of Prairie Grove in 1862, set the conditions for the defeat and capture of Confederate strongholds north of Vicksburg, Mississippi, and ultimately Vicksburg itself. The outcome would deny the critical center of gravity of the Mississippi River to Confederate control and lead to the collapse of the Confederate defense perimeter, increasing the difficulty of supporting and transferring Rebel forces along the Mississippi River system.

Appendix II

Initial Organization of the Missouri State Guard

At the outbreak of the Civil War, it was difficult at times for the people of Missouri to know if a local militia or guerrilla force was actually an organized unit or a collection of horse thieves, robbers and criminals. It would be common back then to use identical terms when referring to units on either side. By 1862, "bushwhacker" or "Border Ruffians" denoted pro-Southern marauders, partisans or guerrillas, and "Jayhawkers" denoted pro-Union marauders or guerrillas. We have strived to make these distinctions clear.

The organization of Missouri's state militia was originally bounded by state statutes passed in 1854. In 1861, the state legislature passed a Military Bill proposed by Governor Claiborne Jackson that reorganized the state militia into the Missouri State Guard. The Missouri State Guard was initially organized into the following geographical departments and districts.

1st District/1st Division: St Francois, Ste. Genevieve, Perry, Cape Girardeau, Bollinger, Madison, Iron, Wayne, Stoddard, Scott, Mississippi, New Madrid, Butler, Dunklin and Pemiscot (Nathaniel W. Watkins, M. Jeff Thompson)

2nd District/2nd Division: Scotland, Clark, Knox, Lewis, Shelby, Marion, Monroe, Ralls, Pike, Audrain, Callaway, Montgomery, Lincoln, Warren and St. Charles (Thomas A. Harris, Martin E. Green)

3RD DISTRICT/3RD DIVISION: Putnam, Schuyler, Sullivan, Adair, Linn, Macon, Chariton, Randolph, Howard and Boone (John B. Clark Sr.)

4TH DISTRICT/4TH DIVISION: Gentry, Harrison, Mercer, Grundy, De Kalb, Daviess, Livingston, Clinton, Caldwell, Ray, Carroll and Worth (William Y. Slack)

5TH DISTRICT/5TH DIVISION: Atchison, Nodaway, Holt, Andrew, Buchanan, Platte and Clay (Alexander E. Steen, Colonel James P. Saunders)

6TH DISTRICT/6TH DIVISION: Saline, Pettis, Cooper, Moniteau, Cole, Osage, Gasconade, Maries, Miller, Morgan, Camden, Pulaski and Phelps (Mosby Parsons)

7TH DISTRICT/7TH DIVISION: Dallas, Laclede, Texas, Dent, Reynolds, Shannon, Wright, Webster, Greene, Christian, Stone, Taney, Douglas, Ozark, Howell, Oregon, Carter and Ripley (James H. McBride)

8TH DISTRICT/8TH DIVISION: Jackson, Lafayette, Cass, Johnson, Bates, Henry, Benton, Hickory, Polk, St. Clair, Vernon, Cedar, Dade, Barton, Jasper, Lawrence, Newton, McDonald and Barry (James S. Rains)

9TH DISTRICT/9TH DIVISION: St. Louis, Washington, Franklin, Jefferson and Crawford (Meriwether Lewis Clark Sr., Daniel M. Frost)—it was never formally organized following the Camp Jackson Affair, and units served with other commands

Appendix III

Timeline of Union Commanders in Missouri

May 31, 1861	Promoted to brigadier general, Captain Nathaniel Lyon assumes command of the Department of the West from Brigadier General William Harney.
June 6, 1861	Missouri is transferred to the Department of the Ohio under the command of Major General George B. McClellan.
July 25, 1861	Major General John C. Frémont, U.S. Army, assumes command of the Department of the West.
July 29, 1861	Brigadier General John Pope, U.S. Army, assumes command in northern Missouri.
August 8, 1861	Brigadier General Ulysses S. Grant, U.S. Army, assumes command of the District of Ironton, Missouri.
September 1, 1861	Brigadier General Ulysses S. Grant, U.S. Army, assumes command in southeastern Missouri.
September 17, 1861	Brigadier General Benjamin M. Prentiss, U.S. Army, is assigned to command along and north of the Hannibal and St. Joseph Railroad.

November 2, 1861	Major General John C. Frémont is relieved by Major General David Hunter.
November 9, 1861	The Department of the Missouri is constituted. The Department of Kansas is constituted.
November 19, 1861	Major General Henry W. Halleck, U.S. Army, assumes command of the Department of the Missouri.

By 1862, the Department of Missouri encompassed not only the state of Missouri but also parts of Kansas and Arkansas and the Nebraska, Colorado and Indian Territories. Geographical responsibilities were modified during the course of the war as the Trans-Mississippi Region theater changed. The Department of the Missouri commanders appointed often changed over the course of the war, as shown in the following timeline. Because of the vast territory and the limitations of Federal railroads only reaching out to half of the state territory, Missouri was subdivided into the Southwest Army and later converted to the Department of the Southwest, Department of the Southeast, Department of the Frontier and Department of the Border. Departments consisted of a mixed hierarchy of units such as divisions, brigades, regiments, battalions and/or companies and batteries organized depending on the type of forces necessary to confront the Confederate threat in each location. There were special districts created, such as the District of St. Louis and District of Rolla, to protect important supply centers, railroad depots and the local population from bushwhackers and roving partisan bands.

September 24, 1862	Major General Samuel Curtis, U.S. Army, assumes command of the Department of the Missouri.
May 24, 1863	Major General John M. Schofield, U.S. Army, assumes command of the Department of the Missouri.
January 30, 1864	Major General William S. Rosecrans, U.S. Army, assumes command of the Department of the Missouri.

December 9, 1864	Major General Grenville M. Dodge, U.S. Army, assumes command of the Department of the Missouri.
June 27, 1865	Major General John Pope, U.S. Army, assumes command of the Department of the Missouri

Appendix IV

Missouri Civil War Prisons

Source: www.civilwarmo.org/educators/resources/info-sheets/military-prisons

Gratiot Prison. The largest prisoner of war camp in Missouri was Gratiot Prison, located in St. Louis, Missouri, in a confiscated school building. Operations began in 1861, and at times, it would house as many as 2,000 prisoners. Often overcrowded, prisoners suffered, as its official capacity was only 1,200. It incarcerated not only Confederate soldiers but also sympathizers, guerrillas protected by General Order No. 100, spies and Union soldiers who had committed crimes.

Myrtle Street Prison. This was originally a two-story brick building slave pen with a capacity for 100 prisoners. In September 1861, Myrtle Street became the first prison to be used by the Union and eventually housed as many as 145 prisoners.

Alton Prison. The Illinois state prison in Alton, Illinois, north of St. Louis that had been closed in 1857. After the Gratiot and Myrtle Street Prisons became overcrowded, Alton Prison was reopened. More than 11,000 soldiers were incarcerated, and the site experienced the highest death rate of Union prisoners due to the harsh conditions and exposure to smallpox and rubella. It is estimated that more than 1,500 Confederate soldiers perished within its confines. The prison site is in the National Register of Historic Places, and a section of the prison wall remains and can be examined on the site.

Local city prisons in use by Federal forces: Jefferson City Prison, Macon City Prison and Springfield Prison

Appendix V

Civil War Veterans Buried at National Cemeteries in Missouri

	Marked	*Unmarked*	*Total*
Jefferson Barracks	8,717	2,906	11,623
Jefferson City	475	334	809
Springfield	874	734	1,608

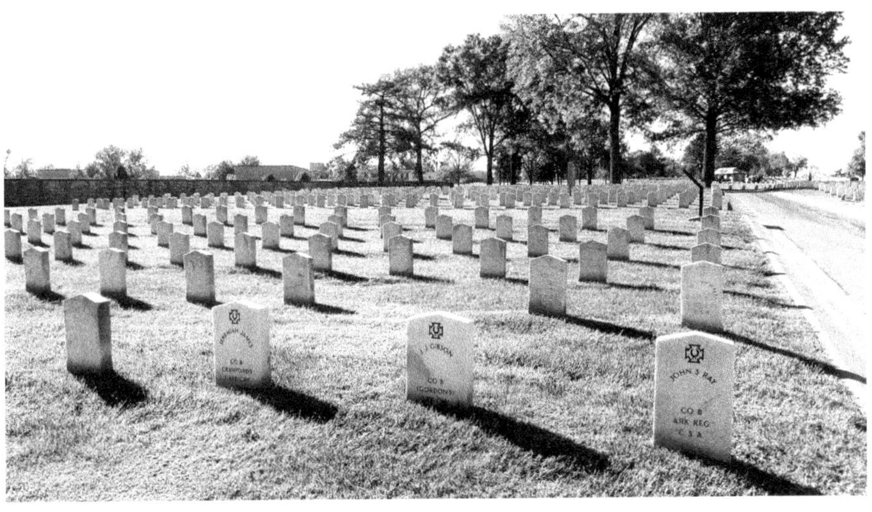

Confederate Cemetery, Jefferson Barracks National Cemetery, St. Louis. *Courtesy of Whit McCoskrie.*

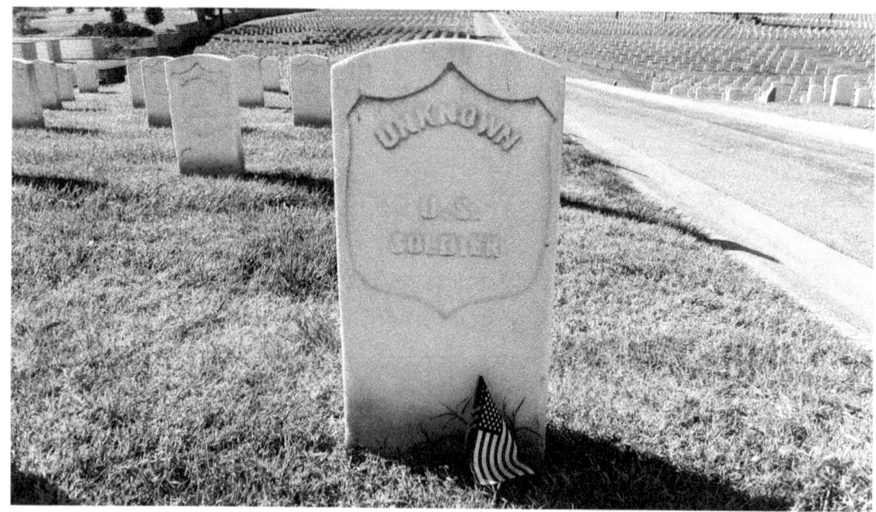

Unknown Soldiers Union Cemetery, Jefferson Barracks National Cemetery, St. Louis. *Courtesy of Whit McCoskrie.*

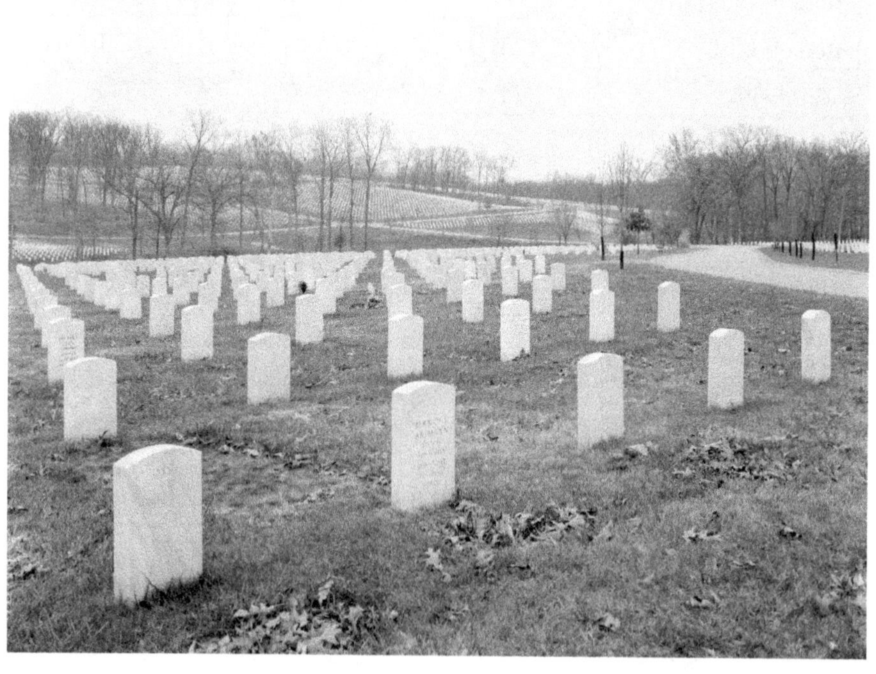

Headstones at Jefferson Barracks National Cemetery, St. Louis. *Courtesy of the Library of Congress.*

Glossary

Border Ruffians: name given to proslavery advocates from Missouri who were involved, often violently, in influencing the outcome of voting for Kansas to become a slave state.

bushwhackers: a common name used during the American Civil War describing guerrilla, partisan-like irregular forces that conducted mostly indiscriminate attacks in rural areas. While usually attributed to proslavery Missouri Border Ruffians, such actions were often nothing more than neighbors settling personal attacks or vendettas of some perceived or real injustice or a quasi-military rationalization of robbery, plunder, murder and arson. Often associated or identified with non-uniformed assailants who attempt to conceal criminal and terrorist attacks, as in the realm of justifiable military attacks during wartime.

Enrolled Missouri Militia: state militia forces authorized by the State of Missouri in 1862 for the primary purpose of acting as a part-time local garrison defensive force but also to augment Unionist Missouri State Militia to conduct offensive operations against guerrilla and other pro-Confederate raiding bands.

Free Soiler: political party active in the presidential elections of 1848 and 1852 that, among other platforms, opposed slavery's expansion into the western territories. Free Soilers broke away from the Democratic Party over its support of popular sovereignty (local control). Initially considered by some as antislavery moderates, the opposition to the Kansas-Nebraska Act persuaded its followers to form an alliance with the Whig Party, giving rise to the Republican Party.

Free Staters: members of a political organization of abolitionists who campaigned and succeeded in gaining Kansas's admission to the Union as a free state.

General Order No. 11: the most controversial of a series of general orders by Union general Thomas Ewing on August 25, 1863, to deprive pro-Southern guerrillas, partisan bushwhackers and raiders support from rural homesteaders along the Kansas-Missouri border. Residents in four counties were given just two weeks to evacuate their homesteads if they could not prove their loyalty to the Union. Pro-Union Jayhawkers assisted in their removal, often causing the destruction of their homestead. The severity of the order and the excesses it caused raised questions by historians of its benefit to Union counter-guerrilla operations. Although repealed in 1864, the psychological damage was irreversible, causing more large-scale massacres and brutal retaliation on both sides.

General Order No. 100 (Lieber Code): the official instructions authorized by President Lincoln outlining the code of conduct for soldiers during the Civil War. Also known as the Lieber Code, it is attributed to the German American legal scholar and political philosopher Franz Lieber. Interpretations varied, and the code was often ignored and misused by both sides during the Civil War. It was particularly difficult to adhere to in Missouri by both sides because of the uncertainties of whether pro-Southern partisan and guerrilla leaders and units were under the control of Confederate leaders. This uncertainty led to unauthorized executions, deprivations and acts of brutality by both sides on a large scale throughout the war, particularly in Missouri. President Lincoln issued a directive that all executions by Union military units required his approval. This was often avoided due to accidental but mysterious deaths that occurred to a prisoner of war during transportation to a detention center by Union forces.

guerrilla units: usually referring to bands of bushwhackers, criminals masquerading as soldiers, murderers and even former Confederate soldiers recruited not officially under the control of the Confederacy but with obvious strong anti-Federal sympathies. Often Union forces considered this designation as being for individuals who were not subject to protection as prisoners of war according to General Order No. 100 and were subject to summary execution if caught. About fifty-one such units were operating at various times in Missouri.

Home Guards: companies and regiments raised by pro-Union supporters, opposing early secessionist Missouri Volunteer Militia and Missouri State Guard. The St. Louis Unionists, many of whom were German Americans, were one of the first units mustered into service in April 1861. Service was initially for a period of three months. The state legislature authorized the creation of Home Guard units to act as organizations for local protection. Later, the Home Guard became known as the Missouri State Militia, Enrolled Missouri Militia and the Provisional Enrolled Missouri Militia.

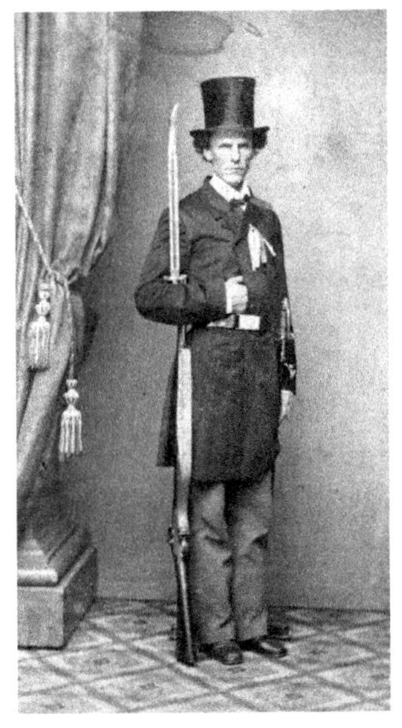

James H. Lane. *Courtesy of the Library of Congress.*

Jayhawkers: considered pro-Union guerrilla fighters from Kansas—the most well-known and violent militant organization of the abolitionists in Kansas. Lawrence was their symbolic headquarters, as it was the home of Senator James H. Lane. Also known as Red Legs, they gained a reputation for conducting most of the raiding, plundering and destruction of western Missouri communities.

"Little Dixie": a section of approximately ten or more counties clustered in mid-Missouri along the Missouri River whose culture resembled the Upper South, where most of the pre–Civil War migrants came from. The culture brought along its architectural, political and economic practices, including slavery. By 1860, slave populations in Little Dixie counties varied between 20 and 50 percent, depending on the nature of the agriculture practices. Major cash crops were hemp, tobacco and cotton. Some counties developed plantations with large estates of five hundred to two thousand acres or more, with slave populations ranging from a dozen to fifty or more.

Missouri State Guard (MSG): authorized by the Militia Act in May 1861 for the initial purpose of opposing a Federal invasion of Missouri. After the Federal commander General Lyons and Governor Jackson could not agree on its purpose, Governor Jackson called out the Missouri State Guard for service in the Confederacy.

Missouri State Militia (MSM): although its existence predates the Civil War, it is the name given to pro-Union units replacing Home Guard units. By November 1861, provisional Missouri governor Hamilton Gamble had been authorized by President Lincoln to organize a permanent standing state militia, financed by the United States but under state control. The state militia coordinated operations with the Federal forces but with the intentions of not serving outside the state. Primarily, a mounted force was required to pursue the elusive raiding forces of pro-Southern guerrillas, bushwhackers and Southern recruiters. Although Congress would limit the state militia to ten thousand soldiers, Missouri's state militia at one time consisted of as many as fourteen cavalry regiments, plus numerous other artillery, infantry and independent organizations.

Missouri Volunteer Militia: although sometimes confused by some historical reports regarding whether a unit was pro-Union or pro-Confederate, this is the designation given to state militia the governor would call out for emergencies or annual training authorized by the Missouri State Statutes of 1854. Many of these militia units wore distinctive, uniquely ornamented uniforms reflecting a local military esprit de corps. During the initial secessionist crises in Missouri, pro-secessionist General David Frost usurped this authority to call out state militia to Camp Jackson, St. Louis, with the generally believed intent of raiding the St. Louis Arsenal.

OR: designates information that was found in the *The War of the Rebellion: A Compilation of the Official Records.*

partisan rangers: officially recognized as units in the Confederacy under Confederate control (twenty-one units were operating in Missouri) who technically would be protected under Union General Order No. 100 as combatants entitled to treatment as POWs.

Bibliography

Ambrose, Stephen E. *Nothing Like It in the World: The Men Who Built the Transcontinental Railroad 1863–1869*. New York: Simon & Schuster, 2000.

Anders, Leslie. "The Blackwater Incident." *Missouri Historical Review* (July 1994): 416–29.

Arthur, Anthony. *General Jo Shelby's March*. New York: Random House, 2010.

Banasik, Michael. *Cavaliers of the Bush, Quantrill and His Men*. Iowa City, IA: Camp Pope Bookshop, 2003.

Bartels, Carolyn M. *The Civil War in Missouri, Day by Day, 1861–1865*. Independence, MO: Two Trails Publishing, 1992.

———. *The Forgotten Men: Missouri State Guard*. Independence, MO: Two Trails Publishing, 1995.

Bradbury, John F., Jr. "This War Is Managed Mighty Strange: The Army of Southeastern Missouri, 1862–1863." *Missouri Historical Review* (October 1994): 28–47.

Brownlee, Richard S. *Gray Ghosts of the Confederacy, Guerilla War in the West, 1861–1865*. Baton Rouge: Louisiana State University Press, 1958.

Castel, Albert. "Kansas Jayhawking Raids into Western Missouri in 1861." *Missouri Historical Review* (October 1958).

Catton, Bruce. *Centennial History of the Civil War*. Vol. 1, *The Coming Fury*. New York: Doubleday, 1961.

Chief of Record and Pension Office of the War Department. *Missouri Troops in Service during the Civil War.* Washington, D.C.: Government Printing Office, n.d., 246–56.

Civil War Centennial Commission of Missouri. "The Civil War in Missouri, 1861–1865." Circa 1965.

Civil War Roundtable of Western Missouri. Civil War Monuments and Memorials in Western Missouri, 2016.

Dick, Jimmy R. "Porter's 1862 Campaign in Northeast Missouri." *Saber and Scroll* 5, no. 1 (April 2016). American Public University System.

Dyer, Frederick H. *A Compendium of the War of the Rebellion.* N.p.: Dyer Publishing Company, 1908. In 1908, Frederick H. Dyer prepared an 1,800+ page compendium of the war that is easily accessible online or on CD. It is divided into three sections: Number and Organization of the Armies of the United States; Chronological Record of the Campaigns, Battles, Engagements, Actions, Combats, Sieges, Skirmishes, etc., in the United States, 1861 to 1865; and Regimental Histories.

Eakin, Jeanne Chiles. *Confederate Records from the United Daughters of the Confederacy.* N.p.: Missouri Division, 1996. www.shsmo.org.

Eanrgey, Bill. *Missouri's Roadsides: The Traveler's Companion.* Columbia: University of Missouri Press, 1995.

Edwards, John N. *Noted Guerillas, or the Warfare of the Border.* Independence, MO: Two Trails Publishing, 1996.

Erwin, James W. *Guerilla Hunters in Civil War Missouri.* Charleston, SC: The History Press, 2013.

Farley, James W. *Forgotten Valor: The First Missouri Cavalry Regiment, CSA.* Independence, MO: Two Trails Publishing, 1996.

Fellman, Michael. *Inside War: The Guerilla Conflict in Missouri during the American Civil War.* New York: Oxford University Press, 1989.

Freedoms Frontier National Heritage Area. Brochure, National Park Service, 2011. www.freedomsfrontier.org.

Gerteis, Louis S. *The Civil War in Missouri: A Military History.* Columbia: University of Missouri Press, 2016.

———. "The Civil War in Missouri: An Overview." *St. Louis Post Dispatch*, June 2, 2014.

Gilmore, Donald L. *Civil War on the Missouri-Kansas Border.* Gretna, LA: Pelican Publishing Company, 2005.

Goman, Frederick W. *Up from Arkansas: Marmaduke's First Missouri Raid Including the Battle of Springfield and Hartville.* N.p., 1999.

A Guide to Trans-Mississippi Civil War Sites. Oklahoma Historical Society, n.d.

Hollingsworth, John Hampton. *The Battle of Blackwell.* Independence, MO: Two Trails Publishing, 2007.

Hurst, Jack. *Men of Fire: Grant, Forrest and the Campaign that Decided the Civil War.* New York: Basic Books, 2006.

John Brown of Kansas, 1855–1859: Prelude to the Civil War. A Territorial Kansas Heritage Alliance Guide. N.p., 2001.

Kingdom of Callaway Historical Society. "133rd Anniversary of the Battle of Moore's Mill." 1995.

McGhee, James E. *Missouri Confederates: A Guide to Sources for Confederate Soldiers and Units, 1861–1865.* Independence, MO: Two Trails Publishing, 1996.

McGhee, James E., and Richard C. Peterson. *Sterling Price's Lieutenants: A Guide to the Officers and Organization of the Missouri State Guard, 1861–1865.* Independence, MO: Two Trails Publishing, 2007.

McLachlan, Sean. *Ride Around Missouri: Shelby's Great Raid.* Osprey Raid Series no. 25. Oxford, UK: Osprey Publishing, 2011.

Missouri Civil War Heritage Foundation. "A 'Desperate and Bloody' Fight: The Battle of Moore's Mill, Callaway County, Missouri, July 28, 1862." Prepared by Douglas D. Scott, Thomas D. Thiessen and Steve J. Dasovich. St. Louis, MO, March 2014. American Battlefield Protection Program, GA-2255-12-012, National Park Service, Washington, D.C.

———. Grant Trail Map brochures. St. Louis, MO.

———. Gray Ghost Trail Map brochure. St. Louis, MO.

———. *U.S. Grant Trail Missouri Kentucky.* Brochure, n.d.

———. *U.S. Grant Trail Missouri Northeast Segment.* Brochure, n.d.

———. *U.S. Grant Trail Missouri Southeast Segment.* Brochure, n.d.

Missouri Life. "Top 50 Civil War Sites" (May 13, 2011).

Monaghan, Jay. *Civil War on the Western Border, 1854–1865.* Boston: Little, Brown and Company, 1955.

Monnett, Howard N. *Actions before Westport, 1864.* N.p.: Westport Historical Society, 1964.

Mudd, Joseph A. *With Porter in North Missouri: A Chapter in the History of the War Between the States.* N.p.: National Publishing Company, 1909.

Muench, James. *5 Stars: Missouri's Most Famous Generals.* Columbia: University of Missouri Press, 2006.

Nichols, Bruce. *Guerilla Warfare in Civil War Missouri.* Vol. 2, *1863.* Jefferson, NC: McFarland, 2007.

Northway, Martin. "1861, Civil War Comes to the Kingdom." *Gates Camp Gazette,* spring 2009.

Parrish, William E. *A History of Missouri.* Vol. 3, *1861 to 1875.* Columbia: University of Missouri Press, 1973.

Rhodes, James Ford. *A History of the Civil War, 1861–1865.* New York: Macmillan Company, 1917.

Shea, William L. *Fields of Blood: The Prairie Grove Campaign.* Chapel Hill: University of North Carolina Press, 2009.

Sheeley, Andrew. "The Current River's Civil War Legacy Remembered at Round Spring." *Salem News,* June 28, 2016. salemnewsonline.com.

Soltysiak's, Harry A. "The Battle of Fredericksburg." *The Marketplace* (June 1989).

Stark, David. "Deadly Skirmish in Daviess County." Daviess County Historical Society, March 6, 2004.

St. Louis Post-Dispatch. "125 of St. Louis' Top Stories: No. 3 General Sherman's Funeral." December 14, 2003.

Ulysses S. Grant Personal Memoirs. New York: Random House Publications, 1999. Reprint of the 1885 edition edited by Mark Twain.

The War of the Rebellion: A Compilation of the Official Records of the Union and Confederate Armies. Prepared under the direction of the secretary of war, Brevet Lieutenant Colonel Robert N. Scott. Washington, D.C.: Government Printing Office, 1883. This is the most extensive primary source, with 128 volumes.

Wolk, Gregory. *Friend and Foe Alike: A Tour Guide to Missouri's Civil War.* St. Louis: Missouri Civil War Heritage Foundation, 2012.

Woodworth, Steven E., and Kenneth Winkle. *Atlas of the Civil War.* New York: Oxford University Press, 2004.

Online Sources

Almost Unabridged Guide to the Civil War in Missouri. www.almostunabridgedguide.com.

American Civil War Archive. "Union Regimental Histories: Missouri." www.civilwararchive.com/Unreghst/unmoinf5.htm.

———. www.civilwararchive.com.

Callaway County Historical Society. www.callawaycivilwar.org.

Camden Point, Missouri Civil War Information. www.civilwartalk.com/threads/the-battle-of-camden-point-july-13-1864-near-camden-point-missouri.92301.

Carthage Missouri Civil War Information. www.mostateparks.com/park/battle-carthage-state-historic-site.

City of St. Louis, Missouri. www.stlouis-mo.gov.

Civil War Battles 1861–1865. www.mycivilwar.com/battles.

Civil War Blog. http://civilwartalk.com.

Civil War Information. www.civilwarindex.com/battles.

The Civil War in Missouri. www.civilwarmo.org.

The Civil War Museum. www.thecivilwarmuse.com.

Civil War on the Western Border. www.civilwaronthewesternborder.org.

Civil War Roundtable of Kansas City. www.cwrtkc.org.

Civil War Roundtable of St. Louis. www.civilwarstlmo.org.

Civil War Roundtable of Western Missouri. www.cwrtwm.org.

Civil War Trust. www.civilwar.org.

Cornell University Digital Library of the War of the Rebellion. ebooks.library.cornell.edu/m/moawar/index.html.

Dayton, Missouri Civil War Information. www.civilwaronthewesternborder.org/timeline/raid-dayton-mo.

Fayette, Missouri Civil War Information. www.civilwarguide.info/battles/battle-fayette.

Gray Ghost Trail Map Brochure. www.civilwartraveler.com/maps/moremaps/MO-GrayGhosts.pdf.

Helena, Arkansas Civil War Information. www.historyofwar.org/articles/battles_helena.html.

Huntsville, Missouri Civil War Information. www.sites.google.com/site/historichuntsvillemissouri/home.

Lanes Prairie Civil War Information. www.ozarks-history.blogspot.com/2014/07/affair-on-lanes-prairie-maries-county.html.

Lexington, Missouri Civil War Information. www.mostateparks.com/park/battle-lexington-state-historic-site.

Lone Jack, Missouri Civil War Museum. www.historiclonejack.org/museum.html.

Military Order of the Loyal Legion of the United States (MOLLUS). Missouri Chapter. www.suvcw.org/mollus/mo.htm. This organization and its chapters in each state offer considerable information online regarding the American Civil War. It is a fraternal organization started at the conclusion of the war to recognize, among other things, the patriotism of those who fought in the war. Many distinguished officers have led the order since its founding in 1865.

Missouri Civil War Battles Alphabetical List. www.researchonline.net/mocw/battlesalpha.htm.

Missouri Civil War Heritage Foundation Website (Download Map Brochures). www.mocivilwar.org/travelers.

Missouri Civil War Map of Battles. www.americancivilwar.com/statepic/missouri.html.

Missouri Civil War Museum at Jefferson Barracks. www.mcwm.org.

Missouri Civil War Sites. www.missouricivilwar.net.

Missouri Civil War Units and Information on Requesting Individual Records. www.familysearch.org/wiki/en/Missouri_in_the_Civil_War.

Missouri Home Guard Information. home.usmo.com/~momollus/MOREG/HG.htm.

Missouri Sons of Confederate Veterans. www.missouridivision-scv.org. This organization's website provides one of the most informative resources regarding all things Confederate, such as details about leaders, soldiers and units who served in Missouri. It has many active local organizations, called Missouri Division Camps, dedicated to providing historically accurate information regarding the Civil War in Missouri. The site also provides helpful information for those seeking individual military records from the National Archives and Records Administration in Washington, D.C.

Missouri State Parks. www.mostateparks.com/park/missouri-state-museum.

Missouri War Memorials. www.americanmemorialsdirectory.com/missouri.html.

Mr. Lincoln and Friends. "Members of Congress: John B. Henderson (1826–1913)." www.mrlincolnandfriends.org/members-of-congress/john-henderson.

National Park Service Civil War. www.nps.gov/civilwar/index.htm.

National Park Service History of Battle Units. www.nps.gov/civilwar/search-battle-units.htm.

National Park Service Soldiers and Sailors Database. www.nps.gov/civilwar/soldiers-and-sailors-database.htm.

Newton County Civil War Information. www.newtoncountymotourism.org/civil-war-mines-mills.php.

Official Records of the Union and Confederate Armies. www.simmonsgames.com/research/authors/USWarDept/ORA.

Ohio State University Digital Library of the War of the Rebellion. ehistory.osu.edu/books/official-records.

Ozark Missouri Civil War Information. thelibrary.org/lochist/periodicals/wrv/V1/N5/F62e.htm.

Ozarks Civil War. www.ozarkscivilwar.org.

Pea Ridge, Battle of Arkansas History. www.encyclopediaofarkansas.net/encyclopedia/entry-detail.aspx?entryID=509.

Plattsburg, Missouri Civil War Information. www.plattsburgmo.com/History/1864BattleofPlattsburg.htm.

quantrillsguerrillas.com/en/biographies.

Springfield, Missouri Civil War Information. www.springfield1863.org.

State Historical Society of Missouri digital collections. digital.shsmo.org.

State Historical Society of Missouri research and publications. www.shs.org.

St. Louis Public Library. indexes.slpl.org/Pages/BATTLES.aspx.

University Civil War Official Records Sites. "Dyer's Compendium of the War of the Rebellion: Battles." www.perseus.tufts.edu/hopper/text?doc=Perseus%3Atext%3A2001.05.0140%3Astate%3DMissouri%3Ayear%3D1861.

Washington County Civil War Information. www.carrollscorner.net/WashCoCW2.htm.

Washington Missouri History. http://www.washingtonmo.com/History+of+Washington+MO/historychap4.htm.

Westport, Battle of Civil War Information. www.battleofwestport.org/VisitorCenter.htm.

Wilson's Creek National Battlefield Information. www.nps.gov/wicr/index.htm.

Index

C

D

G

H

L

M

N

O

P

Q

R

S

V

W

Y

Z

About the Authors

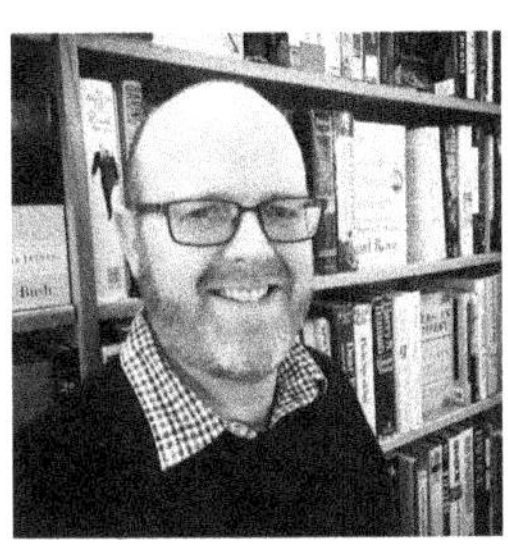

Brian Warren, a native of Southern California, studied history at California State University–Northridge. After a fifteen-year career in the technology business in California's Silicon Valley, Brian opted for a quieter life, settling in rural central Missouri. He is the proud owner of Well Read Books in Fulton, Missouri, and enjoys reading, following the Los Angeles Dodgers and writing fiction.

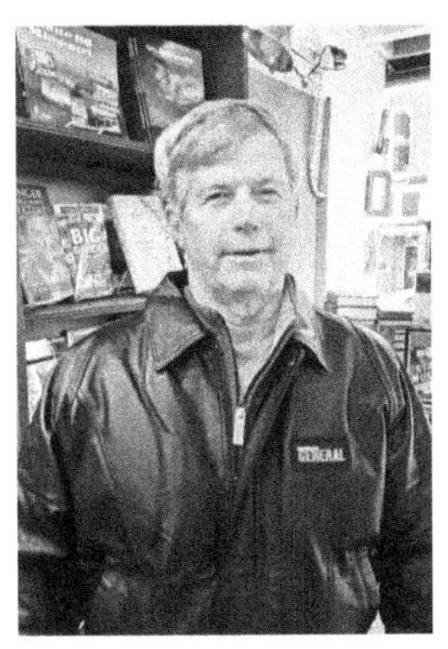

Joseph W. McCoskrie Jr. is a Midwest native who graduated from Virginia Military Institute and subsequently served in the United States Army for twenty-eight years, retiring as a lieutenant colonel. After more than twenty-five years as a Midwest banking executive, Whit was hired to become an instructor in Leadership and American Military History for the Army ROTC program at Illinois State University and the University of Missouri. Whit and his wife have two sons, Brian and Robert, and reside in Fulton, Missouri, where he currently spends some of his time as a volunteer tour guide at the National Churchill Museum.